The Faith Factor in Fatherhood

The Faith Factor in Fatherhood

Renewing the Sacred Vocation of Fathering

Edited By
Don E. Eberly

LEXINGTON BOOKS
Lanham • Boulder • New York • Oxford

LEXINGTON BOOKS

Published in the United States of America
by Lexington Books
4720 Boston Way, Lanham, Maryland 20706

12 Hid's Copse Road
Cumnor Hill, Oxford OX2 9JJ, England

British Library Cataloguing in Publication Information Available

Library of Congress Cataloging-in-Publication Data

Eberly, Don E.
  The faith factor in fatherhood : renewing the sacred vocation
of fathering / Don E. Eberly.
      p.   cm.
  Includes bibliographical references and index.
  ISBN 0-7391-0079-3 (alk. paper). — ISBN 0-7391-0080-7 (pbk. :
alk. paper)
   1. Fatherhood—Religious aspects—Christianity. 2. Church work
with men—United States. I. Title.
BV4529.17.E24   1999
261.8'358742'0973—dc21   99-37771
                                                            CIP

Printed in the United States of America

⊖™ The paper used in this publication meets the minimum requirements of American
National Standard for Information Sciences—Permanence of Paper for Printed Library
Materials, ANSI/NISO Z39.48–1992.

Contents

Contents

Part Three
Fatherhood and Faith in the American Public Debate

Part Four
Faithful Fathers: The Journey Back

Acknowledgments

There are many people to thank in a project like this, starting with the chapter contributors themselves. The 19 contributors to the *The Faith Factor in America's Fatherhood* represent, without doubt, the leading organizers, scholars, and practitioners of the faith-based wing of the fatherhood movement. They exemplify in their ideas, their programs, and their lives what committed, God-centered fatherhood is all about.

I would also like to thank two exceptional people who have worked with me on several previous book projects and who made time available again for this one: Deb Strubel, who is a master at turning average copy into superbly edited and readable material; and Cliff Frick, a ten-year colleague who has also brought his considerable professional talents to bear on this manuscript, all to the reader's benefit.

I also wish to acknowledge the outstanding service of the entire National Fatherhood Initiative staff who, every day, help advance what has been a dream of mine, namely creating a society-wide fatherhood movement to renew fatherhood and to thereby improve the lives of kids.

Special thanks as well to the Humanitas Foundation for providing funds to conduct a national interfaith summit on fatherhood, from which some of the material for this book was drawn, and to the Lilly Endowment and Earhart Foundation, which both made the preparation, production, and distribution of this book possible.

The highest form of gratitude must be reserved for my real source of strength for the work of fatherhood, namely the heavenly father and also my earthly family—wife Sheryl, and kids, Preston, Caroline, and Margaret—who shape and nourish my life as a father and give my message both practical and spiritual authenticity.

Introduction

The Spirit of the Fatherhood Movement

David Blankenhorn

When my son was eight years old, brimming with excitement about the game of basketball, I took him to visit the Basketball Hall of Fame in Springfield, Massachusetts. Many of the exhibits are interactive—one lets you measure your highest jump against Michael Jordan's highest jump—and most focus on the achievements of basketball's greatest players and teams. But off in a corner, in a room that had few visitors the day I was there, one can find a modest exhibit on the origins and early history of basketball.

The photos and memorabilia told a story that I had often heard before and had already passed on to my son. In the winter of 1891-92, Dr. James Naismith was a young "physical education instructor" at Springfield College. As one pamphlet puts it, his "bored students were young men suffering through a required gymnasium class."[1] Determined to end the boredom, Naismith set out to invent a new winter or indoors game that would be as exciting for his student athletes as football in the fall or baseball in the summer. So he thought up some rules, nailed two half-bushel peach baskets to the lower rail of the gymnasium balcony, one at each end, and . . . basketball was born.

As I reimmersed myself in this great old story, so familiar to anyone who loves the game, one odd detail in one photograph in the exhibit caught my eye. The photograph shows the building in which basketball was invented. Almost all the literature refers to this building as "Springfield College." But the sign above the main entrance of the building in the photograph clearly says "School for Christian Workers." What's that? Looking a bit more carefully through the exhibit, and also searching through the footnotes and fine print in the main literature on basketball, one can find occasional references to this building, the forerunner of today's Springfield College, as the "International YMCA Training School."

It seems that, in the case of basketball's origins, there is a story behind the story. Or more precisely, an actual history that has been largely displaced by a sanitized, "official" history. Dr. James Naismith, it turns out, was an ordained Presbyterian minister. In 1891, he was just beginning a ministry that was to evolve into a lifetime of service to the church. His job at the "School for Christian Workers" was not, it turns out, simply to instruct "bored" college kids in "physical education." His job was to help train young men to become professional leaders of the then-burgeoning Sunday School movement and the similarly growing YMCA (Young Men's Christian Association) movement. And the goal of those two closely allied movements, both led by large and denominationally diverse groups of pastors and church-based volunteers, was to build character and inculcate Christian virtue in young people.[2]

Yes, Naismith invented basketball. Moreover, the entire early history of basketball is part and parcel of the YMCA movement. (The first basketball league, for example, consisted of YMCA clubs playing one another.) But for Naismith—and for his students, and for his fellow faculty—basketball was not an end in itself. Playing basketball was one pathway toward solid character formation, one good activity for young men who aspire fundamentally to spiritual fitness.

The YMCA movement in Naismith's time promoted "the fourfold program" for fitness: physical, social, mental, and spiritual development, with the spiritual being the highest and ultimate form of personal fitness or strength of character. Accordingly, the emphasis on physical development was understood to be directly connected to the cultivation of civic and religious virtues. For example, YMCA leaders first opened gymnasiums largely in order to give young men an alternative to socializing in saloons. In 1895, this concept of balanced or integrated character development was altered slightly, and was symbolized by the Y in the form of a red triangle, which denoted the Y's holistic focus on the three sides of a man's nature: physical, mental, and spiritual.

Interestingly, this YMCA formula directly influenced the leadership of the American Boy Scouts, who in this period added a clause to the Boy Scout oath by which Scouts would pledge to keep themselves "physically strong, mentally awake, and morally straight." Similarly, the Scout law obligated boys to be trustworthy, loyal, helpful, friendly, courteous, kind, obedient, cheerful, thrifty, brave, clean, and reverent.[3]

The key idea in each of these formulations is that building character in children and young adults is a multidimensional task, requiring a focus on "the whole man" that integrates various aspects of personal development, but also a task that culminates in the "spiritual condition" (YMCA) or in being "morally straight" and "reverent" (Boy Scouts). This religiously informed view of character-building reflects one important way in which evangelical Protestants in this era sought to introduce and bring young people to Christian faith and to influence the larger society on behalf of Christian principles.

Most of this, of course, is ancient history. Today, the "Y" as an organization is about as centered on spiritual goals as McDonald's or Starbucks. Indeed, YMCA facilities in most communities have become virtually indistinguishable from any other mildly upscale private health club. The Sunday School movement still remains, but has been in decline for at least several generations. Basketball today has become largely integrated into our growing entertainment culture, driven by money and focused on international celebrity—athletes such as Michael Jordan and Shaquille O'Neil.

But for those who worry about the crisis of fatherlessness in the United States, perhaps this little piece of basketball's social history is less ancient, and more relevant, than we might first imagine. For if this valuable collection of essays on "the faith factor" in American fatherhood tells us anything, it tells us that the renewal of fatherhood in our society, if it is to occur at all, will be instigated in large measure by people of faith and will be premised in large measure on what Don Eberly and others call a renewal of "God-centered masculinity."

At the turn of the last century, the character-building movement in our society, led by Dr. Naismith and his colleagues at the Y and in the Sunday School and Scouting movements, was based explicitly on moral and religious ideals. The YMCA did not improve the lives of millions of young people and place its stamp upon the American character because its leaders believed in the ideal of guys playing basketball. It did not even achieve its remarkable (if historically short-lived) success because its leaders upheld a secular or purely civic ideal of character formation. Yes, the character-building movement successfully taught the liberal and civic virtues of good citizenship, compassion, patriotism, and duty to community. But the movement's success in transmitting these social values to young people—an irony that we see often in the history of social reform—clearly hinged upon its ultimate aspiration toward something greater.

Successful social movements frequently, in this sense, point beyond themselves. Their core values run deeper and aim higher than the movement's immediate worldly goals. Why do successful movements so often possess this trait? One explanation, for people of faith, is divine providence. Another, more sociological explanation is that big changes in individuals and in societies—a troubled kid who decides to get her life straightened out, a society that decides that every child deserves a father—come from big changes in our hearts and in the way we think, not small changes.[4]

For these reasons, as we enter the next century, a successful movement to reverse the trend of fatherlessness in our society is not likely to draw its essential inspiration from the worlds of professional social work, interest-group politics, or legislative lobbying, or from any other set of principles that is confined solely to the existing material world, the current social "is." If it is to be successful, this new movement's underlying inspiration will almost surely come from elsewhere: from the larger moral "ought" and from principles of life that are essentially spiritual.

Consider the case of Dr. Wallace O. McLaughlin, the young executive director of the Father Resource Program in Indianapolis, Indiana. This recently established community-based organization works primarily with young, unmarried, poorly educated African Americans. Echoing Dr. Naismith and the earlier character education movement, Dr. McLaughlin's project is multidimensional, focusing on "the whole man": employment skills, job opportunities, parenting skills, whatever is needed to help the father reconnect with his child and the mother of his child. With his Ph.D. in family studies, and informed by several years of practical experience in working with young fathers, Dr. McLaughlin particularly emphasizes what he calls the "mental health dimension" of fatherhood-building. For this reason, the young fathers in his program often begin by discussing their own fathers. Was he there for me? Did he hit my mother? If I was not properly fathered, how can I break the cycle with my own child?

But in addition to his academic degree, Wallace McLaughlin is an ordained pastor. His work with fathers is essentially a ministry. Many of the guys enrolled in the Father Resource Program visit and attend his church. Dr. McLaughlin also observes that many of these young fathers are in "spiritual arrested development." So he pastors them, helping them to discover for themselves the integral connection between being a good father and being spiritually fit.

Dr. Wallace McLaughlin and Dr. James Naismith are separated in time by about a century. They are also separated by race, region, and, no doubt, any number of theological and denominational fine points. And for all I know, Wallace McLaughlin does not even play basketball. Yet I am certain that these two men—and their two movements—are much more alike than different. They are kindred in spirit because both are ultimately anchored in things of the spirit.

Moreover, Wallace McLaughlin is no anomaly. Across the country, in today's emerging fatherhood movement, many (though certainly not all) of the leaders are people of faith, and much of the movement's energy and most effective grassroots activity is based in churches, synagogues, and other faith-based organizations. Surely this is more than coincidence.

Of course, some of the influence of "the faith factor" in today's fatherhood movement can be explained in practical and institutional terms. Years ago I worked as a community organizer. Whenever we wanted anything done, my first step was to contact at least some of the local churches. After all, they had social halls to meet in. They regularly took up collections of money. They were often led by clergy who were sympathetic to community concerns, and sometimes by pastors like Dr. McLaughlin who themselves were known and admired as community leaders. Most of all, the churches had people. People who were already organized for a collective purpose. People who tended, on the whole, to be decent, self-respecting, neighborly, and compassionate. People who tended to show up when something important was happening. The kind of people, in short, who will tend to support any worthy social initiative, from coaching Little League to building houses for the poor.

But with fatherhood, just as with character education, "the faith factor" in the movement is not primarily a matter of convenience, logistics, or available leaders. It's also and most importantly first a matter of principles. Indeed, one of the main conclusions of this provocative book of essays is that hands-on human fatherhood is ultimately a spiritual calling, intimately linked to the search for transcendence.

As several contributors point out, nurturant fatherhood is not a necessarily predictable or even likely result of male sexual embodiment. Instead, true fatherhood in any society is largely a cultural creation, particularly the creation of a culture's basic ethical system. Put differently, true fatherhood is not a natural fact. It becomes a material reality only when viewed with a moral squint. In this sense, fatherhood is a metaphysical idea, decisively dependent on things unseen. Fatherhood is especially dependent on norms of male submission and giving of self that are usually honored by flesh-and-blood men at least as much in the breach as in the observance.

Responsible fatherhood moralizes natural masculinity. It leads adult males toward loving intimacy with at least a few other people, and more broadly, encourages them to put other people's needs before their own. It guides men toward understanding certain acts of obedience and submission as acts of heroism. It fundamentally transforms aggression—what Martin Luther King Jr. called the "drum major instinct," or the desire to lead the parade—into servanthood, an ethic of demonstrating strength through sacrificing for family.

In short, true fatherhood teaches men, in the face of much evidence to the contrary, that they are taller when they bow. Surely such a root-and-branch moralization of male behavior can finally be understood only in spiritual terms—as the fruit of a spiritual vocation or calling, or perhaps even better, as grace, a spiritual gift. The core mystery of fatherhood, in my view, is that a bare biological act can produce such a transforming personal reality.

For this reason, I believe that "the faith factor" in today's fatherhood movement will ultimately prove to be the most important factor of all. Nearly ten years into the modern fatherhood movement, this is the first book produced by that movement that gets us to the heart of the matter.

Notes

1. "Basketball Was Born Here," (Springfield, MA: Springfield College, 1998).

2. See David I. Macleod, *Building Character in the American Boy: The Boy Scouts, YMCA, and Their Forerunners, 1870-1920* (Madison: University of Wisconsin Press, 1983); and Anne M. Boylan, *Sunday School: The Formation of an American Institution, 1790-1880* (New Haven: Yale University Press, 1988).

3. Macleod, *Building Character*, 29, 45, 72-73, 118-129.

4. C. S. Lewis and others have described what has been called the principle of indirection or inattention: There are certain wonderful things that we get mostly by pursuing something else. For example, to put it negatively, few people find happiness by dedicating themselves to the goal of being happy. The pursuit of creativity as an end in itself often leads to the foreclosure of creativity. Humility is a rare trait among people who constantly draw attention to their modesty. People who flaunt their patriotism, or who embrace it as an absolute value, are often potential dangers to their society, and so on. Putting it positively, this is what the poet Richard Lovelace (1618-1658) means when he says, "I could not love thee, dear, so much,/Loved I not honor more." This is also what many people believe Jesus means when he says (Matt. 7:33), "But seek first the Kingdom of God and his righteousness, and all these things shall also be given to you." These authors are here speaking of our personal life journeys, but I believe that this same basic insight—especially the idea that turning what are (in spiritual terms) worthy but relative goals into absolute goals make those goals themselves harder to attain—might also help us to understand the logic of many successful social movements, especially in the United States.

Part One

The Story of
American Fatherhood

Chapter 1

The Collapse and Recovery of Fatherhood

Don E. Eberly

The Old Testament Scriptures end with a remarkable warning to a nation caught in the grip of fatherlessness. The writer Malachi speaks of the need for a prophet whom God will send to "turn the hearts of the fathers to their children, and the hearts of the children to their fathers" lest the land be struck "with a curse" (Malachi 4:5-6).

Like never before America's attention is focused on the plight of fathers and the social curse brought about by their growing absence. Nothing would do more to improve the well-being of children, women, communities, and the nation than strengthening fatherhood. So many men are in trouble and are struggling as fathers.

This book is dedicated to today's and tomorrow's dads. It is not written for individual fathers as much as it is for the communities of faith in which they gather. It is specifically a call to action for denominations and congregations to recover the heritage of fathering that has nearly been lost. Committed fathering once enjoyed wide support in America's churches, but in recent decades churches have become, much like the wider society, silent on the rapidly spreading epidemic of fatherlessness. Great opportunities for renewal exist.

As the founder and chairman of the National Fatherhood Initiative (NFI), a national civic organization aimed at mobilizing a society-wide response to the problem of father absence, I am regularly called on to speak to general audiences, policy makers, and the media. My mission, and that of the NFI, is to improve the well-being of America's children by increasing the number of kids who are raised by committed, engaged fathers.

One incident several years ago brought home to me just how far the faith community had drifted from its own traditional commitment to fatherhood. I was invited to appear on the radio program of Cardinal Bevilacqua, a popular broadcast in Philadelphia that the Cardinal uses to address issues of concern to the Catholic laity as well as the community at large. I talked at length, as I usually do, about how father absence was harming the condition of children and the well-being of society. After the program, Cardinal Bevilacqua embraced me with a long bear hug and said, "Please keep up what you're doing in the culture to renew fatherhood. It has become difficult for us in the church to confront this issue directly, and what you're doing in the culture will make our job a lot easier."

I was startled! I grew up thinking that the world worked the other way around—that the church set the pace for values in the culture.

I assumed that if the tradition and practice of fatherhood was either ignored or roundly ridiculed in the wider society, surely the church would be doing its job to keep it alive.

Not so. The Cardinal's admission suggested something about how powerful the culture has become in setting the agenda for the church as well as society in general. Vast changes have come to our culture, but it turns out that something has gone seriously wrong in the church as well. On the decades-long collapse of fatherhood, the church has not put up much resistance until recently.

Fatherhood has lost its valued place in society. The United States is in the midst of what one hopes is the final stage of a decades-long cultural revolution carried confidently along by the myth that children do just fine without fathers. The social premise underlying vast realms of American society, from popular culture to family sciences, psychology, and public policy, has been that fathers are superfluous. The tacit assumption, and in many cases the firm conviction, of social experts for at least the past three decades was that fathers make no gender-specific contribution to the lives of children.

What fathers do as parents, the theory held, is interchangeable with what mothers and adults in general do generally, which meant that father absence was no great loss for children or society. The only loss of any real consequence was perhaps the father's paycheck, and that could be remedied through a mammoth child-support bureaucracy to chase down the dollars of "deadbeat" dads. The father had become emasculated—reduced to little more than a walking wallet.

Such an experiment was bound to produce tragic consequences, as most objective observers now admit when they look honestly at the evidence of profound social tragedy before them. Mountains of social science data tell the story of children living in deep disadvantage and disappointment. Even the child support enforcement machine, which employs an army of 33,000, has generally been regarded as a failure.

Why are we surprised?

A society that did nothing to preserve the institution of fatherhood was bound to get increased fatherlessness. Preserving and enforcing the norms of responsible fatherhood is the job of culture and its many character-shaping institutions, chief among them religious institutions. Anthropologists and social historians have always contended that fatherhood is a social institution to roughly the same degree that motherhood is biologically determined.

Fathering, says family sociologist John Miller, is "a cultural acquisition to an extent that mothering is not." Given that there are few biologically compelling reasons for the male to care for his offspring, "a set of overlapping largely cultural developments" is required. When a culture "ceases to support a father's involvement with his own children (through its laws, mores, symbols, models, rituals) powerful natural forces take over in favor of the mother only family."[1]

Miller is essentially describing what has happened in America over the past several decades. Drift and disintegration occur when a culture turns against fathers: "Powerful natural forces take over in favor of the mother only family." History records no example of a society in which mothers abandoned their children in large numbers. Physically and emotionally engaged mothering requires little social encouragement. Some mothers may need coaching from older women. Others may need extensive help in developing effective parenting skills. But mothers, as a group, do not abandon their biological offspring. They never have.

By contrast, when societies fail to reinforce the unique and irreplaceable role that fathers play in the lives of children, fathers steadily disappear, leaving large numbers of children vulnerable to poverty, emotional suffering, and behavioral problems. The late Margaret Mead said, "The primary task of every civilization is to teach the young men to be fathers." In other words, the job of society is to resist and overcome those powerful natural forces that permit fathers to drift away.

Whose job is it to teach the young men to be fathers? The responsibility falls to an entire society, meaning those who lead, teach, or serve in any capacity. First and foremost, individual fathers and grandfathers must pass along the skills and personal devotion of fathering. But even that private role is couched in and encouraged by an assortment of institutions, including schools, media and entertainment, and the community. Most importantly, this work must be carried out by places of worship.

The Free Fall in Fatherhood

How far American society has fallen from what was once a fatherhood norm, and how fast the descent has occurred, is hard to comprehend. The number of children living with only their mothers in 1960 was 5.1 million.[2] Today the number of children who go to bed at night in a household in which the biological father does not live is pushing 24 million, or almost 40 percent of all children. America passed Sweden in the mid-1980s as the world leader in families headed by single mothers.[3]

No social transformation has had more tragic results for children, been more fiscally costly for governments at all levels, or increased more dramatically such social pathologies among youth as teen pregnancy, adolescent crime, and drug abuse. Few things can be asserted with greater confidence based upon settled social science findings than the fact that children of father-absent households, on average, do more poorly at just about everything. They are five times more likely to live in poverty, three times more likely to fail at school, two to three times more likely to experience emotional or behavioral problems, and three times more likely to commit suicide.

To some extent society has always struggled to keep families together and fathers engaged. The work of building and protecting strong families has always been difficult, even before the arrival of the modern influences that have proven hostile. Family life is challenging. Fatherlessness has always presented itself as a problem to one degree or another, leaving the struggle of caring for the unfathered to others. If God himself includes in his self-description "a father to the fatherless" (Psalm 68:5), then certainly his people should welcome that mission as well.

Nevertheless, the father absence of today is very different than that of the past: It is dramatically larger in scale, and it is distinctly different in nature. The source of father absence throughout most of American history was overwhelmingly the father's death, not desertion. The father would go away to work or to war, and not return, in which case the father himself was permanently gone. His absence was tragic, but because the absence was beyond the father's control, it was understood and excused. The father was missed, but his memory lived fondly on in the minds of his children.

By the 1960s, father absence was generated predominantly through divorce, separation, or nonmarital childbearing. In other words, the father absence of more recent vintage is voluntary and volitional. Father absence today is explained almost entirely by the lifestyle choices of adult men and women. And those choices are not easily understood or excused by children.

Not only have fathers disappeared in historically unprecedented proportions, but also the very meaning and identity of fatherhood has come perilously close to disappearing. America has almost lost what David Blankenhorn, author of *Fatherless America: Confronting Our Most Urgent Social Problem*, calls "the idea of fatherhood."

Family Relativism and Personal Autonomy

The erosion of the fatherhood ideal has come in many forms. Even the very discussion of family in recent years has had the effect of eroding support for father-involved families. The vagueness of our description of "family" reflects society's desire to accommodate a steep rise in separated, divorced, blended, and never-formed families headed predominantly by single mothers. To some, the term family is now so elastic that it means little more than a collection of adults bound together by temporary needs and agreements.

This relativization of the family fits comfortably with the broad tendency within the culture to expand the sphere that is considered exclusively private, where decisions are made entirely on the basis of personal choice by autonomous individuals, far removed from social scrutiny. This privatization of personal choice in matters of family has been a huge boon to individualism and an equally great bust for society. Society is forced to accommodate greater demands by individuals for personal freedom while, in the case of fatherless families, having to pick up the cost and consequences.

Society becomes obligated to bear the huge financial costs and social burden of caring for fatherless children and their impoverished mothers, and has little choice but to cope with their often destructive influence in public institutions such as schools. Most of the costs for compensatory programs in schools and communities have to do, directly or indirectly, with broken, father-absent households.

In spite of this widespread social burden, society has almost completely lost its capacity to voice a disapproving attitude, even in the case of adult behavior that is undeniably hurtful toward children. Remarkably, adult decisions—even those involving the welfare of the most vulnerable citizens—are assumed to be private and protected from public scrutiny. Society is forced to watch in silence.

Because all family circumstances do not lend themselves equally to engaged fathering, this dilution of the meaning of family is not inconsequential; the broader, fuzzier definition of family that has gained acceptance will likely make married, full-time fathering harder to attain. Little in the modern cultural script consciously and deliberately favors the father, in the same way that one might describe a culture that favors avoiding drugs, keeping the environment clean, driving safely, or staying in school.

Ever since the rise of the omnipresent media and entertainment culture, Americans have been overwhelmed with messages deemed by their social betters to be important: Don't smoke; don't drink and drive; don't pollute; be sure to exercise; be a volunteer, and so on. Ironically, the message that is heard most consistently from every corner of society is our need to rescue children, so many of whom are now in trouble.

One would think that a society that is overcome with concern regarding the state of children would mention the problem of missing fathers at every opportunity. Instead, entire sectors of the government are dedicated to alleviating the consequences of father absence rather than addressing the causes. Some of our largest civic organizations see mentoring troubled children, not enlisting their fathers, as the cure. We admonish each other to take care of the needy children around us, which of course we should, but we fail to demand that fathers take care of their own by denying themselves some personal freedoms for the good of their children.

The best example of the effort to escape the call to responsible fatherhood was at the so-called "Presidents Summit on Volunteerism," which took place in April 1997 in Philadelphia. The primary purpose of the summit was to enlist armies of volunteers to rescue the tens of millions of American children who are now described as "at risk." Who are these children? Overwhelmingly, they are children who have been neglected, if not abandoned, by their fathers. And where were these fathers? No one bothered to ask. Except for a panel that I organized and moderated, there was not one mention of fathers.

The point here is not to fault calls to compassion, but rather to challenge a society's unwillingness to subscribe to a "parents-first" policy, which in the vast majority of cases means connecting fathers to their children. Volunteering, mentoring, and finding quality father-substitutes where necessary is important work. But there are no examples in history of large numbers of people volunteering to raise other people's kids. Most movements to renew America in the past took dead aim at renewing parenting, not merely attempting to compensate for its absence.

A society either places a premium on fatherhood or it doesn't. For decades, the cultural message was at best neglectful of fathers, at worst denigrating. In the vast majority of cases, cultural institutions have simply been silent regarding the unique and valued role of fathers, which is perhaps the least harmful response. More frequently, the cultural response is one merely of indifference; occasionally it is one of hostility. Dad is presented in popular culture as an extra set of hands, a deputy mom, a provider of child support payments, possibly "the nearby guy," more akin to a relative than a devoted nurturing father.[4]

Popular entertainment portrays the father as a dunce, a guy lacking brains or character who is reluctantly permitted to be around children. Still worse, popular literature attacking domestic abuse often uses statistical falsehoods to raise the ugliest specter of all: dad as a danger. In truth, the male least likely to engage in the abuse of women and children is the married, biological father. In the vast majority of cases, abuse is carried out by a live-in acquaintance or an estranged boyfriend.

Only recently has a countertrend begun to emerge as films, books, and corporate advertising capture positive images of fathers playing a vital, healthy role in the lives of children. For example, Madison Avenue is increasingly portraying men having tender moments with their children in order to sell products. The movement to revive fatherhood in the entertainment culture has received powerful support from the National Fatherhood Initiative's public message campaign through the Advertising Council in New York, which has generated over $100 million in donated broadcast time, produced tens of thousands of calls, and led to the creation of hundreds of grassroots fatherhood projects.

How could an entire society ignore what anthropologists have long considered its most important job and instead waste decades trying to normalize alternative and amorphous family arrangements which in the large majority of cases exclude the biological father? To preserve fatherhood, a society must make responsible fatherhood one of its most important social goals. The keystone in preserving the family in every society has always been the "capturing of male energy into the nurturance of the young," Blankenhorn says. In short, "the key for men is to be fathers. The key for children is to have fathers. The key for society is to create fathers."[5]

"Capturing the male" was a task society once confidently faced. Up until the nineteenth century, much of the instructional material for children and most parental guides to the discipline and moral cultivation of children were prepared for fathers. Fathers were seen as integral to the child's physical growth, character and skills, and general preparation for life. Religious organizations offered opportunities for men to encourage and challenge each other based upon deeply ingrained traditions of male responsibility for children. Male rites of passage and various communal rituals served as important guideposts to young men as they assumed the duties of adulthood.

Today, those religious and cultural supports are largely gone, and true to the patterns of history, large numbers of fathers are missing in action. When fatherhood dies, men do a disappearing act. One in every two children being born today will spend a portion of his or her childhood in a father-absent household. Thirty-three percent of newborns now enter the world as members of a father-absent household. In some urban communities, the number goes as high as 90 percent.

Father absence has been gathering force and momentum in the culture. Fatherlessness, says National Fatherhood Initiative president Dr. Wade Horn, is approaching the point of critical mass in society—meaning a near majority—which would make achieving a reversal exceedingly difficult. Fortunately, at the time of this writing, the relevant statistical indicators of father absence, such as out-of-wedlock birth rates and divorce trends, have stabilized and even declined slightly.

The Multiple Forms of Missing Fatherhood

The most common means of measuring fatherhood involvement is the physical presence or absence of fathers from their children. While most would agree that increasing the number of households in which the married, biological father is present and active is an important goal, it is not the only goal. That single aim ignores what is going on in certain communities. For one thing, many nonresidential fathers are doing heroic jobs as fathers in spite of divorce or separation, and many unmarried fathers in the low-income community make important contributions to their children through informal interaction in the neighborhood. For another, such a goal too easily dismisses the problem of physically-present but emotionally-absent fathers.

Father absence takes many forms. While many fathers are missing altogether, many more who are physically present are not living up to their potential. The loss of a strong fathering heritage has produced negative effects even for those who are physically present and reasonably active as fathers. Tens of millions of American fathers struggle as adult parents because they have not had a model of effective fathering in their own lives.

Many baby boomers were raised by fathers who were physically present, but emotionally absent. These fathers were products of war and depression, and became excessively strict in their discipline and personally detached. Their sons' pain was not due to physical separation but the lack of affirmation and emotional connection with their dads. The baby boom generation, in turn, became the most divorce-prone group in American history, producing the largest crop of sons whose fatherhood experience was strained by family breakup.

The pattern during this century has moved from strict and emotionally detached fathering to divorced or separated fathering, leaving the entire heritage of fatherhood in a fragile state. Many of today's young fathers are consequently either absorbed in their own strained father-relationship or searching for the means to rise above their own past and break the pattern.

The outcome for these fathers remains uncertain. Some will confidently break the chain of ineffective or absent fatherhood and build a positive new fathering heritage from which future generations will profit. Others will return to the pattern of brokenness and ineptitude that they experienced in spite of their best hopes and intentions to the contrary. Few things are more disheartening to witness than the pattern described in the Scriptures as "the sins of the father being visited on the third and fourth generation" (Exodus 20:5).

Dr. Ken Canfield of the National Center for Fathering captures it well: "The hearts of many fathers ache." According to Canfield, men learn to father by watching their dads, but "a crisis of fatherlessness has removed the models for many men and distorted them for others." He adds that although many fathers want to break the cycle and give something better to their children, their "best plans can go awry, because sheer determination is not enough."[6]

Canfield and other fatherhood experts such as Gordon Dalbey stress the importance of preparing fathers for fathering by first helping them overcome the bankrupt relationships they had with their own fathers. Dalbey, an early and prominent contributor to the fatherhood movement and author of *Father and Son: The Wound, the Healing, the Call to Manhood*, maintains that the key to becoming a father isn't merely commitment or motivation. It is about "the prior and primal step of manhood in becoming a son."[7]

Canfield maintains that for those fathers who grew up with physically absent or emotionally disengaged fathers, this won't happen instantly. He says, "You will need to allow time and effort for grieving, healing and restoring your heart." Once the father wound is healed, most fathers are ready to move forward.

So if individual men need to grieve and heal, why write a book about that for religious institutions?

The answer is simple. What better institution to undertake this work of renewal than our houses of worship? Is there an institution that compares in its power to restore? Places of worship can nurture this healing process and repair the blueprint for healthy, successful fathering. Local gatherings of men, organized and assisted by local churches, can recover the lost rites and rituals of turning a father's heart toward his children and passing along blessing and affirmation.

The Factors Behind Fatherlessness

There was a time in American life when the challenge of fathering was widely recognized and met. How did we arrive at our current crisis, and what were the major contributing factors? Obviously, no one factor is ever responsible for massive social change, and the rise of father absence is no exception. A combination of economic and cultural factors played leading roles.

The demise of fatherhood in America has economic, cultural, and moral causes. In pinpointing the date of modern culture's departure from involved fathering, social historians point specifically to the onset of industrialization, and more generally to the process of modernization, which removed male employment from the home and farm, and in turn separated fathers from the nurturing role they previously played with their children. Prior to the industrial revolution, and throughout the whole of prior history, men might be separated from their homes for war or extended periods of hunting, but otherwise were present and involved in all aspects of their children's lives. Changing economics started a process of severe role differentiation among mothers and fathers.

"At the heart of this change was the decline of the corporate household economy and the emergence of a commercial-industrial world in which increasing numbers of men became breadwinners who commuted to work while their wives assumed direction of the household," says fatherhood historian Robert Griswold. In short, he says, "the restructuring of American capitalism refashioned fatherhood."[8]

The corporate household economy during seventeenth and eighteenth century America was exemplified by the family farm or the small artisan shop, which "helped promote fathers' influence over their children," according to Griswold. Fathers worked in close proximity to their children and presided over all aspects of the child's preparation for life. This economic system began to erode in the late eighteenth and early nineteenth centuries, and was steadily replaced with a factory-dominated culture. Growing numbers of urban and even small town residents found, according to Griswold, that "the bond once uniting men with their children had been broken."[9]

Whereas nurturing and breadwinning roles were previously combined on the farm, changing economics compartmentalized life to the detriment of involved fathering. The story of fatherhood since the industrial revolution until the present has been an enfeebled tale of a one-dimensional male, reduced to little more than breadwinner and an end-of-the day disciplinarian.

Providing materially for one's family is an essential and honorable role, but its emergence as the primary male contribution to family life had the effect of crowding out other important contributions fathers had to offer. Much of the current tendency to view the father as the source of child support payments emanates directly out of this view of the father as the fountain of financial provision and little else.

With this social transformation, the paternal functions previously carried out by fathers were increasingly absorbed, first by a maternal culture of the home, and then even by the state as the twentieth century progressively expanded the social benefits available to women and children. In many ways the logic of the welfare state took root in the myth that fathers possess no meaningful moral or psychological content of value to children, but rather serve a utilitarian function as income-producers, a function which can easily and efficiently be replaced by check-writing bureaucracies.

Beginning in the post-World War II period, the breadwinning function became glorified as the preeminent form of male achievement. By mid-century, the ideal father was the company man who prized hard work and loyalty to his employer. Postwar prosperity only fueled the drive by fathers to bring home the bacon—more and more of it. The cultural script portrayed images of happy times with dad securely employed returning to a house busy with full-time mother and children.

Fatherhood became synonymous with the quest for family financial security. Men worked hard, saved more than any generation before or since, and heaped conveniences on their families thought unimaginable by previous generations as rapidly as the emerging mass consumer culture made them available.

A period of stability and continuity followed the time marred by war and depression. Things were perceived to work to most everyone's advantage. Not surprisingly, these hard-fought social conditions produced a strong tendency toward conformity to social rules. For fathers, this meant a certain emotional detachment from the children combined with a parenting role that frequently did not extend beyond discipline. Some argue that this concept of the father—the rule-driven, emotionally flat, and authoritarian male—symbolized what the most rebellious generation in history turned against.

If severe role differentiation had relegated fathers to the margins of childrearing, it had similarly confined women exclusively to the world of children, partitioned off from achievements in higher education and the rewards of professional contributions. Much of the advice on parenting by now assumed that men's lives existed outside of the home and further "assumed that mothers were the primary child rearers and that to fulfill this responsibility they needed knowledge of hygiene, nutrition, child development, and the like."[10]

Rarely in history had a division of labor become so strictly gender-based, both in the home and the workplace. These vast economic changes with their severe role differentiation had fairly dramatic effects on women and men alike. For working-class fathers, the pressures and problems that accompanied the breadwinning role, such as unemployment, low wages, or occasional disruption through depression, only further marginalized the male as a source of paternal nurturance. His primary contribution, and in turn his source of identity and self-worth, was now tied to the vicissitudes of the market. Suddenly, in the late twentieth century the tables turned as the American economy entered its next great transition, this time out of the industrial revolution which favored men and into a technology-driven economy that increasingly favored women.

It would take a decades-long women's movement to broaden the contribution of women beyond childrearing, combined with a reassessment by baby boom men, weary of materialism and shallow definitions of success, to bring greater flexibility to roles.

Cultural Shifts

The changes in family life wrought by shifting economic trends were soon reinforced by the culture. Trends far more destructive to fatherhood and family than economic restructuring would take root in the 1960s, manifesting themselves first in an explosion in the rate of divorce, followed by a steep rise in out-of-wedlock birth rates. Industrialization merely separated the father from his children for days or weeks at a time. These more recent trends removed fathers completely and permanently from their children in the vast majority of instances.

These social phenomena, however, were rooted in far deeper changes that were affecting the moral attitudes and beliefs of individual Americans. A society awash in consumerism was bound to extend the ethic of personal choice ever more deeply into human relationships such as marriage and kin.

The family was buffeted by urbanization, materialism, individualism, the sexual revolution, and a host of forces that promoted the self at the expense of the family. The ethic of self-sacrifice steadily yielded to a new cultural ethos that celebrated emotional release, greater personal freedoms, and the relaxation of social standards generally.

Daniel Yankelovich, a prominent national pollster who has studied subtle changes in American attitudes about moral values, finds important and consequential shifts in such norms as duty, obligation, and willingness to sacrifice. "Throughout most of this century," he says, "Americans believed that self-denial made sense, sacrificing made sense, obeying the rules made sense, subordinating the self to the institution made sense. But doubts have now set in, and Americans now believe that the old giving/getting compact needlessly restricts the individual."[11]

Most of the destructive developments in the culture have their roots in subtle shifts in the way we view the individual self and his or her obligations to others. The American society has always been strongly oriented toward individualism, which in its gentler and moderate forms has supplied the nation with great strength in the form of an ethic of self-help and entrepreneurial drive. The individualism of today, however, is widely regarded as far more extreme: self-absorbed and too frequently indifferent to sacrifice for the good of the group, whether the larger society or even the more intimate unit of the family. Yesterday's individualism was grounded in and guided by moral principle; today's is tied to a radical vision of human autonomy, severed from moral norms and social obligations.

This radical vision of human autonomy operates largely outside Western Judeo-Christian tradition, and is perhaps the most powerful challenge to it. An individualism in which a person is autonomous and encouraged to act on his own preferences, tastes, and passions, is one that is deeply hostile to the family.

As University of Chicago professor Don Browning tells it, Christianity took men and husbands and "humbled and modeled them after the sacrifice of Christ."[12] It was this self-subordinating servant mentality that distinguished the Christian male from the more egoistic patterns of the surrounding Greco-Roman world. The Christian ethic moves people in the direction of love as mutuality or equal regard, according to Browning. One is not neglectful of oneself, but neither is one preoccupied with self. A person "respects the selfhood, the dignity, of the other" and works to advance the welfare of others.[13]

The Christian Scriptures are filled with warnings against narrow self-interest. The apostle Paul admonished the believers of his day to "do nothing out of selfish ambition or vain conceit, but in humility consider others better than yourself." He did not encourage love of others to the neglect of one's own needs, but he did stress that each should "look not only to your own interests but also to the interests of others" (Philippians 2:3-4). The picture that emerges is of an individualism tempered by Christian morality and the ethic of love and service.

The apostle Paul warns of a rampant self-love that could describe conditions in American today, in which this ethic of mutual regard is thrown on its head. He spoke of "terrible times" to come in which people become "lovers of themselves . . . . lacking self-control . . . . not lovers of the good

.... conceited" (2 Timothy 3:2-4). Essentially, Paul is describing the rise of an autonomous, self-absorbed individualism.

Numerous movements in the popular culture arose over the past quarter century, including entitlement, victimhood, and self-esteem ideologies that viewed the person, not as a unique blessing of God with inherent worth and dignity, but as a little divinity, a virtual godlet. Misguided notions of the self create narcissistic self-love, which breeds anger and bitterness at the slightest provocation, and produces men without chests as C. S. Lewis put it, incapable of heroic virtue on behalf of others.

Many other cultural influences emerged and contributed to the pressures on families and fatherhood. For example, the settled life of caring for children while men made their mark at the factory and office struck more and more women as intolerable. Children became increasingly more immersed in their own nascent youth culture, the divorce revolution gained momentum, and the general fracturing of society all contributed to weakened family bonds.

The Rise of a Fatherhood Movement

Today, American society is drowning under the flood of social consequences of these economic and moral trends that have combined to separate fathers from childrearing. Fortunately, numerous positive signs that did not exist five years ago point to possibilities for the restoration of fatherhood. "Father hunger" has arisen out of our social convulsions. Father hunger can be heard in the violent and misogynous lyrics of rap musicians, gang members, and prison inmates. It can also increasingly be seen in the images of quiet despair and alienation among children who live in small rural hamlets and golf-course-lined suburbs.

This hunger is now acknowledged and verbalized through popular movements such as Promise Keepers, the National Fatherhood Initiative, and hundreds of local projects and programs, which are increasingly showing potential for restoring fatherhood.

The national media have suddenly discovered fatherhood; policy makers are stepping forward to promote its renewal; and there appears to be a genuine cultural shift under way in television, film, and corporate advertising that, once again, points to the importance of fathers.

Religious denominations and places of worship, which one would assume should play a central role in this process of renewal, have been surprisingly slow in responding. The movement to renew fatherhood started largely outside of the church. By contrast, the most dynamic social movements in the past were born in the churches and were carried along by religiously grounded civic associations. Similarly many periods of social renewal focused on family fragmentation and the need to recover responsible parenting. The Promise Keepers movement and the more secular fatherhood movement represented by the National Fatherhood Initiative seem to operate in that tradition.

Many in the church have responded to political appeals based vaguely on campaigns to strengthen the family through policy reforms. Yet it is doubtful that changes in governmental statutes will do much to prompt more people to marry or to turn the hearts of fathers toward their children. Throughout American history, the most promising social change has not come from the political sector but rather through social movements aimed at restoring individual responsibility and restraint, strengthening families, and renewing the parents.

The nineteenth century, for example, witnessed an explosion of voluntary associations and organizations aimed at social reform and moral uplift. Spiritual awakenings and temperance movements were dynamic movements that transcended politics and assumed that the greatest need was to change people's moral beliefs, personal attitudes, and individual behaviors. This was the work of society, and it provided a special place for churches and faith-based civic initiatives.

Leading social scientist James Q. Wilson, who has tracked social reforms in history, has said, "The institutions that have produced effective male socialization have been private, not public." Accordingly, says Wilson, our policy ought to identify, evaluate, and encourage those local private efforts that seem to do the best job at "inducing people to marry and persuading parents, especially fathers, to take responsibility for their children."[14]

In the past churches led and society followed. Today society is trying to lead and churches are dragging their feet. Perhaps this is so because churches lack guidance and information.

The Need for This Book

No systematic instructional guides exist for religious institutions to assist in charting this new course of action. Self-help literature and books that speak directly to individual fathers continue to proliferate, but they exist in isolation from the religious institutions in which fathers gather to receive moral and religious instruction. The market is flooded with fathering books to equip individual dads to navigate their way through every imaginable circumstances and stage of life.

This book, by contrast, encourages and equips churches, denominations, and religious social agencies to recover and institutionally pass on their own heritage of positive, effective fathering. If local congregations are going to play a key role in socializing a new generation of committed, effective fathers rather than deferring to popular movements, which come along periodically and fill stadiums, every church and denomination needs this book.

Secular society is beginning to acknowledge that churches, synagogues, and faith-based agencies are in a position to bring about renewal that no other institutional players are capable of producing. Such groups are being called upon like never before to care for the poor, mentor youth, and do the work of renewal in the communities of America, especially reaching, training, and encouraging fathers.

By wide acknowledgment, religious denominations and places of worship once strongly shaped male attitudes about their responsibilities for the nurture, moral discipline, and spiritual development of children. Also widely recognized is the fact that religious institutions have drifted away from this role, often leaving parishioners lost in a sea of confusion over gender roles, parenting responsibilities, and family life generally. The challenge today is for the faith community to recover the heritage of fathering. We must return to strengthening fatherhood, whether through theological instruction, rites of passage, celebrations, stories, marriage and family preparation, or mentoring and community outreach.

Part two of this book examines what denominations are presently doing to recover the heritage of marriage and fathering. Part three addresses the wider social context and public debate that so powerfully shape the church. Approaches to renewing fatherhood in places of worship cannot be separated from the political and social currents that mold the attitudes and decisions of parishioners. The faith community must not refrain from participating in an increasingly dynamic and promising debate outside the church over fathers and family life. Those issues include strengthening marriage in our communities, dealing with changing gender attitudes and responsibilities, finding common ground around models of marriage, and building social movements to renew men, marriage, and fatherhood.

This is not a theological text on fatherhood. I am neither a trained theologian nor an ordained minister, and that is generally true of the book's contributors. The theological fine print will be left to individual churches and denominations. The purpose of this book is to motivate and equip religious institutions—from whole denominations to religious social agencies and family ministries to local congregations—to recover their earlier role of preparing young men for committed and responsible fatherhood. The book draws from many, though certainly not all, of the major Judeo-Christian traditions operating in America. It addresses the historical as well as practical aspects of supporting fatherhood and how the ideal of fathering should be carried forward both in the faith community and through local religious bodies, to the wider society.

Naturally, the issue of fatherhood is wrapped up in an assortment of other important topics involving men, such as gender roles, changing approaches to leadership, and a host of theological questions having to do with God's purposes for men and women. These issues will not be directly confronted, as important as they are. Each would require a separate volume. The focus of this book is not the role of men, per se, in church or society but rather the importance of men as fathers. The focus is on men as they stand in a long tradition of fathering, or more correctly a tradition that has come under enormous strain and in some locations in America almost disappeared.

The circumstances—cultural and economic—under which fatherhood takes place have changed dramatically. But what has never changed, and is unchanging, is the need of children to be raised by responsible fathers, to know their fathers. We have seen vast changes in society, economic conditions, the rise of divorce, all of which have affected the relationship of fathers to their children. But the needs of children have not changed one iota. Children need fathers, and the faith community can play a critical role in bringing that about.

Notes

1. John Miller, *Biblical Faith and Fathering: Why We Call God Father* (New York: Paulist Press, 1989), 2.

2. Wade Horn, *Father Facts*, second edition (Gaithersburg, Md.: National Fatherhood Initiative), 4.

3. Horn, *Father Facts*.

4. For further analysis of the cultural scripting of fatherhood, see David Blankenhorn, *Fatherless America: Confronting Our Most Urgent Social Problem* (New York: Basic Books, 1995), 65-185.

5. David Blankenhorn, "Fatherless Society," *Quadrant Magazine*, December 1997, 9.

6. Ken Canfield, *The Heart of a Father* (Chicago: Northfield Publishing, 1996), 11.

7. Gordon Dalbey, *Father and Son: The Wound, the Healing, the Call to Manhood* (Nashville: Thomas Nelson, 1992), xii.

8. Robert L. Griswold, *Fatherhood in America* (New York: Basic Books, 1993), 13.

9. Griswold, *Fatherhood in America*.

10. Griswold, *Fatherhood in America*, 33.

11. Quoted in Alan Wolfe, *One Nation After All* (New York: Viking, 1998), 282.

12. Don S. Browning et al., eds., *From Culture Wars to Common Ground: Religion and the American Family Debate* (Louisville: Westminster John Knox Press), 132.

13. Browning, *Culture Wars*, 153.

14. James Q. Wilson, "Culture, Incentives and the Underclass," in *Values and Public Policy* (Washington, D.C.: Brookings Institution, 1994), 74.

Chapter 2

Making Great Men and Fathers

Don E. Eberly

Like never before, the state of men is emerging in the public debate in America as a leading concern. Large numbers of men, quite obviously, are in trouble, and they are in trouble because the institution of fatherhood, the means by which morally and spiritually mature masculinity is transmitted, has fallen into misuse or dysfunction. The demise of strong fathering has led to many maladies of contemporary masculinity because men lack a model of what constitutes a real man.

The journey to mature manhood is a spiritual one that requires an understanding of true masculinity. Most men, despite their behavior, long for personal significance and direction, and they desire to be connected to their offspring. Churches stand in a unique position to capitalize on those desires and to orient men toward the source of true manhood.

The Search for Masculine Mending

When the subject of men comes up, some wonder what is so unique about men that they deserve this sudden attention. Haven't we as a society already focused far too much on separate categories of the human race, whether ethnic, gender, or religious, instead of focusing on the far more important business of strengthening the social units of family, the church, or the community as a whole?

The short answer to that is yes; we have focused on parts to the exclusion of, and even detriment of, the whole. In one sense, there is nothing particularly unique about the condition of men. All members of the human race have suffered since man's fall from grace in the garden. But in another sense, if the male was specially created by divine design to be unique, then it only follows that the male is uniquely broken in his natural fallen state, and that this brokenness has unique social consequences that must be taken into account.

If God gave us gender-specific qualities for the proper harmonizing of parenting and family life, it follows that fathers have unique gender-specific struggles in their role as parents. Certainly roles stretch as social conditions change. But from brain research to best-selling books like *Men Are from Mars, Women Are from Venus*, modern inquiry is only proving what we already know from God's creation: Men and women were made remarkably, splendidly different. These differences are again being widely acknowledged and affirmed, as a growing number of voices call for gender harmony and complementarity.

God made us wonderfully male and magnificently female. Modern science, whether social research into the developmental differences of boys and girls, or brain research that maps the contours of gender differences, has produced indisputable evidence of what might have been considered obvious all along. While men and women are equal in God's eyes, and should be just as equal in our own, God is not into androgyny; it was never a part of his creation, and no amount of social engineering will change it. God is undoubtedly displeased by our discontent with his design and our striving to radically alter it.

Men and women fell from a state of perfect harmony with God in all of their gender uniqueness and thus must be restored and made new as well in all their gender distinctions. Much is peculiarly ugly about the male outside of fellowship with God—so much potential for hurt and for destruction. Similarly, there is much that is peculiarly beautiful about the male who has been restored by faith and is increasingly being conformed to the image of the Heavenly Father. In short, the condition of fathers and fathering has as powerful an influence as any other factor in shaping social well-being.

Equal numbers of dysfunctional women and men may exist, but the consequences of male dysfunctionality can be terrifyingly different. Most mature men feel a painful embarrassment in representing the male gender before their wives, daughters, and female associates when they reflect on the full scope of disorder, heartache, and pain that is directly attributable to psychologically and spiritually wounded men. How much less scarred human affairs would be—less violence, abuse, gross injustice, and war there would be—if it were not for an out-of-control and chaotic masculinity?

The Male Problematic

The state of men has become the topic of popular debate. In a *Time* cover story entitled "Are men really this bad?" the magazine chose to depict what it considered the average male with a picture of a well-suited, prosperous middle-class white male with a dirty-snouted pig's head. The essence of the story was that men are hopelessly boorish—that men are basically swine. The story suggested that now that the cold war was over perhaps it was time for the media pick up the "men are awful" motif, implying that world conflict itself is mostly rooted in out-of-control men.

The writer, Lance Morrow, declares that "any honest male admits, in the privacy of his heart, that he considers men to be pretty awful sometimes." He admits that he has known guys "that were so rotten that . . . well, women don't know the half of it." If he were a woman, he states, he would be disgusted by "men's preoccupation with sex, which makes them alternately clumsy and dangerous; by their selfishness and egotism, by their bullying and insecurity; and above all by their potential for violence."[1]

With the inevitable and understandable movement of women's concerns to the front burner of society's agenda over the past several decades, attention to the development of boys and men simply fell off society's menu. The problem is, societies have never had to make a special effort to steer girls and women away from crime and violence, abandonment or neglect of their children, or generally acting out against the social order.

Many of these same concerns, however, do present themselves in bold relief in the raising of sons, and societies have been forced to confront them from the beginning of time. This difficulty that civilizations have consistently had in socializing males is often referred to in shorthand as the "male problematic."

The tendency on the American scene in confronting masculinity has been to ignore it or negate it, not to confront it. We have so emasculated contemporary masculinity that the dictionary doesn't even describe its function or content. It merely defines masculinity as "having qualities that are appropriate to a male." But it doesn't say what those qualities are. The social and emotional damage, not to mention the monetary costs, of wounded masculinity can hardly be tabulated.

Finally, after decades of neglect, society is turning its attention to the plight of boys. In a five-part series published in the *Washington Post*, staff writer Megan Rosenfeld describes the trouble that boys are in:

The case begins with numbers. Boy babies die in greater numbers in infancy, and are more fragile as babies than girls. Boys are far more likely than girls to be told they have learning disabilities, to be sent to the principal's office, to be given medication for hyperactivity or attention deficit disorder, to be suspended from high school, to commit crimes, to be diagnosed as schizophrenic or autistic. In adolescence, they kill themselves five times more often than girls do.[2]

Rosenfeld goes on to describe the tremendous neglect that has occurred toward boys and the confusion that prevails over how best to help them develop emotionally and socially in a world that isn't sure what it wants to expect of boys and men.

The picture, not surprisingly, does not improve for older males. Men account for two-thirds of all alcoholics, 90 percent of all arrests for alcohol and drug abuse, 80 percent of the country's homeless population, 60 percent of high school dropouts. The suicide rate is four times that of women. Men are responsible for the vast majority of gangs, antisocial behavior, violent crimes, rape, and physical abuse of children.

Just as remarkable is the positive difference men can make as fathers to the well-being of children. If the picture of dysfunctional masculinity is ugly, the picture of mature masculinity is beautiful. There are few things more magnificent than a mature man, rich in character and self-control, secure in his masculinity, confident in his fathering, and able to lead and serve with compassion and tender-heartedness. Such a man makes a huge difference in his world.

Much has been done to bring about equity in society among men and women, most of which has been welcomed by most people. But there is a role that remains man's alone. A man's power, for good or ill, will never be reduced in that place, and that is his role as father. So long as children are brought into the world—whether to loving two-parent households, through the accident of teen pregnancy, or by way of a test tube for a "single parent by choice" mother—children will have origins in a biological male, and they will have a deep, almost unspeakable need for his love and affirmation.

Every child carries the full biological and social contribution (or lack thereof) of his father, and each child bears a powerful longing to have an intimate relationship with the father—to know him and where he came from, to be with him and experience all that he represents in his manhood, to either live and walk in his heritage or to reject it, but at least to experience the father as a living reality. Whether absent or present, whether good or bad, there is such a thing as the father factor in every child's life. This will never change.

Sadly, while there are many examples in today's world of outstanding fathering, the largest percentage of children in history are being raised apart from their fathers. Father absence is by far the most socially consequential problem of our time. It contributes directly and powerfully to every negative outcome among children today in American society. Over the past decade, a voluminous body of data has documented the ill effects of growing up without a father.

Several caveats are appropriate here. First, children who are raised in mother-only households are not bound by some immutable law to fail in school, turn to drugs, or commit crime. Kids from father-absent households can and do become merit scholars, all-star athletes, and professional successes, and even if they don't excel, many turn out well enough. Good single mothers and good nonresidential fathers can make a huge difference.

That said, few would deny that children are who they are by virtue of the quality and strength of their family life. When we look at the children and youth around us, we typically evaluate them on the basis of whether they came from good families. When we say good families, what are we talking about? In some cases, we are referring to whether the parents possess character or competence. But in other instances, we are talking about whether or not the family has a father present.

Society must affirm the important contribution that single parents make every day under trying circumstances, but without denying the basic evidence confirming that a host of bad outcomes for kids are strongly tied to the presence or absence of fathers.

The second caveat is that the news about fathers is not all bad. Recently, a Gallup Poll (see chapter 3) evaluated the state of fathering, not by interviewing a team of experts, but by gathering views from those for whom parental performance matters most—kids. As judged by America's kids, a large majority of American dads are getting pretty good grades. Seventy-one percent of children believe their dads are doing as well or better than a generation ago, especially in light of the widely held view that fathering is harder today than a generation ago (a view held by 63 percent of kids, not to mention most fathers themselves). Remarkably, 70 percent of kids report being "extremely close" or "very close" to their fathers. In a society where everyone seems to be running short on time, 82 percent of kids report having had conversations with their dads over the past week.[3]

But once again, even the good news must be understood in light of distressing trends. Even though there are a lot of good, even great dads today—perhaps more than ever—the story of fathering in America is increasingly a story of the fathering "haves" and "have nots." For those kids whose fathers live in the home and are actively engaged, fathering may be better than ever. By contrast, those who lack strong fathers or are growing up entirely fatherless, the picture is probably bleaker than at any time in American history. According to the Gallup Poll, only 63 percent live with their biological father, with only a fourth of those in fatherless households reporting having regular contact with their fathers.

The results for all too many kids in this category could not be more unfortunate, for them as well as society.

Poverty

No factor is more powerful or disturbing than the undeniable tie of father absence to poverty. A father-absent society is a society in which growing numbers of children are poor. Poverty has many root causes, but none so decisive or powerful as father absence.

Tragically, fatherless children are five times more likely to be poor, with all of the stark disadvantages that come with that status. It is worth considering just how much better shape our children would be in if we had prevented the trend toward fatherlessness. Child poverty rates today would be one-third lower if family structure had not changed so dramatically since 1960. According to the National Commission on Children, almost 75 percent of America's children who live in single parent families will experience poverty before turning 11 years of age, whereas the vast majority of kids from father-present families will never experience poverty.[4]

Much of the difference in poverty rates between black and white households is explained by family structure. Conversely, the family income of black two-parent households is almost three times the family income of white single-parent families.

Social Disorder and Crime

Fatherlessness contributes to crime. American society is paying a huge price for failing to heed the warning by Daniel Patrick Moynihan in 1965: "A community that allows a large number of young men to grow up in broken homes, dominated by women, never acquiring any stable relationship to male authority, never acquiring any rational expectation about the future—that community asks for and gets chaos."[5]

Male acting out against the social order is widespread and comes in numerous forms, from behavior that is merely obnoxious to that which is socially menacing. Evidence of its impact can be found among numerous categories, from criminals to rich athletes and world-famous entertainment celebrities.

Consider the case of Dennis Rodman, the profane and outrageous

Chicago Bulls basketball player. Rodman attributes his rather perverse performance as a sports celebrity to the example of his father. He hasn't seen his father, who now lives overseas, in 30 years. Rodman Sr. has fathered 27 children by various women and reports to be "shooting for 30."[6]

Or consider the case of Howard Stern, the "shock jock" radio host who looks for new ways to titillate and offend each day, usually through degrading sexual references to women. Stern talked about his father in an interview with *Rolling Stone* magazine: "The way I was raised my father was always telling me I was a piece of (expletive), I think I'll go to my grave not feeling very positive about myself or that I am very, very special."[7]

Bill Stephne, who runs an entertainment company in New York and tracks trends and issues within the music industry, reports that the vast majority of gang members and misogynous violent rappers live in violence and rage because of missing fathers. In fact, the theme of anger toward the father they never knew is emerging as a major new trend in rap music. In the rap song "Father," LL Cool J sings, "All I ever wanted, all I ever needed, was a father." LL Cool J told a *Newsweek* reporter that he went to see his kids, and his son asked, "Daddy, are you going to marry Mommy?" He added: "That was deep to listen to. That told me he was yearning for a family unity and how important it was."[8]

The most socially destructive form of aggressive acting out which is tied to father absence is crime. Although the serious crime rate has stabilized recently, many social experts predict a dramatic rise in adolescent crime committed by unfathered young males. Seventy-two percent of adolescents serving sentences for murder are from fatherless households. Juvenile detention centers are filled with males who lacked the firm guidance and caring example of a devoted dad. Sixty-two percent of convicted rapists are from fatherless homes.[9]

Michael Singletary, who serves on the advisory board of the National Fatherhood Initiative, has spoken frequently in prisons and reports that when he asks audiences of inmates how many of them had caring, involved fathers, he rarely if ever sees a hand raised.

Unfathered males are the overwhelming source of society's grief and heartache. Recent studies indicate that the chief predictor of crime in a neighborhood is not poverty or race, but the proportion of households in which fathers are missing. When one takes the presence or absence of fathers into account, the relationship of crime to income as well as to race disappears.[10]

Sexual Misconduct

Fatherlessness is also a factor in the sexual misconduct of young women and young men. The tendency in focusing on the male problematic is to neglect the serious consequences of father absence in the lives of girls and young women. As any experienced father knows, one of the most vulnerable persons in the world is the adolescent girl. With compassionate attention, involved fathers can guide girls to maturity. They can provide an understanding of the dangers of having the wrong kind of contact with males, especially older males.

Poorly fathered girls, by contrast, often fall victim to poorly fathered young men who prey on the vulnerabilities of girls who carry within them a hunger for the father's affection and who confuse it with false and costly alternatives. Girls turn to older men in search of the fatherly affection they never received.

Many persons wrongly think the problem of teen sex among girls is, strictly speaking, a teen problem of raging hormones mixed with ignorance. But here again, father hunger plays a part. Fatherlessness leads frequently to premature sexual involvement by girls. Girls of father-absent households are 164 percent more likely to have children out of wedlock, often starting in their teens.

A recent example of father-hunger-related sexual misconduct is the sad and sordid case of 20-year-old Nushawn Williams, a shiftless HIV-infected drug dealer who succeeded in seducing dozens of adolescent girls, infecting many of them with the deadly AIDS virus. He managed all of this because, as one girl put it, Williams resembled a father and treated her like a princess.

Poorly fathered males are also the leading source of domestic abuse. Nothing casts a darker shadow over men generally than the fact that they abuse millions of American women and children every year. But it is a mistake to permit this hideous social problem to create the impression that men are generally a problem. They are not. It is a particular kind of male and particular circumstances that produce domestic violence. The least likely person to abuse anyone is the married husband and biological father. The most likely source of abuse is the cohabiting male—live-in boyfriends and male acquaintances.

Only 3.2 percent of the boys and girls who were raised by both biological parents had a history of maltreatment, compared to upwards of 20 percent of children in other family situations. No community in America, large or small, has been spared frequent news reports of grisly violence and death at the hands of live-in boyfriends and other unattached males.[11]

The Social Costs of Chaos

If fatherlessness is at the root of social chaos, it follows that it is overwhelmingly the source of our nation's social costs. Untold billions are spent each year providing for the direct and indirect consequences of fatherlessness. Whether it is the federal government, states, or cities or dozens of welfare programs, hundreds of categorical programs for children and youth, child support enforcement, and family courts, it is father absence that lies at the root of spiraling expenditures. Many of these costs would be seriously reduced if a solution were found for missing or incompetent fathers.

Recently, the National Fatherhood Initiative formed a partnership with a bipartisan Congressional Task Force on Fatherhood Promotion to elevate the nation's awareness of fathers and of their importance. At one Capitol Hill event featuring boxing superstar, Evander Holyfield, the task force leaders and I visited with then Speaker of the House Newt Gingrich. The Speaker at the time was considering competing plans for a balanced budget. I asked him if he had considered how much easier the job might be if decades ago we had slowed or reversed the increasing trend toward fatherlessness. Fifty-three percent of the cost of AFDC, Medicaid, and food stamp programs are attributed to fatherless households begun by teens.[12]

Through a similar task force involving states, the National Fatherhood Initiative was invited to participate in a conversation involving over a dozen governors. Each attributed his own success in public life to a strong father. One governor was the product of a divorce, but his father remained deeply, passionately committed to him. The meeting turned especially somber when one governor after another reflected on the costs, socially and financially, of father absence. One asked his colleagues to imagine the excess funding they would all have if they didn't need to spend 15-20 percent more each year on prison construction.

America is living with the aftermath of a massive social experiment that, among other things, ignored everything we know about men from just about every chapter of history. James Q. Wilson, the noted social scientist, has said: "Every society must be wary of the unattached male, for he is universally the cause of numerous social ills. The good society is heavily dependent on men being attached to a strong moral order centered on families, both to discipline their sexual behavior and to reduce their competitive aggression."[13]

Curbing the aggressive impulses of young males is perhaps the greatest challenge that falls to fathers. As the national news regularly reports, there is today in American society an unusually large number of young people who are very, very angry and volatile, who appear wound up like tightly coiled springs waiting to explode at the slightest provocation. They seem perpetually agitated and are quick to see even the most everyday forms of human conflict as a sign that they have been "dissed."

The nation has been served a stream of shocking reports of brutal school-yard shootings by young males. In defiance of stereotypes, all of the shootings have occurred in small, rural communities, by young white males from average, middle-class backgrounds. Shawn Johnson, a California-based forensic psychologist who has conducted over 6,000 evaluations of adult and juvenile criminals states: "This is the price we are paying as a society for the number of fathers who have bailed out on their children." He adds that the extent to which fathers have abandoned socializing young males "is just mind-boggling."[14]

Obviously, only a small minority of troubled kids will turn to slaughtering others in cold blood. Nevertheless, the alienation among youth and even young children today is widespread. Never before have children been so far removed from the things that give life a sense of direction, meaning, and purpose. Where do we get these things? Through connection to one's heritage, place, and people. In no case is this alienation deeper than in the fraying of family bonds, and the separation of children from their fathers.

The Spiritual Journey Toward Mature Fatherhood

When masculinity lacks positive form and substance, men are adrift. Every period of renewal in history has focused on the pressing spiritual needs and social conditions of that period. The greatest challenge today is to piece together the scattered strands of broken masculinity.

The journey toward true masculinity requires that we ignore the various models of manhood that are frequently offered. We must journey farther upstream to the true headwaters of masculinity, says author Stu Weber, "to the true taproot of masculine health," to the God who designed man.

On this journey back to our roots that Weber describes, we trudge through the shallow murky waters of contemporary men's movements of the 1980s and 1990s with its drum beating self-absorption, up through the turbulent rapids of the sexual revolution in the 1960s and 1970s with man sexually liberated and uncommitted, well past the tributary of pseudo-masculinity of the flint-faced, gun-toting stoic of John Wayne and Sylvester Stallone, back farther past the calm and tempting but still polluted waters of the 1950s where men had authority but were emotionally frozen, continuing farther upstream until we get to the headwaters of God-centered masculinity.[15]

Here, we find the man as he was meant to be, mirroring the true character of God. Here we find the paternal male who generates, not destroys life—the benevolent provider and defender, not the aggressor or predator. Here we discover the man who finds his strength and purpose as a father and friend, a protector and provider, and mentor and a moral example. Here we find the husband who builds up, nourishes, and honors his marriage partner.

Anthropologists have found throughout the world that almost every culture has placed a great emphasis on properly raising young males. The exceptions are in Western secular and industrial societies, especially the United States. And this unfortunately became true of the church as well. There was a time prior to the turn of the nineteenth century when the nurturing role of men was thought to be supremely important.

What are we offering our young today? Do young men get the clear sense that they are under masculine apprenticeship? Do they know they are on a path toward joining the company of men—men who are comfortable in fellowship with each other, who know each other and are accountable to one another, men grounded in the tradition of confident fathering, men who are partners in passing on the spiritual heritage of healthy, responsible masculinity?

Our sons need to see examples of the confident male turning his energies toward affirming life and nourishing character, not the pseudo-masculinity of power and self-advancement. Our daughters need our attention no less than our sons, but it is our sons who are on their way to becoming men and fathers, a passage that can only be navigated by fathers and other mature males.

Those who have studied masculinity frequently remark about its fragility. David Gilmore, who has studied how boys become fathers in various cultures, says that in most cultures, to be a man, "one must impregnate women, protect dependents from danger, and provide for kith and kin. . . . Manhood is a kind of male procreation; its heroic quality lies in its self-direction and discipline."[16]

Even in this portrait one senses opportunity and danger, contradiction and ambivalence. The physical strength that makes man a protector can also turn him into an aggressor and predator. The impulse toward self-discipline and leadership can easily degenerate into a hunger for domination and control.

It is all too easy for masculinity, which is held together tenuously by societal norms and functioning institutions, to fall out of kilter, especially when few fathers are there to model it in all of its complexities of strength and tenderness, initiative and restraint. When these supports are not in place, society suffers not from too much genuine masculinity but from far too little of it. A society of too few mature fathers ends up with what Dr. Frank Pittman calls "toxic masculinity," where essentially weak, insecure, and poorly fathered men chase after a socially destructive masculine mystique. This mystique robs men of the capacity to be close to their fathers and denies them the freedom to talk about masculinity and its roots. It instead glorifies masculinity and subjects men to "impossibly unachievable myths of masculine heroics."[17]

Men who have not fully felt the love and approval of their fathers are men who live in masculine shame. "Men without models don't know what is behind their shame, loneliness, and despair, their desperate search for love, for affirmation, and for structure, their frantic tendency to compete over just about anything with just about anybody," says Dr. Pittman. "Even if they do know that the pain is caused by the missing father, they don't know what they can do to ease the pain."[18]

Men without a strong fathering heritage grow up faking masculinity and acting out a form of "pathologically exaggerated masculinity." Boys who want to become men have to "guess at what men are like" which usually turns out to be a hypermasculine display of machismo that pursues macho things like women, wealth, toys, or fame. Most men spend their lives trying to be what they think a man is supposed to be, only making "a tolerable approximation of masculinity."[19]

In reality, the passion is not for these things, as much as it is a passionate search for true masculinity. These men are in a battle not with women, whether their mothers, wives, or girlfriends, as much as with their own fathers. The average philanderer is not really chasing women; he's chasing after the fatherly affirmation of a real dad. Whatever the challenge, men are never "man enough." And that is because they are "locked into a struggle to somehow finally get their fathers to anoint them, and declare them man enough."[20]

What is the way out of this trap of shrunken, shame-filled masculinity?

"Ultimately," says Pittman, "we're not going to raise a better class of men until we have a better class of fathers, fathers who don't run out on the job."[21] The answer, he says, is to rediscover "the forgotten profession of fatherhood."[22]

The Search for Spiritual Masculinity

Far more is involved in confronting the American problem of fatherlessness than delivering admonishments regarding its dangers and consequences. Churches and other religious gathering places must make real efforts to renew men, which will often involve specific programming and, in the case of fathering, assistance in skill-building. Many contributors to this volume offer suggestions for program initiatives.

What are the access points that places of worship and other religious agencies might consider as a means of reaching and renewing fathers? What exactly are men striving for today? How, in other words, can programs be developed to meet the needs and desires that are already there?

Connect Fathers to Children

Most fathers have powerful longings to be more deeply connected to their kids. God appears to be "turning the hearts of fathers to their children, and of children to their fathers." The sense of separation and loss described earlier is creating, in children and fathers alike, a passion to reconnect and grow deeper.

The term "father hunger" has entered the public conversation to describe this phenomenon. The so-called "X" and "millennial" generations show evidence of more commitment to mending the child-parent relationships than the baby boom generation, which recklessly abandoned them. For its part, the baby boom generation is reacting to its own excesses and neglect of family and is rediscovering the joys and rewards of family life.

Churches can channel these longings with programs designed to nurture healthy family relationships.

Guide Toward True Significance

Men long for a sense of personal meaning and significance in their professional as well as home arenas. They want their lives to count for something, so they work hard at being busy. But there is a danger in this. We live in a culture of action. Meaning and accomplishment are found in action, we believe, not in rest, reflection, or contemplation. Quietness is hard for men: The most common measurement of male character usually has something to do with productivity. And this can be healthy, of course. The suggestion here is not greater approval for unproductivity or sloth. But this obsession with productivity often translates into endless and pointless motion, and a quest for status and achievement in the places least likely to fulfill.

In truth, without the satisfaction of family life many men feel insignificant. They somehow know that most of what they have poured their energies into, except for their families, will be forgotten the moment their life is over. They verbalize these feelings with humor, saying, "No one will read your resume at your funeral" or "When was the last time you saw a hearse pulling a U-Haul?" Men, not merely women, sense that too much has been made of the male role as provider. They know it is a core responsibility, but it should not entirely define our lives.

Churches have the ultimate answer to our desire for significance: We are important to God; we matter to him. Men who believe they are significant to God can translate that inner strength and health to their children.

Blossom Individuals

Men want to live as *they* were meant to live. Most of us sense that the life God designed for us is unique, and we want to have the peace and satisfaction of knowing that we are in harmony with God's purposes. A man feels glad when his gifts and the world's needs intersect. He blossoms. The application of one's best strengths and gifts to improving family life meshes with the grand scheme. He becomes useful to the world and for posterity because his children, and their children, will live on after he's gone.

Churches can help men think through how to use their gifts for enriching the family experience. Men gathered together could challenge each other to develop life plans that set clear goals in the areas of social responsibility and family life.

Reduce Regrets

Men want to live without regrets. One of the worst things that can happen to a man is to wait too long to discover the rewards and joys of his own family—and end up living with, or dying with, regrets. Men all across America are scrambling to make up for lost time. Churches can help men examine and challenge each other to make sacrifices for their families before it's too late and can provide compassion and nurturance for those who already have pain and regret for failing to invest in their families.

Men struggle with their own mortality, feeling that life is rapidly ebbing away. Our culture, with its obsession with youth and physical vitality does not prepare us for aging, dying, or death. How sad it is to attend the funeral of a friend or relative in which there was serious unfinished family business. The surviving members are haunted by "if only" ghosts. Churches can guide men to turn the brevity of life into an opportunity to live life as God intended. Men can challenge each other on how to live, and for what to live, especially in reference to their spouse and children.

Bring Balance

Many men are not in control of their time or priorities, which usually means they're not in control of anything, including their homes. Life lacks harmony and balance, and what's worse, men feel powerless to do anything about it. They are out of control and overwhelmed.

Nothing is more paradoxical than the widespread sense today that we lack control over our schedules and our lives. The entire enterprise of modernity, which has been swallowed whole, was premised on the idea that mankind could gain greater control over life through knowledge, science, and technical advancements. But it hasn't worked out that way. We are now slaves to a culture of consumerism and technology. Worse, we are blind to our slavery.

We believe that by filling our lives with more conveniences we will be free to do the things that matter. But this hasn't panned out. Time saved is not transferred to the family, leisure, or the inner world of the soul. Research shows that the average household costs far more to supply and furnish today than during our parents' time—which almost always translates into an excuse for a second income—because of dozens of devices that are supposed to make life more comfortable and save time.

The problem is that greater busyness or increased work obligations immediately consume most time saved by costly technology. We eat fewer family meals together, we destroy our Sabbath rest by filling Sundays with youth soccer, and we open our malls all night to ensure sufficient time for shopping. The convenience of facsimile machines and e-mail tempt bosses to get a jump on the work week by giving telecommuters their "to do" lists on Sundays. Workers then feel obligated to interrupt family time to "look" at the message in case it really is urgent. The Internet calls investment professionals from sleep to keep abreast of markets half way around the world. So much for the saving power of technology and modern conveniences.

The things that would strengthen family and fathering most may have little to do directly with parenting and a lot to do with rejecting modern values. It is doubtful that life will be dramatically improved for fathers and families without living in conscious resistance to, or informed questioning of, much of secular culture.

The church could do a far better job in assisting men to examine and fight consumerism, to keep workplace demands from impinging on home life, and to resist the strong pull toward mindless amusement and sensual entertainment.

Consider, for example, the impact of television on spousal intimacy.

Wives frequently complain of the TV-watching habits of their husbands, and for good reason. One reason men become unhappy with the physical appearance of their wives is because of the daily reminder they get from television of how imperfect she is compared to a standard of perfection that exists only in the fantasies of Madison Avenue executives. Many of our grandfathers and most of our great-grandfathers spent their days working with mules, and the only woman they could fantasize about was their own wife.

The amount of time some men spend watching sports on TV is another impediment to intimacy and is what many wives consider a form of adultery. Frequently, men who freeze up when the subject turns to personal matters of faith, family, or relationships come alive when the conversation turns to sports. A wife concludes her husband's love of sports outshines his love for her. The atmosphere of the home becomes a breeding ground for discontent and faultfinding. And when discontent is full grown it gives birth to divorce.

Churches can teach men how to balance personal time with time for their wives, time for entertainment and sports with time for honest communication.

Teach Core Values

Finally, men are wrestling with a model for who men ought to be. What is the mark of a real man? Here the traditional Judeo-Christian values—patience, tender-heartedness, fidelity, truthfulness, and others—are invaluable. Stu Weber, who wrote about spiritually grounded masculinity in *Tender Warrior*, describes the real father as tough yet tender, strong yet sensitive, fierce yet friendly. The real man, he says, is open and authentic, ready for accountability, vulnerable and honest, seeking forgiveness, and finding power in humility.

The notion of power in humility is worth reflection. Humility may unlock the keys to the other virtues: to give, to forgive, to serve, and to honor. The true measure of the good man is the man who lives in humility before God.

A major cause of male aggression is pride—fear of losing control or looking bad. But the very time when one has lost control or looks bad is an occasion for God-centered masculinity to burst forth. The reason a man can't be tender with his wife, extend a long overdue compliment, or fulfill her emotional needs is often pride. Pride keeps him from being emotionally open with his children and seeking forgiveness for wrongs. Men's morbid fear of disclosure and accountability is rooted in pride.

The antidote to pride is a biblical view of man, full of garbage and glory.

The church can bring the true concept of manhood to men, and in the process bring hope to families.

Making Great Men and Fathers

Great men make great fathers. The basis of a superior man lies in the knowledge of God as his superior. A great father is one who looks to the example of his Heavenly Father and strives to translate that model to his relationship with his children. When men have a sense of meaning, direction, and purpose for their lives, they bless their families with a heritage of love that permeates everything, including society.

For the church not to be involved in such a mission and a ministry would be treason.

Notes

1. Lance Morrow, "Are Men Really That Bad," *Time*, 14 February 1994, 55.

2. Megan Rosenfeld, "Little Boys Blue: Reexamining the Plight of Young Males," *Washington Post*, 26 March 1998, A1.

3. George H. Gallup International Institute, *Youthviews* 5, no. 9 (May 1998).

4. Wade Horn, *Father Facts*, second edition (Gaithersburg, Md.: National Fatherhood Initiative), 52.

5. David Broder, "Beware of the Unattached Male," *Washington Post*, 16 February 1994.

6. "Perspectives," *Newsweek*, 9 September 1996, 25.

7. "Interview with Howard Stern," *Rolling Stone*, 10 February 1994, 28-53.

8. Veronica Chambers, "Family Rappers," *Newsweek*, 19 January 1998.

9. Horn, *Father Facts*, 32-33.

10. Horn, *Father Facts*, 32.

11. Horn, *Father Facts*, 43.

12. Horn, *Father Facts*, 18.

13. David Broder, "Beware of the Unattached Male," *Washington Post*, 16 February 1994.

14. Elizabeth Kastor, "When Kids Kill," The Washington Post, in *Lancaster (Pennsylvania) Sunday News*, 5 April 1996, P1.

15. Stu Weber, *Tender Warrior: God's Intention for Man* (Sisters, Ore.: Multnomah, 1993), 35-36.

16. Frank Pittman, *Man Enough: Fathers, Sons, and the Search for Masculinity* (New York: Berkley Publishing Group), xiv.

17. Pittman, *Man Enough*, xvii.

18. Pittman, *Man Enough*, xx.

19. Pittman, *Man Enough*, 4.
20. Pittman, *Man Enough*, 13.
21. Pittman, *Man Enough*, 25.
22. Pittman, *Man Enough*, xxi.

Chapter 3

What Americans Believe About Fatherhood and the Role of Religion

George Gallup Jr.

It is a sad irony that while most U.S. adults prize fatherhood and say they themselves have had a positive experience with their fathers, many youngsters in our nation today never experience the warmth of a father's embrace.

Yet, fortunately, the populace seems to recognize fully the importance of fatherhood to a healthy society. One survey shows that 79 percent of Americans say father absence is the nation's most significant problem. In addition, no fewer than 85 percent of Americans say that "the number of children being born to single parents" is either a critical or a serious problem, putting this problem at the top of the public's agenda for the future.

Seven in ten Americans, furthermore, believe a child needs a home with *both* a father and a mother to grow up happily, yet four in ten children are not so blessed. Wade Horn, president of the National Fatherhood Initiative writes: "Every child deserves the love, support, and nurturance of a legally and morally responsible father, because fathers are different from mothers in important ways and the father-child bond is important to the healthy development of children."

The key predictor of crime is not education or income, according to one objective study, but whether or not a child lives with his biological father. The public would concur: Eight in ten agree with the statement that "the absence of fathers in the homes of young people" is a critical or very important reason for crime in this country. (Other key problems named as causes were lack of moral training in the home, alcohol and drugs, lack of jobs for young people, lack of punishment, availability of guns, lack of role models, and influence of television.)

Fatherhood in Context of Family

It may be helpful to examine the status of fatherhood in the United States in the context of the family. Here we uncover some encouraging findings, based on a 1997 survey on "Family Values," conducted by The Gallup Organization for Edelman Communications on behalf of the Church of Jesus Christ of Latter-day Saints.

A large majority of Americans express happiness with their family life. Most likely to express a high level of happiness are adults who are married, have graduated from college, have children under age 18, and who say religion is "extremely important" in their lives.

Money and lack of family time top the list of American families' *concerns*, while health and financial security lead the list of *wishes* for their families.

The vast majority (89 percent) believe there is a link between how well families work in America and how well society functions. The family is viewed as extremely important in teaching values, educating children, and providing emotional support. In this connection, it is interesting to note that the *Journal of the American Medical Association* reported in the fall of 1997 that "teens with strong emotional connections to their parents are less likely to engage in early sex, experiment with drugs and alcohol, commit suicide or behave violently," as determined by a federal study titled the *National Longitudinal Study of Adolescent Health*, which surveyed 90,000 students from seventh through twelfth grades across the country.

A majority of persons in the survey for the Church of Jesus Christ of Latter-day Saints, describe their family as "extremely" or "very close." Yet a sizable minority (17 percent) characterize their own family as only "somewhat close." Four percent say "not close."

Even though time is paramount, families appear to be making time. Asked how many hours in a typical day they spend doing things together as a family, respondents with families say they spend an average of one hour together. Two-thirds of persons responding to the survey say they eat at least one meal together each day. Religion, outings, and eating meals are seen as activities that strengthen families. Half of those interviewed have an optimistic outlook for families, although a large majority believe America's moral direction is worse than when they were children.

Experience of Fatherhood Has Been Positive

A Gallup Poll revealed that adults with living fathers (about half of the adult population) are generally having a positive relationship: described as "easygoing" rather than "tense" (74 percent to 21 percent), "fun" rather than "boring" (72 percent to 18 percent), "warm and affectionate" rather than "cold and restrained" (71 percent to 20 percent), "close" rather than "distant" (69 percent to 24 percent).

Despite a great deal of discussion about the sexual revolution and the loss of family stability in America today, another Gallup Poll shows that a number of basic aspects of childrearing have changed very little over the years. In fact, parents believe they are spending more time with their children than their parents spent with them. Parents generally tend to give themselves good grades as child rearers.

Parents Grade Themselves

Today's parents generally feel that they are doing a good job raising their children. When asked to grade themselves, parents of children under age 18 give themselves almost exclusively "A" (31 percent) or "B" (58 percent) grades, with only 10 percent grading their performance as parents at "C" or below. Virtually no parents give themselves an "F."

Despite the high grades parents give themselves, Americans are less certain about the job being done by parents in general. About as many Americans say that parents do a poor job of preparing their children for the future as say that they do a good job, although this has changed only slightly since the question was last asked in 1967.

There is also widespread agreement that it is more difficult today than in the past to raise children.

Still, about six in ten parents today say they spend more time with their kids than their parents spent with them, with only two in ten saying that they spend less time.

There is no dramatic evidence in the Gallup Poll that today's families are so widely pulled apart by their various activities that they "eat on the run," as has often been asserted. Over 70 percent of parents with children under age 18 say that their family eats dinner together at least five out of seven days a week, with over a third indicating that their family eats dinner together all seven days.

The Gallup survey also shows evidence of a significant increase in piety at these family dinner gatherings. Almost two-thirds of parents of families with children under age 18 assert that their family says grace or gives thanks to God aloud before their meals. This represents a significant change from 50 years ago, when only 43 percent of parents said that their families prayed or said grace before meals.

Still Optimistic About Children's Futures

Despite discussion about the loss of the American dream and opportunities to get ahead in this country today, significant majorities of both men and women say that their sons and daughters will have a better chance of succeeding than they themselves had when they grew up. For men, this positive outlook on the future for their sons has not changed since 1946. About 62 percent of men now say that their sons will have a better chance of succeeding than they did, compared with 64 percent in 1946.

For women, positive perceptions of the opportunities for their daughters have climbed significantly over the years. Today 85 percent of women say their daughters will have a better chance of succeeding than they did, compared with 61 percent of women in 1946 who gave this same answer.

Now, the Bad News

The findings reported thus far in this chapter paint a generally healthy picture of families and childrearing in the United States. At the same time, however, surveys document an alarming condition of fatherlessness in this country.

Columnist Michael McManus writes vividly about this situation in one of his weekly articles:

> Society is coming unglued. Look at the faces of children:
> In three decades, teen suicide rates tripled and SAT scores fell nearly 80 points. A million teens get pregnant a year, 350,000 of whom give birth. Since 1970, child poverty grew by 42 percent. "Children are the fastest growing segment of the criminal population in the United States," reports the Justice Department.
> What's the cause of these trends? Close your eyes and guess.
> Did you guess America's soaring fatherlessness?
> It is driven by two trends. Only 5 percent of children were born out-of-wedlock in 1960, vs. 32 percent in 1995—a *six-fold* growth. And divorces tripled since 1960. This year 1.3 million kids are born out-of-wedlock; another million see their parents divorce.
> The tragic result is that nearly four of ten children—24 million kids—do not live in homes with their fathers. . . .
> Such abandonment is unprecedented in any nation. Three-fourths of

those children will live in poverty before age 11. They are more likely to fail in school, engage in early sex, have drug or alcohol problems. And 70 percent of juvenile felons have absent fathers.

More Hard Facts

By way of background, let's examine some additional hard facts about children. One in five children live in poverty; ten million do not have health coverage. Homicide and suicide kill almost 7,000 children every year. One in three children are born to unmarried mothers, many of whom are children themselves. And 135 children bring guns to school each day. Children from every social strata suffer from abuse, neglect, and preventable emotional problems.

In cities and suburbs alike, America's teens are meeting violence in their schools and their homes. The twin threats of unwanted pregnancy and AIDS make teen sexuality more complicated and dangerous than ever. Bad eating habits, poor attitudes toward exercise, and too much fatty food combine to make America's teens among the least healthy of developed nations. Drug and alcohol abuse, pervasive among teens in this country, are linked with juvenile crime, as well as higher rates of teen suicide. Too many Americans lack the one weapon they need to confront the risks they face: solid values rooted, for many, in religious faith. Young people caught in risk behaviors are unlikely to attain the level of education required for survival and success in a world that is growing increasingly complex and competitive. School failure too often leads to lives of chronic crime, unemployment, or welfare dependency.

Fear at Home and School

The sad fact is that many young people in the homes of both the privileged and underprivileged worry daily about their physical well-being. One teenager in four is worried about his or her physical safety at school each day. So concern about safety is found not only in the streets, but also in the schools and even at home.

Young people are apprehensive about the future and a host of problems that are relatively new on the scene: the threat of AIDS, the availability of potentially deadly drugs, and random death and violence, to name a few. Gone for many are the key support systems that have been important to childrearing and a young person's sense of security: strong families, with both parents; friendly and supportive neighborhoods; and a society generally in agreement on vital, core values. What can be predicted as a result of such problems? A report from the Carnegie Council on Adolescent Development states, "All together, nearly half of American adolescents are at high or moderate risk of seriously damaging their life chances. The damage may be near-term, or it may be delayed, like a time bomb." The report notes that these conditions exist among families of all income levels and backgrounds, in cities, suburbs, and rural areas. But they are especially severe in neighborhoods of concentrated poverty, where adolescents are more likely to lack two crucial prerequisites for healthy growth and development: a close relationship with a dependable adult and the perception of meaningful opportunities in mainstream America. One should add that, while a dependable adult is a major step, nothing replaces a mother and father for providing a caring environment.

Victims of Physical Abuse

One of our studies conducted in 1995 indicated that more than three million children were victims of physical abuse inflicted by their parents, and another one million were victims of sexual abuse perpetrated either by an adult or an older child. These estimates are 16 times the number of cases of physical abuse and ten times the cases of sexual abuse than are actually recorded. Because we can get into homes through telephone surveys in a way that social workers and others can't, we can presumably come closer to getting an accurate fix on the number of cases of abuse, and the number is staggering.

The urgent need for a powerful, pervasive, societal response now is underscored by two trends. America is continuing to polarize into a land of rich and poor. So the number of children who are at risk will grow at a shocking rate, especially in view of the projection that America's teen population will top 30 million by the year 2000, the highest number since 1975. Second, predictions are that juvenile crime will get worse. A report from the Commission on Violent Crime warned of a coming storm of juvenile crime that will be more random and more brutal than anything Americans have confronted.

Deprived Family Life Key to Alienation

The anger, depression, and even violent or suicidal tendencies of some teens are topics we see daily in our morning newspaper. Those stories are about individuals, and the circumstances that may have led them to stray from a more positive or fulfilling path.

The Gallup Youth Survey is designed to reflect what is happening with "real teens" as a group. If some American teens are depressed, or alienated, who are they?

We decided to attempt to answer these kinds of questions by constructing an "alienation" index . An index such as this one helps us better understand and predict the behavior and attitudes of teens.

The Gallup Youth Survey's Teen Alienation Index reveals that alienated teens experience a deprived quality of family life, a preoccupation with ideas of death and dying, and a less than optimum ability to make productive use of their time. The survey does not indicate to what extent the high alienation scores are "cause" or "effect."

Here is a summary of the findings for the three categories explored in the survey: family life, attitudes about death, and use of time.

Family Life

A deprived family life seems to be the key "cause" indicator of alienation. Compared with other groups, these teens have less opportunity to discuss their lives with the adults at home. They are less likely to see others reading at home and less likely to remember being read to. They wish they had more help with homework at home. They are also more likely to come from a household with problems getting enough to eat.

Attitudes About Death

Those high in "alienation" are far more preoccupied with thoughts of death and with notions of untimely death. Compared with teens who did not score high for "alienation," this group is more than twice as likely to see itself dying before age 50; and to see itself as "very likely" to die from a car accident, a disease, a terrorist bombing, or a motorcycle crash. This group is slightly more likely to see itself making use of assisted suicide. Friends and television or movies are more likely to be "very important" to this group in forming ideas about death (compared with other influences such as parents or teachers).

Extent of worry over matters concerning death is greater than for less alienated counterparts. Compared with other teens, this group is more likely to express "a great deal" of worry over not having the chance to say they are sorry, the possibility of great pain before death, the thought of "not being alive," what will be said about them at their funeral, and who will talk about them at their funeral.

Use of Time

The "alienated" group (with poorer school performance and lower levels of parental education) is less likely to use time productively. They are more likely than others to "hang out with friends" after school rather than to do homework. They are also more likely to report that they go to the mall or "sit around home and do nothing in particular." This group is twice as likely to report that after-school activities "almost always" get in the way of doing homework.

What Do Teens Tell Us About Fatherhood?

The preceding paragraphs hopefully have shed some light on the world of children, and more specifically of teenagers, as a backdrop to a direct investigation of the status of fatherhood in our society.

The George H. Gallup International Institute, through the Associated Press, and in consultation with Dr. Wade Horn, devoted a 1997 national Gallup Youth Survey of teenagers to exploring the topic of fatherhood. The areas covered are below:

1. How many teens have no father at home?
2. How many teens live with both parents?
3. Who lives in the household with teens?
4. What makes for a good father?
5. How many teens say their fathers match up to this ideal?
6. Which teens are likely to have a good father?
7. Do teens feel close to their fathers even when living apart?
8. How do teens feel about fatherhood—is it harder to be a father today?

Many Teens Have No Father at Home

In America today, one-third of teenagers cannot talk about life with father. When asked what relatives live at home with them, although 91 percent of teens mention mom, only 67 percent say that their father lives with them.

Having a father at home is least likely to be true of teens living in large cities and in rural areas. Only 57 percent of the young people who live in large cities and 65 percent of rural teens have a father at home, according to the findings of the latest Gallup Youth Survey. On the other hand, 74 percent of teens in small towns and 70 percent of suburban teens report having their fathers living at home.

This does not necessarily mean that these young people are without a male role model in their daily lives. Eleven percent have a stepfather, 3 percent a grandfather or great-grandfather, 2 percent an uncle, and 1 percent a boyfriend of their mother living at home with them. This suggests that, apart from their own father, 17 percent of teens have an adult male at home.

Rural teens are more likely than others to live with a stepfather, with 19 percent reporting this to be the case compared to 12 percent of suburban teens, 11 percent of large city teens, and 8 percent of teens living in small towns.

Having an adult female relative living with teenagers is not as frequent an occurrence, because teens' mothers live at home more often than do their fathers. Only 9 percent of teens say that an adult female relative other than their mother lives at home with them, with their grandmother (5 percent) most often mentioned. Two percent name an aunt, 1 percent a stepmother, and another 1 percent a great-grandmother.

While the most often reported group of relatives living at home with teens are their parents and siblings, the survey indicates that a fair number of teens share living quarters with an assortment of relatives. Half report a brother and/or sister living at home with them, while 3 percent name a half-brother, and another 3 percent a half-sister. Two percent say that a cousin lives with them, and the same percentage of teens report an aunt and/or an uncle to be in their homes. One percent list a stepmother, great-grandmother, their own child, their mother's boyfriend, and/or a great-grandfather.

Only Half of Teens Live with Both Parents

The Gallup Youth Survey confirms what we have been hearing for a while; only slightly more than half (57 percent) of America's teenagers live with both of their parents. "Parents" in this survey include two biological parents married to one another (54 percent) plus a few adoptive parents and parents who are together but unmarried.

Younger teens (ages 13-15) and those with higher academic credentials are more likely than those in other groups to live with both their married biological parents. Nearly four of ten surveyed (39 percent) live with only one of their parents. The majority of teens in this group live with one single, divorced, widowed, or separated parent who did not remarry (26 percent). Also counted here are teens living with one of their biological parents who has remarried (13 percent).

Black teens are more likely than those in other groups to live with only one parent. A few teens (4 percent) live in some other situation, such as with grandparents or foster parents.

Teens Say Divorce Is Too Easy to Get

On the issue of divorce, American teens appear cynical. And given that so many teens do not live with two parents, their cynicism is not surprising.

A strong majority of American teenagers (77 percent) say that divorce in this country is too easy to obtain. Those teens of higher academic standing and those who attended religious services last week are even more likely to consider it to be too easy to get a divorce.

Almost two teens in three (65 percent) also say that people who get divorced failed to try hard to save their marriages. Older teens (ages 16-17), teens of higher academic standing, and teens who attend religious services are even more likely to hold this opinion than those in other groups.

The level of education of one's parents might have an effect on attitudes about divorce as well. Teens without a parent who attended college are less likely to say that divorce is too easy to get. And these teens are also less likely to agree that most couples who became divorced did not try hard to save their marriages.

What Makes a Good Father?

Most teens believe that their father tries to be a good dad.

Teens were read a series of statements about fathers and asked first whether "a good father definitely does this." Then they were read the same series and asked to answer with regard to their own father. Does he definitely do the things they think make for a good father?

Teenagers think a good father is a person who shows respect for and cares for others. Statements on the survey about affection and caring for others drew strong consensus from teens.

Nine teens in ten say a good father shows respect and care for his children's mother (91 percent) and that a good dad teaches his children to be polite to neighbors and older people (90 percent).

Their fathers fall considerably short of perfection, however, as only three-quarters of teens believe their own father shows their mother respect (75 percent) and teaches them to be polite to others (79 percent).

Fathers have a way to go in their affection for teens. Most think a good father tells his children he loves them at least once a week (85 percent) and that he hugs his children at least once a week (75 percent).

But only two-thirds of teens say their own father tells them often that he loves them, and just slightly more than half of teens (55 percent) say dad hugs them at least weekly.

One other area in which fathers seem lacking, according to their teenage children, has to do with schoolwork. While a majority of teens (71 percent) say a good father helps children with their homework, only 45 percent report that their own father does so.

With regard to communication with a teen's teachers, four in ten (41 percent) say a good father should have such contact, yet only one teen in ten (10 percent) says his or her dad actually is in touch with the teachers.

In some traditionally "dad" areas, teens seem to think their father is measuring up. For example, discipline often has been perceived as a father's responsibility, and teens agree that it should be. A good father is one who punishes children who have broken a rule at home (71 percent) or at school (68 percent), according to teens surveyed.

As for a classic fatherly role, that of teaching a child to ride a bike or play a sport, teens say their dad has done well. Eight out of ten teens think a good dad teaches bike riding or sports to his children, and nearly as many (76 percent) say their own dad has so instructed them.

Which Teens Are Likely to Have a Good Father?

Teens whose parents attended college are more likely to say their dad has traits they perceive to be important to good fatherhood. Being white, religious, younger (13-15), and having good grades in school also are traits or conditions found in teens who think their fathers are doing a better job than most.

Good fathers, as noted, teach their children to be polite to neighbors and to older people, say America's teens, and eight in ten of them say their own father does so. Among boys and younger teens, though, the percentage is even higher.

Three out of four teens say their father taught them how to ride a bike or play a sport, another one of the traits they associate with "good fatherhood." Fathers of white teens and those whose parents attended college are even more likely to give their dad credit here.

Three-fourths of teens say their father shows respect for and is caring of their mother. This proportion is higher among teens with above average academic standing.

Two-thirds of teens say their father tells them he loves them at least once a week. This figure is higher among younger teens, whites, and teens whose parents are college educated.

More than six dads in ten (62 percent) ask their children how their day went, according to their teenage kids. The number of teens who recognize this trait in their own dad is higher among better students, whites, and teens whose parents went to college.

About the same percentage of teens (61 percent) say their father punishes them when they have broken a rule. This figure rises among younger teens, whites, and teens who attended religious services the week prior to the survey.

Slightly more than half of teens (55 percent) say dad hugs them at least weekly; these numbers increase among better students, whites, younger teens, and teens whose parents went to college.

And "good fathers" help their kids with homework, although fewer than half of teenagers surveyed (45 percent) say they are recipients of such assistance. Teens who are better students, younger, worshiped last week, and whose parents attended college are even more likely to say they get homework help from dad.

It is hard to say whether these teens experience desirable traits in dad because of favorable social circumstances (which presumably lead to higher paying jobs and the associated benefits to home life), or because those circumstances enhance their perceptions that dad is doing a good job.

Teens Feel Close to Dads Even When Living Apart

Approximately four out of ten American teens (39 percent), as noted previously, are living with only one of their parents. More than eight times out of ten, the absent parent is the father.

Among American teenagers 13 to 17 years old, 63 percent live with their biological fathers. While this is a majority of teens, it is not a large one. Whites, those with higher academic standing, those with two parents who attended college, and those who consider themselves Republican are more likely than other teens to live with their biological fathers.

Teens whose racial background is nonwhite, and black teens in particular, are less likely to live with a biological father.

Nearly another fourth of teens (24 percent) have contact with their biological father even though they do not live with him. This means that most teens (87 percent) have contact with their fathers even when they are not together all of the time.

Among teens who do not live with their biological father, those in rural areas are less likely to have father contact than are teens living in other settings.

One-fifth of teens live with a stepfather or another adult male such as their mother's boyfriend. However, nearly as many (17 percent) do not live with any type of male adult.

Teens were asked how close they feel to their father or to the person most closely filling that role for them. It is gratifying to learn that a solid majority of teens (70 percent) say they feel "extremely" or "very" close to their father.

Those more likely than their counterparts to say they feel "extremely close" to their fathers are boys, teens from white-collar households, and those who attended religious services last week.

Also, as the number of parents in the household who attended college increases, so does the likelihood that teens report feeling "extremely close" to their fathers.

American dads should take note that their teenage daughters are not as likely to feel especially close to them as do their teenage sons. Much recent research indicates the importance of fathers in raising confident, competent daughters.

Teens Believe It's Harder to Be a Father Today

When they consider fatherhood of 20 to 30 years ago, American teens conclude it's more difficult to be a father today. In our survey we asked American teenagers 13 to 17 years old to tell us how they feel about fathers and fatherhood.

A majority of American teens (63 percent) say it is more difficult to be a father today than it was 20 or 30 years ago. Another three teens in ten say the difficulties facing the two generations of fathers is much the same.

How well are fathers doing today as compared with the efforts of their own fathers? More than half of teens (53 percent) say their dads are doing much the same job as parents as their own fathers did for them.

And nearly two in ten (18 percent) say their fathers are doing a better job than grandpa did for dad.

However, nearly three teens in ten (29 percent) say their fathers are doing a worse job today than grandfather did a generation ago.

Black teenagers, who are more likely to grow up without a father present than are other racial groups, and those living in the west are more likely to say fathers today are doing a worse job.

What are dads doing to set a good example? Most teens say their father had a conversation with them in the past week (82 percent). This is more likely to be the case for white teens and for those in households where both parents attended college.

Two-thirds of teens say their father "always" or "very often" attends their important events. Teens who attended religious services last week, teens who live in suburbs or small towns, white-collar teens, and teens with two college-educated parents are more likely to say their dad "always" or "very often" attends important events.

Dad "frequently shares important ideas" say nearly half of teens surveyed (47 percent). This is more likely to be said by boys than girls and for teens whose parents both attended college.

One teen in five (21 percent) has a father who spends time doing something with him or her everyday. Better than a third of teens (37 percent) say they spend time with dad two or three times a week. Younger teens (ages 13-15), boys, and teens who attend religious services are more likely to report spending time with their fathers on a daily basis.

A hot issue today in the homes of two-career parents is the role dads play in sharing housework. A large minority of teens (45 percent) say their father is doing chores at home every day. Nearly one-fourth of teens (23 percent) say dad does chores around the house two to three times a week.

The perception that dad does daily chores increases among teens whose parents both went to college and among boys.

Teens and Fatherhood

The Gallup Youth Survey on "fatherhood" reveals the following:

- A majority of American teenagers (63 percent) live with their biological father, but as many as one-third do not. Whites, those with higher academic standing, and those with two parents who attended college are more likely than teens with other characteristics to live with their biological father.
- A solid majority of teens (70 percent) say they feel "extremely" or "very" close to their father. Yet three in ten do not. Those more likely than their counterparts to say they feel "extremely close" to their fathers are boys, teens from white-collar households, and those who attended church last week.
- A majority of American teens (63 percent) say it is more difficult to be a father today than it was 20 or 30 years ago. Another three teens in ten (30 percent) say the difficulty of being a father is the same as it was a generation ago.
- Fully half of teens (53 percent) say their fathers are doing as well as parents as their own fathers did 20 or 30 years ago. Nearly two in ten (18 percent) say their fathers today are doing a better job.
- A large majority of teens agree that "a good father definitely"

shows respect and caring for his children's mother (91 percent), teaches his children to be polite to neighbors and older people (90 percent), tells his children he loves them at least once a week (85 percent), hugs his children at least once a week (75 percent), and asks his children how their day went (70 percent).

What Can Be Done to Restore Fatherhood?

The restoration of fatherhood to American society depends on many factors—economic, social, and spiritual. The hurdles are great. The rite of marriage as a passage to fatherhood, for example, may be in question in the minds of the next generation. Less than half of American teens ages 13-17 (48 percent) consider marriage to be "extremely important" to men before they become fathers.

At the same time, however, another 30 percent do consider marriage a "very important" precursor to fatherhood, bringing the proportion considering it "extremely" or "very" important to nearly eight in ten (78 percent).

Younger teens (ages 13-15), teens from blue-collar households, churchgoers, and teens living in rural areas are more likely than their counterparts to consider marriage "extremely important" before fatherhood. Those teens considering themselves politically "independent" are less likely to consider marriage "extremely important" prior to fatherhood.

Most teens (93 percent) do expect that they will marry someday. There are no differences in this result based on personal characteristics such as age, race, or education level of the parents.

Likewise, most teens (88 percent) expect to have children. This proportion is higher for boys than girls.

A Basis for Being Hopeful?

Despite the fact that fatherlessness is a fundamental flaw in our society—that "such abandonment is unprecedented in any nation," as McManus puts it—there would appear to be a basis for believing that fatherhood can be restored in this nation. Here are some factors that could provide a basis for overcoming fatherhood inattention, alienation, and absence:

1. Broad and deep support is found for family and fatherhood in America. For most adults today, the experience of family and fatherhood has been positive.

2. There is widespread awareness of the problem, namely, fatherlessness is identified by many as the most severe social problem we face. And vast numbers of U.S. citizens would welcome efforts from governmental, corporate, and nonprofit sectors to strengthen family ties and encourage fatherhood.

3. Most fathers acknowledge that they could be doing a better job than they are presently doing.

4. Most teens (who have fathers living in the home) have good things to say about them. And even among those whose fathers are absent, a fairly sizeable proportion say that they still feel close to their fathers.

5. Most teens seek enduring relationships in their lives and look forward to getting married and having children. Most think divorces are too easy to get.

6. The role of religion and churches is fundamental to any turnaround in the present fatherless situation. Numerous surveys have shown that religion plays a major role in healing family relationships and in encouraging closer relationships between parents and children.

In one survey, for example, more than seven in ten adults said that religion in their home has strengthened family relationships "a great deal" or "somewhat." Relatively few say either "hardly at all" or "not at all."

Churches and other faith communities play a key role. There are more than 300,000 churches in the United States, which reach 60 percent of the populace in a given month. This is the way to reach the American people and to deal directly with father inattentiveness, alienation, and absence.

Churches are in a position to meet head-on one of the most destructive trends in our society—that of divorce. More than half of new marriages will break up, spreading dysfunction throughout society. Yet churches too often are "blessing machines" and do not require adequate marriage preparation.

Christian churches should underscore the biblical basis for fatherhood. A man's love for his son or daughter is akin to God's love for us. God loves his sons or daughters unconditionally. He may be disappointed by certain things his children do, but nevertheless loves them deeply. God the Father is always ready to forgive his children. He longs for his children to follow a righteous path. It is surely God's desire to see his children grow into full and responsible adulthood.

The book, *The Blessing* (Smalley and Kushner), reminds us of the importance of the earthly father blessing his son or daughter, picturing a special future for them, and making an active commitment to helping them reach their goals. The father occasionally and reluctantly may let adversity cross the path of his children—letting them "learn the hard way."

Such love of an earthly father is, I believe, akin to God's love for us. God the Father loves his sons and daughters, who feel this love and out of this love do not want to disappoint Him.

There are few steps a father can take that are as powerful as his dedicating at least a few minutes each day with each child at dinner or bedtime, asking the question, "How did things go today?" and then listening, followed by a hug and three words: "I love you," accompanied with prayers and reminders to children that they are loved by God.

Going Forward

Surveys clearly show that most Americans place high importance on family and fatherhood. Those among us who have had the blessing of a loving father must reach out to the four in ten children in our society who come home each day from school to fatherless homes. In fact, each of us at this moment might well ask ourselves this question: Is there a child out there somewhere who deserves the same blessings I received from a father and who needs someone to walk alongside him or her through the travails of youth? Shouldn't we all be mentors of one kind or another? If we do not reach out to fatherless children in our nation, we can count on confronting severe societal problems for years to come. More importantly, as people who have experienced the love of an earthly father, and the love of God of the universe, can we do less?

Part Two

The Heritage of Fatherhood in America's Faith Communities

Chapter 4

Fatherhood in the African American Church

Bernard Franklin

James's Story

Dear Dad:
You make me so #@&%$ sick. Some nights I be wanting to kill you with
my bare hands. The evil things you done to me makes me want to kill you
even more. I blame you for the *&%$#@ thoughts I have. Sure enough my
life is better then what you said it was going to be. The way you treated me
makes me sick. You almost win, but I guess you didn't lose. I should've
been worser, but I have a stronger mind than what you thought pussy. All
you done was made your son more stronger and wittier. Love from your
son, you @#$%&*, and your mothers mother a *&%$# too.

James's mother was killed in a drive-by shooting, while he watched. He
cradled her bloody body until the authorities came to take her to the hospital
where she was pronounced dead. He was eight years old.

James then went to live with his father. When his father left to go to
work on summer mornings, he bolted James inside so he could not go out.
His father often left him a piece of fried chicken and some beer to eat and
drink during the day. James spent much of the day watching TV and looking
through his father's adult magazines. When his father came home in the
evening, he usually spent his time in his bedroom with beer, drugs, and
women. One night his father had consumed too much to involve himself

with the women, so he demanded that James perform with the women. James resisted at first, but his father said he would beat him if he refused. That night James began the insidious lifestyle of sexual promiscuity. James was 12.

James attended a fathering class conducted by the Kansas City based National Center for Fathering through the Drug Court Diversion Program of the County Prosecutors Office. The 24-week class focused on identifying and addressing the underlying causes of the enrollees' substance abuse, especially those related to their family of origin. The men were also assisted in becoming more appropriately involved in their children's lives.

As James discussed his life with the class, he announced, "I am a freakin' pervert, and I hate it." He is the manager of a fast food restaurant where he is in charge of hiring new employees, most often young women. He admitted it usually took him about two to three weeks to seduce the new employees to have sex with him. In addition, he confessed he has had sex with women too numerous to count. When asked about his spiritual life and his church attendance, with a look of pure disgust he replied, "Shi-! Why would I go there! They ain't living no better than I am." Today James is a 22-year-old father of three little girls by three different women, and he represents the world of many urban African American men who have little or no involvement with their children.

This story is repeated all over the country in various forms. It is the tale of a once strong family unit that has dwindled to broken elements of hurt, pain, and confusion. It is also the tale of a once strong family support system, the African American church, and how the perception has developed that the church is more interested in Sunday morning social gatherings of wonderful music, "whooping" messages, and fine fashions than it is in supporting men and families.

African American Men and the Church

How can the faith community encourage African American men like James to be more involved in the lives of their children? In addition to James's fathering class, I have worked with fathers through two elementary schools where nearly 80 percent of the children do not live with their biological fathers, with fathers in an urban church fathering class, with fatherless juveniles facing adult charges in Orlando, and with teen fathers. I have also conducted fathering seminars in several major U.S. cities. This chapter highlights what I have learned about restoring the honor of African American fathering and provides a framework for the faith community to consider in restoring men and fathers.

From my work, I have found that the mental, spiritual, and emotional condition of many African American men is extremely fragile. Many men have a great deal of bitterness and anger. I have observed great despair and hopelessness among many African American men, especially among young men. But no other group of men has faced the subjugation that African American men have encountered and continue to face. There are more African American men in prison than there are on American college campuses,[1] and, according to the American Council on Education, the number of African American men graduating from college has declined steadily since 1976. The NAACP has predicted that unless there is major intervention, by 2010, 70 percent of all African American men will be hopelessly hooked on alcohol or drugs, in prison or on probation, or dead. When I have spoken at churches, many pastors have advised me not to "beat up on my men," or they have asked me to "go easy on these brothers," acknowledging that many men are in a fragile state. These men have grown weak and faint toward their responsibility to themselves and their family.

In addition to my academic training, I have had personal experience in dealing with my own anger and bitterness and some complex family issues following a divorce, so I feel qualified to discuss the condition of African American fathers. The African American faith community needs to step up to the plate and support men and fathers. The church has been a dynamic support to the African American community, but despite some communities having churches on every corner, this faith group has not been as successful in its delivery of services and support to African American men and fathers as it has been to women and children. This chapter should be seen as a preliminary and not an exhaustive analysis of how the African American faith community can be inspired to focus on men and fathers.

The Importance of Fathers

Fathers are essential in the lives of children. God never intended for mothers to give birth to a child, alone, and then raise a child, alone. When God created the first parents, he made one male and one female with unique talents and attributes that complement each other in the care of children. At Creation we see the first family, and we come to understand the critically important role of marriage. The family began as the fundamental unit of society. In fact, family life has been upheld as God's norm for any society throughout the Bible. The Bible is filled with stories and accounts of instructive family life and provides a model for faith communities to use in supporting mothers and fathers in caring for children.

Fathers matter! Along with mothers, fathers are better socializers than schools, clubs, or neighborhood organizations. Caring, loving, involved fathers are linked to children's destinies. More than any other factor, a biological father's presence and active involvement in a child's life will determine that child's personal happiness and his or her success and productivity in the larger society. Middle class or poor, inner city or suburban, children of divorce and those born outside of marriage struggle through life at a measurable disadvantage. While children know that they are loved by their mothers, they yearn, even crave, for the other half of the devotion God designed for them. They will desperately look for the love they never received from their fathers with an overwhelming intensity that often leads to perverse addictions, as well as other inappropriate behavior as they look in all the wrong places.[2]

An astonishing 70 percent of African American children will go to bed tonight without their father present. Further, the November 1997 issue of *Essence* reported that the U.S. Census Bureau has indicated that 91 percent of African American boys do not live with their fathers. While you may consider this figure to be high, it is reasonable for some neighborhoods. Certain housing projects in Kansas City and in other major cities have no fathers living as residents. If we consider that only 1.2 percent of all teachers in America are African American men and that fewer black children are attending church regularly, then it is understandable that many children have little to no contact with an appropriate father or father figure in any given week.[3] There are neighborhoods in America where responsible fathers—usually the best hope for socializing boys—are so rare that bedlam engulfs the streets. Teachers, ministers, police, and other authority figures daily fight losing battles against preteen and teenage male gang members. The result is all too often agonizing levels of violence and incomprehensible incidents of brutality. Thirty years of black father dislocation has moved us from the rhythm and blues lyrics of "Ain't no woman like the one I've got" to such rap lyrics as "Bitches ain't nuthing but hoes and tricks."[4]

The absence of fathers is linked to most social nightmares—from boys with guns to girls with babies. About 46 percent of families with children headed by single mothers live below the poverty line, while about 8 percent of those with two parents do so. Studies show that less than 30 percent of prison inmates grew up with both parents and that a missing dad is a better predictor of criminal activity than race or poverty. Growing up with both parents turns out to be a better antidote to teen pregnancy than any sex education program. Young women reared in disruptive homes are twice as likely to become teen mothers. The data show that children raised with little or no contact with their fathers are likely to drop out of school, join gangs, be sexually active and become teen parents, use drugs and alcohol, commit crimes, and have lower earnings as adults. In fact, recent studies have found that single parenting correlates with violent crime more strongly than does poverty alone.[5] And these measures focus only on physical fatherlessness. The prevalence and impact of emotional fatherlessness are equally alarming.[6]

For a growing number of young African American men, particularly those from low-income, single parent homes, the odds of their achieving a stable family life, being contributors to strong families and neighborhoods, and having an excellent career are dwindling right before their eyes.[7] This is not to deny that fathers matter for girls as well, but in some ways fatherless boys face greater social problems than girls face. For this generation of young fatherless men, the rates of unemployment, teen fatherhood, educational dropout, and death far exceed those of any other demographic group at any point in history. Of young African American men between the ages of 20 and 29, increasing numbers find themselves in prison, on probation, or on parole, according to the Sentencing Project, a not-for-profit organization that is bent on prison reform. Couple this with prejudice, racism, and ignorance, and you have young men who face almost insurmountable odds.[8]

In a world where being a man or a father is a role laden with status and expectations, many young African American males' heroes are sports stars, rap music artists, and street hustlers—not their fathers. Consequently, when these young men grow up, they want to be like their sports and street heroes, not their fathers.

Our community is losing a generation of its young men, and women, to gangs, crime, poverty, drugs, and despair, and our world will be devoid of their talents and abilities. Very few young African American children have a father or significant male role model with whom they can process life's issues. An army of involved fathers and father figures and mentors can reverse these trends. But many of today's African American fathers have grown up in fatherless homes or had a distant father who focused mainly on his role as a provider. Fathers are in desperate need of help in fulfilling their role as fathers: Dads who are out of the home need help reconnecting with their children, and dads who are in the home need help becoming more actively involved in the lives of their children.[9]

The Historical Context of Fatherlessness

Before we discuss solutions to fatherlessness, we must first analyze how we came to be where we are today. We can better define solutions when we take the time to understand where men have been. To objectively discuss the African American father, we should review the beginning of black family life in America. In *Chains and Images of Psychological Slavery*, Na'im Akbar states:

> In order to fully grasp the magnitude of our current problems, we must reopen the books on the events of slavery. Our objective should not be to cry stale tears for the past, nor to rekindle old hatreds for past injustices. Instead, we should seek to enlighten our path of today by better understanding where and how the lights were turned out yesterday.[10]

In looking back, however, we shouldn't stop at slavery. It is important that we go even further back to examine the historical African concepts of fathers and families. I believe it is important to this discussion to understand the concepts of being a father which African men brought to the New World. A community is on a journey toward healing and wholeness when it tries to recollect its own history and begins to compare its present state with its past state, when it seeks to learn from the past to approve or disapprove of inappropriate customs and traditions, and when it encourages progress toward that which is for the good of the community.

On a recent research trip to West Africa (Ghana and Ivory Coast) to learn more about pre-slave fathers and families, I interviewed a wide age range of fathers in remote villages, as well as in the cities. I learned what "family" means in Africa, and I discovered the rich heritage of African fatherhood.

The Meaning of Family

First, I heard about the traditions of the African family. The family in Akan culture, which may best represent the ancestry of most African Americans, is the entire network of kinship. Most African cultures believe that the family includes all members, the unborn, the living, and the dead. Throughout the Akan culture, and many other African cultures, there is no language to describe the nuclear family: a set of parents and their offspring. During the period prior to slave trade, the African family was a stable, secure group subjected to the mores of its particular tribal or kinship unit.

In the last several years we have heard many references to the African proverb "It takes a village to raise a child." In West Africa, the village is another way of saying it takes the entire family to raise a child. Most often a village is a kinship arrangement. To use the proverb in its original context, we should say, "It takes a family to raise a child." In America, we have moved from "It takes a family to raise a child" to "It takes teachers, policemen, the clergy, businessmen, and others to raise a child." That is not its original context. In Africa it took fathers and mothers and aunts and uncles to raise and support children. Absent in our family picture today is the father, and we have accepted his absence.

The Rich Heritage of African Fatherhood

The other significant aspect of African history is the role and function of the father. Here are some of the key themes:

First, fathers were *committed* to the family. Fathers had a deep and abiding commitment to their family. It was socially unacceptable for a man to avoid or disregard his role as a father. It was a man's highest role to be a father, a father of a village. If a father abdicated his responsibility to his family, the men in the village would take him off into the bush to discuss his lack of responsibility. Most men responded positively, but if they did not, they may have been sent out as an outcast.

Second, fathers were religious/spiritual men. Fathers were considered on a level of a god or priest. He performed spiritual rituals, and as such when he was away from his children, the mother covered the children at night with a cloth of the father's, signifying comfort and protection. Scholars agree that religion was and is a distinct aspect of African family life.[11] No one has expressed this better than John Mbiti:

> Wherever the African is, there is his religion: he carries it to the fields where he is sowing seeds or harvesting a new crop; he takes it with him . . . to attend a funeral ceremony; and if he is educated, he takes religion with him to the examination room at school or in the university; if he is a politician he takes it to the house of parliament. Although many African languages do not have a word for religion as such, it nevertheless accompanies the individual from long before his birth to long after his physical death.[12]

To African fathers, religion was as essential as the air they breathed. Their religion consisted of sacred symbols, ritual practices, particular divinities, and ancestral spirits.[13]

Third, fathers represented strength, energy, hardness, toughness. As strong men, fathers were strong leaders. Mothers represented softness and gentleness. The two parents balanced the child's developmental equation.

Fourth, fathers were providers. This age-old role of fathers is not distinct to African fathers. Like many men around the world, African fathers were concerned about the needs of their families and they worked hard to provide shelter and food for the family.

Fifth, fathers "married" for their sons. No, fathers did not exchange vows with their son's betrothed, but they acted for their son's best interest. In West African culture, the act of marrying is an extended process, not simply one day of activity. The son's father was the chief negotiator with the woman's family regarding her "bride price." The father made sure the young woman was healthy and suitable for his son. When all the necessary concerns were satisfied, the father gave his son permission to marry.

Sixth, fathers were the village judge, or magistrate. Fathers settled disputes in the family. He was the first court. If he couldn't settle the dispute, then it may have gone to the head of the clan.

Seventh, if an African father did his job well, he earned a great deal of respect from his family and the rest of the village and/or clan. Children learned not to disrespect their father. They understood they would bring shame on him if they did. If a child did disrespect his father, he may have been beaten by the father's brothers, or had a finger cut-off, or some other consequence as a means of satisfying the gods who may hold this shame against the father. Several of the men I visited had fathers who had several wives and many brothers and sisters with whom they had to share their father. Even with sometimes limited contact, these men still respected their father.

Eighth, fathers honored marriage. In those tribes where polygamy was accepted, if a man wanted to have a relationship with another woman, he would not disgrace her by having a relationship with her outside of marriage. He would marry her to give dignity to their relationship. In monogamous marriages, fathers were committed to their marriage and would consider divorce only under very strict guidelines. During the period of the slave trade, divorce was very, very rare.

Ninth, fathers lived not just for their current generation, but they lived to preserve life and to pass on life to the unborn, to future generations. One young man told me his life today was the chief reason his ancestors had lived. He felt a keen responsibility to carry on his father's and his ancestors' tradition of living for future generations.

These are concepts of fathers and families that the slaves brought with them to the New World. It was generally the young and the strongest African men who were captured and shipped to the New World in accordance with the demands of the slave markets. The settlers and traders to the New World believed that compared to Indian and European slaves, African slave men were hard, strong workers.[14]

The Forces That Crushed Fatherhood

We cannot imagine the intense pain slave fathers must have experienced in being cut off from their cultural traditions as men and fathers. Yet, most slave fathers went to great efforts to provide a positive male image, leaning on the concepts and values they learned in Africa.[15] Marriage was not often permitted. Fathers were usually separated from their families, and many of their women were raped by white men who later denied fathering racially mixed babies. Resisting these conditions verbally, physically, or legally could be punished by death.[16] Yet, fathers still played a vital role in slave family life. Slave fathers gave meaning to young boys' lives and passed on a strong sense of family commitment, often demonstrated when they were forced to cope with the breakup of their families. Some men simply wept, while others expressed sentiments as brutal as cutting off their arm or mutilating other body parts to avoid separation.[17]

The ties of "kinship" formed in the "church in the woods" ended up being the most valuable form of human association the slaves could create. The early slave church was a refuge that gave them a way to express their deepest feelings and at the same time achieve status and find meaning in a cruel and hostile, alien world. Religion offered them a means of catharsis for their pent-up emotions and frustrations. The church became an "invisible substitution" for the family left behind in Africa.[18]

For decades after slavery, African American fathers, influenced by the black church, attempted to marry and raise their families the same as other Americans. Most couples sought to legalize their "informal" marriages, and two parent households represented the norm.[19] They thought they would have acceptance and freedom following slavery, yet they found new contempt and discrimination. Especially in the South, a new white supremacy emerged, and the former slaves were segregated or excluded from participation in the white man's world with separate and unequal conditions. The public schools provided to them were a travesty. The courts set up one standard of justice for white men and another for "colored" men. Many men were subjected to brutal and often fatal violence, being lynched and burned alive by white men who formed the Ku Klux Klan in 1865 as an organization dedicated to preserving the rights and values of white Christian America.[20]

As African Americans migrated from the agrarian South to the urban, industrialized North, increasing numbers of men experienced temporary separation from family and kin networks. This migration demonstrated the commitment of many men to provide and care for their families. It also represented the negative influence of separation. African American women often fared better in the new job markets due to the demand for unskilled and domestic female labor, while men typically had to compete for jobs as skilled and manual laborers.[21] Thus, even in this migration, the dreams of many African American men for their family's economic independence (off the farm) faded under the pressure of economic competition in ethnically polarized, urban industrial centers.[22] Yet, despite this hostile environment, in 1925 more than six out of seven black homes in Harlem had two parents.

By the 1930s, the United States was in the grip of the Great Depression with unemployment rates far beyond 25 percent in most African American communities. During this period, persistent male unemployment took its toll as reports of individual and collective despair, family disruption, widespread homelessness, and even suicides increased. The enduring nature of the African American family caused members to make great attempts at keeping the larger family together, primarily for group survival. It was not until after World War II that the historically high rates of marriage and two parent households among African Americans began to decline and the formerly low rates of out-of-wedlock births and consensual relationship dissolution began to increase.[23]

After World War II, African American men returned to find a shortage of single-family structures in most large, northern cities. This, coupled with discriminatory housing practices, forced many families to move into crowded tenements and housing projects. Inadequate education, lack of employment opportunities, and lack of political clout combined to disenfranchise thousands of African American men eager to find work that could help them establish and support their families. The consequences for African American men who attempted to improve the lives of their families could be extremely harsh, with retribution in the South from groups like the Ku Klux Klan.[24]

The ability to adapt and survive became increasingly challenging as the United States shifted from an industrial to a service economy during the second half of this century. The African American workforce made this transition more slowly than other groups primarily due to the lack of vocational skills and continued hiring and promotion discrimination. As African American men increasingly competed for fewer manufacturing jobs, African American women were more successful in gaining entry-level access in the growing service market. This net effect brought about increased pressure on the relationships of many men and women. The expanding technology-driven economy created more unemployment, household disruptions when men moved to find work, divorce, separation, abandonment, and hopelessness.[25] At the same time, a limited number of highly educated men who had the skills to enter white-collar and professional careers could move their families into the emerging black middle class. Even here, though, it typically took both parents as wage earners to maintain middle-class status. But the continued decline of blue-collar employment, particularly for men, eroded and decimated many men and their families. Families in which men were chronically unemployed or underemployed experienced relationship conflict, and financial distress increased over time, and the family continued to suffer.

Eventually, government and policy makers created the welfare program, which further undermined the African American father. The welfare program was an attempt at supporting urban families and mending a family system that had suffered greatly as a result of slavery and the racism that followed. Conceptually, the mother had a "contract" with the government that ensured her a monthly check if she fulfilled two conditions: (1) she did not work, and (2) she did not marry an employed male, most often the father of her children. Critics on both sides of the welfare program agree that it undermined urban fathers. Eventually, there was a dramatic increase in marital disruption among African Americans from the middle to late 1960s through the late 1980s.[26] In his book *Climbing Jacob's Ladder*, Andrew Billingsley writes: "It is perhaps ironic that the traditional family system that slavery could not destroy during 200 years may be dismantled in a few short years by the modern industrial transition."[27]

The Crisis of African American Men

Once considered hard working and strong, African American men have been rendered broken and bruised by American social conditions. Ted Dobson, a Catholic priest, describes, in Gordon Dalbey's book *Healing the Masculine Soul*, the general condition of most men. However, I think his words eloquently summarize the crisis of African American men:

> Often they [African American men] are not active members of their own families, unable to have effective relationships with significant others, and unknowledgeable about how to rear their children. They often separate themselves from religion—that is, from developing a relationship with the center of the universe. They are often emotionally undeveloped, and their ability to care for and be cared for is stunted. They often recoil from personal growth.[28]

This condition described above is often attributed to a father-wound: Men grew up with an inadequate amount of appropriate contact with their fathers or father-men who could guide them into a healthy self-image. This inadequate contact with their genetic self-image causes deep psychological and emotional pain. While I do believe absent and unengaged fathers have contributed to this condition, the underlying causes appear to go beyond a father wound.

I regularly ask the men I work with about their family backgrounds, about their fathers, their father's father, their father's brothers and sisters. I have them describe the health of their family, marriage patterns, children, death rates, tragedies, divorces, and so forth. I follow up with the same pattern on the maternal side. Then I ask the same questions about their own brothers and sisters, looking for recurrent themes and patterns, both of blessing and destruction.

I have heard many stories about unengaged fathers and a wide range of father neglect and abuse. And often there have been men who have described their father as being present while they were growing up, but they wished their fathers gave more of themselves. I have heard patterns of rejection, divorce, sexual promiscuity, alcohol and drug abuse, poverty, and brokenness. Many of these men are members of families where the men are either being destroyed or have already died tragically.

The Problem of Anger and Bitterness

Beyond issues in their family of origin, however, I have also heard deep resentment, even hostile anger directed toward European Americans. I have heard patterns of anger and bitterness that I believe have their roots in slavery and racism, and these emotions have been passed down to subsequent generations, genetically and spiritually. You hear it in men's voices. It's on their faces. Their spirits reek of years of unresolved generational bitterness and anger. You can read it in books like *Living to Tell about It: Young Black Men in America Speak Their Piece* by Darrell Dawsey and *Makes Me Wanna Holler: A Young Black Man in America* by Nathan McCall. It is in their music, which describes the culture and attitudes of young urban African American men. Listen to their music: "I ain't a killer but don't push me/Revenge is like the sweetest joy next to getting [sex]," says the late icon Tupac Shakur,[29] who also grew up without a meaningful relationship with his father. It doesn't take a rocket scientist or a spiritual giant to discern that there is something more going on in these men's lives than father-wound issues. Whenever such a pattern of destruction upon males in a family emerges, you can be sure that generational sin is involved.

When I asked some of the nearly 100 juvenile criminals in Orlando (two of the boys were involved in killing European tourists at a rest stop several years ago) why they committed their crimes, most of them looked uncomprehendingly at me and said, "I don't know" or "I was in the wrong place at the wrong time." I also asked how many of them had a strong, positive relationship with their father. Not one of the boys raised his hand. Their chaplain said that all of them, however, had incredible amounts of rage. I do not believe their sordid crimes are simply the results of their fathers not being in their lives. It does not seem plausible to conclude that these boys simply woke up one morning and, because they were fatherless, decided to murder foreign tourists. These boys didn't have a chance! They were conceived in bitterness; anger was passed down generationally; and compounding this mess, their fathers were not present to help them process the anger they may have received from previous generations.

So how did we get to this point? Akbar attributes the social and psychological condition of the African American community to the psychological damage of slavery and unabated racism:

> Slavery was "legally" ended in excess of 100 years ago, but over 300 years experienced in its brutality and unnaturalness constituted a severe psychological and social shock in the minds of African-Americans [men]. This shock was so destructive to natural life processes that the current generation of African-Americans [men], although we are five to six generations removed from the actual experience of slavery, still carry the scars of this experience in both our social and mental lives. Psychologists and sociologists have failed to attend to the persistence of problems in our mental and social lives which clearly have their roots in slavery.[30]

Let me take this further. I believe many men satisfy the diagnostic criteria for post-traumatic stress disorder, as defined by the American Psychiatric Association in its 1987 manual. We have used this disorder to describe the symptoms of veterans of wars or POWs, victims of domestic violence, and most recently some of the men who served in Desert Storm. But we have failed to realize that many African American men have suffered trauma from slavery and racism that followed, and they have not been allowed the opportunity to dump years of pain and humiliation. These men have been forced to be strong. They have stuffed their pain in their chest. Dobson further describes the condition of African American men:

> There is a "tear" in the masculine soul—a gaping hole or wound that leads to a profound insecurity. The German psychologist, Alexander Mitscherlich, has written that society has torn the soul of the [African American] male, and into this tear demons have fled—demons of insecurity, selfishness, and despair. Consequently, [African American] men do not know who they are as men. Rather, they [African American

men] define themselves by what they do, who they know, or what they own.[31]

I have gone beyond calling this a "tear" in African American men's souls to saying there is a gaping wound in their souls. Hebrews 12:15 says, "Make sure that everyone has kindness from God so that bitterness doesn't take root and grow up to cause trouble that corrupts many of you." Many African American men harbor roots of bitterness in their souls that have been passed down for generations.

African American men have been denied an opportunity to speak about the atrocities they have faced. They have not been able to express their anger at being the last hired and the first fired, at being harassed by angry mobs, and at being unable to take direct action about those things which seriously affect their lives, their families, and their community. Fear of physical harm kept many men during slavery and the years that followed from expressing their anger. These men lacked the ability, and consequently the skills, to express anger constructively. Even today, many young men behave as they have seen their fathers behave: stoic, cold, macho, because they don't want to be called a sissy.

Demons of bitterness and anger have entered this gaping wound. Such anger destroys health through heart disease, cancer, and high blood pressure. Professional athletes, politicians, clergy, businessmen, as well as brothers on the street, are victims of unresolved bitterness.

Most black men believe they were born into a hostile world that does not care about them. They have been told: just get on with it; just deal with it; pull yourself up by your bootstraps; stuff your pain and anger. Others have advised them to play the hand they have been given. But in order to live out any of this advice these men have had to go into denial. But the hip-hop generation who claim to be the reality generation appear to be tired of stumbling down the path of denial. Their souls are weak. You see, when you have been dealt a good hand, it takes very little energy to play it, but it takes considerable energy to play a poor hand well for many generations.

Bitter fathers transfer their anger to safer people and objects.[32] When a father passes on his bitterness and anger to a weak and vulnerable child, he passes on a kind of "neurosis," a "tear," a root of bitterness, an intense inner chaos that may drive even a child to horrific crimes in an attempt to soothe or eliminate the pain. This anger and chaos becomes more vile with each passing generation. In fact, if a child never makes a proper attachment to a healthy father-man, he consequently may never know inner peace. A pervasive sense of inner turmoil results, and trying to ease this chaos may become the driving force in a young man's life. He may form inordinate attachments to people, objects, or substances. This chaos may also elicit deep feelings of anxiety. When this is the case, alleviating the anxiety becomes extremely important in the life of the person suffering with bitterness. Unlike the man who is able to repress or shut off his feelings through intellectual and other defenses, the bitter man is unable to repress his negative feelings. To compensate, he may develop addictions—to alcohol, drugs, sex, and violence—that provide pleasure or soothe his pain.[33]

Finally, bitterness prevents those suffering from caring for others. They are little boys in men's bodies, but they don't know how to handle adult male challenges as just that, as adults. All they can concentrate on are their feelings and emotions.

It is through sin patterns of bitterness and anger that demons enter a torn soul and can perpetuate their destruction on fathers and families. Whenever there is such a tear or root of bitterness, demons enter to prey upon physical weaknesses to exploit sinful tendencies—to cause proclivities to become addictions, proneness to accidents to become tragedies, bad examples to become traps—and unmet emotional needs escalate to whirlwinds of destruction. Generational patterns are the handles by which Satan pumps the fiery flames of hell in families. The greatest necessity for urban families today is prayer for the end of the destruction of families, calling for the death of harmful generational patterns and the transformation of blessings in the lives of African American fathers and families.[34]

Part of the untold story is that the brutal pain injected by slavery has gone unforgiven in the lives of many African American men. Imagine seeing your brother or father hanging from a tree with a rope around his neck, body parts missing, face disfigured, covered with tar. This image may be hard to forget, and it may be even harder to forgive.

Carrying around bitterness and anger is like carrying a sack of cement. It weighs men down and makes their journey exasperating. They are left with no energy for parenting and caring for their families. They feel physically, emotionally, socially, and spiritually bankrupt. So why do they hang on to something that drains them of life-giving energy when they know they are doing themselves more harm than they are the one against whom they hold the anger?[35]

Wounded adult African American men often behave as children, and it is characteristic of a child to hold onto things, whether literal objects or emotions. Arrested in their development, the man-child holds onto anger. For some, it is their prized possession, the only defense they know.

The Problem of Bitter Root Judgment

This bitter root judgment has become so ingrained in many families that men who are born into these families often become alcoholic, lethargic, unable or unwilling to support their wives, violent, and, generally, men without hope. Far more descends through our physical inheritance than we may suspect. Not only are physical characteristics passed on, but personality and behavioral tendencies as well. Unfortunately, it is not just good characteristics that descend from our ancestors. The good flows down to each generation as well as the bad. Unless forgiveness occurs, these men become their parents, and in so doing, the bitter root takes on greater manifestations. They become more vile. Happenstance can explain some of this, but in the lives of these men so many happenings seem so interconnected that even impartial observers are forced to admit that it can't all be coincidence.

When men combine the bitter root inheritance with bitterness toward their own father for not being there for them, we often end up with a lethal combination. The effects on the emotional makeup of a man are demonstrated by the following symptoms. This discussion is not exhaustive nor are the elements treated thoroughly. Yet they are typical and clearly describe the wide-ranging effects within many men and include some of the ways in which African Americans are restricted in their ability to function as men and as fathers. Many men express feelings of worthlessness, of wishing they hadn't been born, of inferiority, of an inability to express emotions, of depression, of a lack of self-discipline, of irresponsibility, of worry, of doubt, of fear, of self-condemnation, of self-hatred, of guilt, of oversensitivity, and of paranoia.[36]

We tend to become just like the one we resent or hold bitterness toward. What we cannot forgive in others we are doomed to live out in our lives. Either the frailty that we cannot forgive in another person indicates that we have the same negative condition existing in us, or if we fail to forgive another, then the same area we judge in them will be an area in our own life in which God's grace will be inhibited. If we forgive the weakness in another, this act of forgiveness acts as an antidote to our own weakness, but an unwillingness to forgive promotes and develops an ugly quality in us. Especially significant here are parent-child patterns passed down from generation to generation. Leanne Payne says, "To hate a parent is, in the end, to hate oneself."[37]

To men carrying around bitterness, fathering sounds like life on Mars. Basic concepts of caring and nurturing a child are foreign to them. They never experienced these from their father, and they have no role models or examples to tell them it is acceptable for them to be involved. Since men have been misplaced in many black homes, parenting has become a mother's role. So for these men we are suggesting a "new" role that is quite different from the role they play on the street.

In anger we judge others, especially those who we think have wronged us. When we judge others, we blame them and consequently we condemn them. We hold anger and bitterness within our hearts toward those we believe wronged us. But God has established the law of judging and the law of sowing and reaping. Matthew 7:1-2 says, "Stop judging so that you will not be judged. Otherwise, you will be judged by the same standard you use to judge others. The standards you use for others will be applied to you." In other words, if we judge someone of something, it dooms us to do the same thing. When we judge, we reap the same behaviors within our own lives. Every formula must balance.[38]

Judgments set up expectations about the manner in which we believe life will go. But later that judgment often produces a self-fulfilling prophecy, and we then become even more bitter because our life does not measure up to our expectations. We become frustrated with ourselves, which for many leads to self-hate. These judgments produce two types of expectations:

First, in our wounds and hurts from our fathers, we vow, "I will never be like my father." We expect to be different because we want to be, without realizing that we do not automatically have the tools to change. When a man who has vowed to be different becomes a father, he is horrified to see himself doing and saying the same hurtful things his father did, and he may even be more hurtful to his children. And when that man sees he is just like or worse than his own father, he will hate himself.

Second, we draw out of others around us the same qualities and behaviors that we perceive in the people we judge. When a man says, "White people are devils, mean and hateful. They will never let black people get ahead," that man's bitter roots set in motion within him, and in those around him, events that defile him, and he becomes "devilish." He becomes negative, painful to work with, let alone to live with. His poor attitude and behavior cause the folks he calls devils to keep their distance, to be suspicious, to find fault, to become angry with him. That man then is ripe to be falsely accused or blamed and may lose his job or fail to get hired. His expectations come to pass as the mean and hateful folks render him mean and hateful also. So he despairs and feels hopeless, often not realizing he has become like those he accused.

These bitter root judgments are wreaking havoc in our lives. It is through the sins of bitter root judgments and consequent descending patterns that Satan perpetuates his destruction on men and their families. "A thief comes to steal, kill, and destroy" (John 10:10). Family patterns are the handles by which Satan pumps the bellows of the fires of hell in any family.

It is no wonder that 91 percent of African American boys will go to bed tonight without their fathers. We understand why so many young boys are either dead, in prison, or on probation. And we come to understand why this generation of young black men is angry at the whole world and has succumbed to self-hatred that not only kills others but kills themselves. And we see why African American men have a lower life expectancy.

God wants to give his sons all good things all the time, but our bitter root expectations and eventual self-fulfilling prophecies block God's gifts. The primary need for most all African American men is to be set free from their bitter root judgments and expectations.

One of the things that was so striking to me during my stay in West Africa was the gentle ways of African men. They had no air of anger and toughness. One of the highlights of my trip were the challenging interviews with Dr. James Anquanda, world renowned professor of anthropology at the University of Ghana at Legon who specializes in studying the period of the slave trade, and Dr. Kwame Bediako, considered the leading contemporary African theologian. Dr. Anquanda turned the table on me and forced me to consider a most poignant question. He asked, "Why have African [American] men not forgiven those responsible for slavery and racism and moved on with their lives? You have great opportunities, yet your men appear to be drowning in their anger and bitterness at slavery and racism. That's not African. We have a tremendous capacity for forgiveness. We are resilient." Dr. Bediako spoke in great length about Nelson Mandela and other African leaders who have forgiven their oppressors and have moved on with healing their countries. He concluded by saying, "African [American] men should be our voice of hope. You should be telling us in Africa that God will deliver our war torn, impoverished continent and that if he delivered you from slavery and racism, he can deliver us from our plagues. You should be instructing African men to remain true to their families and their God as African nations are being transformed into industrialized democratic nations. But in your condition, you can't tell us anything!"

Healing the Urban Father

I have come to love the story of Joseph, especially his reunion with his brothers. In Genesis 45:5 and 8, Joseph says to them, "Now, don't be sad or angry with yourselves that you sold me. God sent me ahead of you to save lives. It wasn't you who sent me here, but God." Joseph quickly took all the blame from the shoulders of his brothers for their horrible deed by sharing with them the plan and purpose of God. He wanted them to know that from what they had done to him, God had made good out of it. Even in our sins or the sins done unto us, God wants to bring good out of it. Joseph had armed himself against anger and bitterness, and he was willing to rejoice in what God had done in his life, while he may have trembled at the remembrance of the dangers and destruction from which God had brought him. Sharing his vision of how God worked was his way of centering his brothers' attention on one supreme consideration. The providential purpose of God was more significant than any act of mortal man. That purpose involved preserving a remnant who could be used to complete God's purpose on earth.

I believe God is calling the African American faith community to a higher vision, to put aside our anger and bitterness so that we can "rebuild the ancient ruins and restore the foundations of past generations. You will be called the Rebuilder of Broken Walls and the Restorer of Streets Where People Live" (Isa. 58:12). In order to do so, we must have a higher vision that only comes when we lay down our rights to our feelings of anger and bitterness. As we focus on what the faith community can do to heal fathers, there is an application for us in Joseph's story. I believe God wants to preserve a remnant in the African American community to complete his work in America and perhaps to assist in rebuilding African nations.

Much of this discussion regarding how we can provide healing for fathers is based on my personal experiences growing up in a challenging family and observing my father and other men of his period. When I decided to do the "work" to get my life together, I came to accept that even I, an outwardly cool, calm, and collected young man, had to repent of anger and bitterness. Because of a divorce, I was forced to realize that my life was not what others had done or were doing to me, but what I was doing to myself with unresolved anger and bitterness. I came to see that I had a root of bitterness as sturdy and deep as an old oak tree. As I learned to release this anger and bitterness, I began to feel that God was calling me to a higher vision regarding my life. I began to feel that God was not interested in my complaining, my pity parties, my victimization. But being set free took time and patience.

I went through this process of healing with pastoral counselors and trained therapists. It was one of the most liberating experiences in my spiritual development. I saw with new eyes what I had done by judging my parents and white people, and I saw how those judgments were being played out in my life. I gained a new awareness of the awfulness of judging and holding on to seemingly invisible anger and bitterness. It was difficult to identify and accept that I was an angry man. The habit of hiding and keeping this anger stuffed neatly in my private closet had become so deeply ingrained in my life that it was a reflexive action. I now incorporate this concept as I teach other men to be good fathers, and I refer men to trained counselors who can guide them in this journey of healing. I don't believe you can teach a man the art and science of being a father until you have dealt with his anger and bitter root judgment.

If God can't transform lives and change men, we might as well throw in our cloth, close up the church, and lock the doors. We are fooling ourselves that we are "having church." We are really just leading our people in a cultural and religious experience that has no life-sustaining purpose or meaning.

The crux of life is how we choose to respond to negative situations. It has been said that life is 10 percent of what happens to us and 90 percent of how we respond to those situations. We need to teach this generation of fathers how to deal with life so that they can come to help the next generation live more healthy lives.

The wonderful thing about writing to the faith community is that we have a great opportunity to touch men's lives and apply spiritual solutions in a holistic manner. Secular social programs merely apply a Band-Aid to hemorrhaging men. They can't reach down into the depths of a man and speak healing to deep wounds. We have a special opportunity. Let's respond.

While much of this chapter has focused on men who may not be members of churches, they by no means represent the total population who needs to understand this message. There are many men in churches who look good, work hard, but are also neglecting their families and who are full of anger and bitterness.

African American family renewal must include God and the church. The slave revolts, the underground slave railroad, the abolitionist movement, and the civil rights movement all involved God and the church in their efforts. The church must be included in our family renewal efforts.

Churches must make men and families their number one priority. Men's ministries should become as important as women's ministries. And in order to help men, church leaders need to understand that there must be deliberate and intentional efforts to reach men. They will not come to church because we put up a banner announcing "Men's Day Service! All men welcome!"

As church leaders, we have to ask ourselves: Have we offered African American men the best we have? Have we made available to them all of the twenty-century-old traditions of the church, not least that of the first century when the Christian church was impacted by men like Paul, Stephen, and John? Can it be that men today have not been given all of the possibilities and all of the "good news"—such as the sense of total devotion, of being cut to the heart, of deep symbolism, or of participation of the whole person in worship of a loving God—to enable them to make an appropriate decision, and avoid searching for God in unorthodox rites and elements of other religious experiences? Have they been offered all the wealth and life of the traditions of the first millennium of the church, or have they been presented with only a dry, moralizing type of Christianity?[39]

If we examine the hearts of men God sends our way, we will see that most men have small cancerous spots of anger and bitterness on their hearts. Many men's hearts will even look like they have been through a meat grinder. But like most of us, they will on the outside appear fine. But religious men and men who are eager to please will tend to handle their anger by rushing through it to forgiveness without dealing with their deep feelings.[40] We shouldn't rush to make men well, and we should remember that no two men's work is the same. Their processes of healing will be different.

Paul reminds us: "The weapons we use in our fight are not made by humans. Rather, they are powerful weapons from God. With them we destroy people's [men's] defenses, that is, their arguments and all their intellectual arrogance that oppose the knowledge of God. We take every thought captive so that it is obedient to Christ" (2 Cor. 10:4-6). Dr. Clarence Walker, in his book *Breaking the Strongholds in the African-American Family*, says that much time is lost and a lot of energy is spent because we have come to accept what sounds good in attempting to fight spiritual problems. All of that "whooping," hollering, philosophizing, theorizing is just inadequate. You can't do battle with what sounds good and feels good. We must be intentional, and we must use those weapons that are effective. These weapons are the Word of God, effective prayer, and perfect praise. In his book *Reclaiming the Urban Family*, Dr. Willie Richardson says that "we must face Satan head-on and challenge him for millions of unsaved men. The church cannot build Christian families if we are not reaching our unsaved fathers and sons."[41]

Recommendations for Effective Ministry

Here are some components to consider in creating an effective men's ministry which not only attracts and keeps men in church, but also produces real, intentional, deliberate changes in their personal lives. In reviewing this list, keep your mind on Christ and what he might do today to reach men. He was successful more than 2,000 years ago with 12 men. Do you think he could accomplish the same today in our communities? I think so. The suggestions below are ones we have used in our work with men.

Forgive Through Prayer

First, use prayer to lead men into forgiving others and themselves. All restoration starts here. We should begin our prayers by thanking and praising God for all that he has allowed to come to us through our forefathers. We can thank God for all the good that we inherit daily. We also must pray that even this good be filtered through the cross so that the good can begin to appear to the men as good and, indeed, part of what God is using for their benefit. You may be amazed at how men begin to see the good around them as they pray this prayer.

Instruct men in the power of prayer. Ted Dobson proclaims our hope for African American men and all men: "As we bring our insecurity, unforgiveness, and immature thought/behavior patterns to the Lord honestly and vulnerably, He can free us from our pain and weakness and both lead and empower us to live in a new way."[42]

Call in prayer for the blood of Jesus to flow back, with forgiveness, through the family bloodlines throughout each man's history, washing away the ground of Satan's attack. We ask in repentance for forgiveness for all known sins (some things must wait for conscious repentance and confession).[43]

Whatever sin patterns we have seen and discussed, we need to ask Jesus to destroy and transform on the cross. "The reason that the Son of God appeared was to destroy what the devil does" (1 John 3:8). This may be the most important part of the prayer. The greatest necessity in praying for the cessation of ruination in families is to stop generational patterns, calling for their death and transformation into blessing through the power of the cross and the resurrection of Jesus.[44]

We should name each pattern, describing it, and calling specifically for our Lord to destroy it. In this prayer, we are not merely praying for the counselee, but for him in proxy for his entire family. The counselee is the central focus of heaven's attack upon the powers of darkness, and the land to be occupied is the counselee's entire family. We pray that whatever pattern we describe may be destroyed from the life of every brother and sister, uncle and aunt and cousin, grandparent and great-grandparent, and each adopted or in-law connected to the family.

Focus on releasing judgments. We may want men to write in a journal the names of people they have judged. They may name father, mother, brothers and sisters, grandmothers, aunts, and uncles. The list may be long for some and short for others. There may be nameless people, ethnic groups, or one individual that wronged a man and he included all white people in that judgment.

When men feel they are able to let go of the judgments, instruct them as to how to do so. As with forgiveness, there is no formula whereby they can snap their fingers and make judgments disappear. When a man, after much prayer and teaching, comes to the place when he can and wants to let go, help him. But he will have to work through the pain and anger involved. Most men will need a group, a pastor, or a trained counselor or therapist to lead them through the process.

Most of this work should be done without confronting family members or ethnic groups. Talking to a parent may not be the important thing to do. Cleaning our heart and healing is a personal thing and must be done internally. We must believe that God will answer according to his will and knowledge of what is right.

Create a Safe Atmosphere

We must create an atmosphere of grace, safety, and trust. Men need to feel free to be honest and vulnerable. This must come first from the pulpit and must involve regular teaching on humility, grace, unconditional love, the power of forgiveness, and the centrality of intimacy with the Father to men's Christian walks. Men need to know that God desires and is able to forgive, heal, and restore anyone—no matter what he has done.

Creating this atmosphere requires that ministry leaders be open about their own failings. The dishonest posturing of "sinless perfection" by leaders has been a debilitating phenomenon in the church today. To a broken man, a pastor looks like and sounds like a perfect man whom they cannot relate to. It is only when we shed our Ph.D.'s, and our Right Reverends, and discuss our own past anger, bitterness, and how we overcame them do we appear real to them.

Nearly all of the men I have worked with, including James with whom we began this chapter, have accepted the responsibility of working in groups to improve their condition, and remember these are men who may have never shared their pain and suffering with another man. Counseling, group or individual, is not an acceptable cultural norm in the African American community. As we have said earlier, African American men have never been given permission to seek counseling for their inner wounds. They have been forced to be strong, hard-working men, and admitting hurt and pain of any kind, especially to other men, has been viewed as an indication of weakness. So for some of the men it was tough to open up at first. But most of them began to open up when they heard they were not alone in their struggle with bitterness and pain. I have concluded that there are not enough safe places for men to open up and share their pain. Most places that offer counseling in an acceptable form are available only after men have committed a crime. We make few efforts in churches and other faith organizations to let men share their pain. As Charles Ballard says, "We got to get the hurting father out of him before he can be a father to his children."

Train Resource People

Train resource people to handle specific problem areas of men. Pastors of medium to large congregations cannot possibly see all of the men who may desire their counsel. It is important that a team of men be trained in handling addictions, adultery, anger, finances, leadership, self-esteem, and roots of bitterness. These men will often be ones God has forgiven and healed of similar patterns, but not always.

Also, work to establish a Men's Council that can deal with situations as they arise, creating programs and assigning lay ministers as "accountability partners," peer counselors, prayer leaders, and mentors. Finally, great efforts should be made to pair men with a mentor to help them through the peer pressure of their past.

Use Specialty Ministries

Encourage specialty ministries within the church. You can invite outside parachurch ministries to come alongside to aid men when there appears to be no one in the congregation able to assist. However, your men are going to be most comfortable with men they have come to know and trust. There are many excellent examples of churches ministering to men.

Encourage Men's Groups

Encourage men to attend regular men's fellowship groups. Attendance at men's groups, prayer breakfasts, or other gatherings can provide opportunities for fellowship and spiritual growth. A broken man needs to be integrated into the body of believers. He needs to experience forgiveness and hang around those who can model and encourage him to be a good father and a responsible man. He also must be called into servanthood by the needs of the group so that he can learn to focus on others instead himself.

Be Practical

Be practical, down to earth, and meaningful. As part of the restoration process, give assignments that will not only help men grow, but also will test their willingness to do whatever it takes to be made right with God and with their community. Have them read books on being a good father, watch videos, listen to tapes, attend conferences and counseling or group sessions, write reports, or keep a journal on what they are learning.

Assign appropriate actions for them to carry out in order to restore broken relationships. Teach them practical things such as how to worship, study the Bible, listen in prayer, and how to live by faith.

Provide Resources

Make every effort to provide resources. There are books, tapes, videos, and support group materials available that can aid any church seeking to help men. A good men's library would be a worthwhile investment.

Many urban men have a visual learning style. We have used video movie clips during our class sessions. This has been helpful in teaching men various skills of caring for children and showing them how to handle interpersonal relationships with the mothers of their children. Video clips give a man permission to be an active father and help him form a meaningful mental picture of what methods are good.

We have focused our lesson planning on the belief that many African American men have a sixth grade reading level. They will probably not read a good fathering magazine or a lengthy academic book directed at being a good father. I usually present a one page sheet with bold letters and bullet points. I avoid long sentences and paragraphs. Their reading span is limited. In fact, they are not very comfortable reading to each other, and in most of the settings there has been at least one man who could not read at all.

Maintain Confidentiality

Always, always seek to maintain confidentiality. Keep the knowledge of a man's failures within those structures that have been established—and teach group members to maintain confidential information. Trust is a very real factor in attracting and keeping men.

Trust is a key element in keeping broken men coming to church. Because of their lack of fathering and poor track record with male authority figures, many men are suspicious and distrustful of pastors and ministers. Not only do we have to maintain their trust by keeping their personal business confidential, but we also have to maintain their trust by our own personal behavior. We can forget about getting men to come to church when leaders do not maintain personal integrity.

Focus on Process, Not One Experience

Don't fall victim to the belief that a single spiritual experience will change a man's life. Focus instead on the process of changing through Christ's power and individual effort. Many church leaders believe that men can have a "spiritual experience" of making a decision for Christ, for example, and have instant healing or in that moment take giant steps toward emotional maturity. The truth is that for many men, basic personality is not changed by a single spiritual experience.[45]

A single spiritual experience usually does not give one a new personality type. The apostle Paul, for example, changed from an aggressive Christian-killer to an aggressive ambassador for Christ. His new style was tempered by love, but he did not change his basic personality from an aggressive tiger to a passive pussycat. Standing in a healing line, as another example, does not give a man instant skills for dealing with his anger. Conversion gives one a motivation for change and growth and places one in a setting where growth can take place, but it is rare that God immediately gives a person a new personality. We are "new creatures," born again. We are newborn babes, uninformed and immature. Babies have the capacity to grow and want to grow, but their growth requires knowledge, nurture, and time. Men under our care need the same.

Promote Relationship with Christ

Finally, but not least, we know that the root cause of all bitterness and anger is sin. The antidote to sin is a personal relationship with God through Christ. This leads to hope, reconciliation, and healing. God usually initiates a personal relationship with a man and nurtures it, through his church.[46] But many African American men have no personal relationships with men of faith, black or white. Consequently, they have no believers to love them, encourage them, counsel them, or teach them.

The church should be the source of healing for angry and bitter men. Tragically, much of the church is conspicuously absent from the lives of urban fathers. The church has become more concerned with great choirs and rousing "musicals" and urban renewal of bricks and mortar than with renewing the souls of men and fathers.

There are many good black folks in the urban community who are cowering behind high fences, barred windows, and steel doors. Many believers feel helpless and overwhelmed by mounting problems related to fatherlessness. All too often, they huddle in their places of worship, hoping they can sing, pray, and preach their problems away. The reality is that the problem is too large for the small, storefront churches, which are for many men the only form of God in the urban core. Many of these black church leaders often work full-time jobs, in addition to chasing emergency vehicles, planning and attending funerals, and keeping up with the programmatic events of their church.

African American men are not merely searching for truth—they are searching for how truth can be applied to their personal lives. I believe they want to experience biblical truth in terms of relationships and relevance. All around the urban community men are struggling with anger and bitterness. They are ready to give up on the Christian church and turn to the god of Farrakhan and the Nation of Islam. But Black Muslims as a group are angry with white Americans and use that as their group's central theme.[47]

Our job is not to get these men to be members of our church, but it is to be the church to these men, meeting them at their point of need. It is critical that we guide men to an intentional relationship with the Father who created us and is calling us all into true manhood among fellow men. The key lies in healing the tear in men's soul, which the church has largely ignored and which the prisons can house but not heal.[48]

Include These Aims

We should also make sure to include the following aims or goals in everything we do. By thinking about how each program or activity encourages strong fathers and families and by reinforcing the initiatives below whenever possible, we can help the church and the community understand that unless we change, we are doomed to experience hell here on earth.

1. Restore marriage as the honored institution for strong families and communities.
2. Create effective ministries to men and fathers.
3. Work with employment services and government programs to prepare men to meet the challenges of co-supporting children and families and to make them more marriageable.
4. Encourage members to consider adoption as a means of supporting children.
5. Support single mothers through the men's program. Assist

these mothers by having men act as surrogate fathers and support teams to these at-risk families.

The Hope for the Future

There is no greater time than now for us to lay aside our pleasure, comfort, and luxury and to call for the blood of Jesus to flow back through the family bloodlines of African American men. Despite the past catastrophes and the present problems, healing is possible. Faith leaders need to help African American men come to a place where they can forgive the sins of their fathers, both their biological fathers and their white forefathers, so that the chains of Satan's stronghold can be broken.

By denying the problem of bitter root judgment, leaders abdicate their responsibility to their communities; they abdicate the responsibility given them by their ancestors; and they abdicate their relationship to their great "African ancestor," Jesus Christ.

The process of healing must first begin with pastors and African American faith leadership. Men who have not dealt with their anger and bitterness cannot lead another man to healing. Many faith leaders hide behind a performance-oriented religious facade. They are haunted by the feelings of worthlessness, and they fear if they slow down, those feelings will catch up with them.

I believe deep in the heart of all African American men is the longing for the Heavenly Father to say, "This is my beloved son, in whom I am well pleased." We have lost the central theme of the gospel that enraptured many slave men: a thriving, loving relationship with the Heavenly Father. We have settled for a social gospel, a civil rights message, an empty afro-centric theology. God stands ready, even perched, for us to ask him to do what we can't do for ourselves.

But in some ways the black church has set up a roadblock to the healing God wants to provide. It has become a cultural parade of fancy hats, Armani suits, and expensive cars in the parking lot. The men on the outside feel like they don't fit in.

The black church as we know it must be revolutionized. Truly, there are some fine programs in the country. But then, some neighborhoods are totally without significant and meaningful spiritual influences despite the many, many blocks of churches. Many urban African American churches have wonderful music and some of the best speakers in the world, reminiscent of the oratory style of Dr. Martin Luther King. But many of these preachers spend so much time trying to imitate Dr. King and they major in style and minor in content while their words are full of shallow hope, long on wind and "whoop," and void of the kind of "message" that will take people broken and in despair into the twenty-first century.

The church should become socially relevant to men and fathers. We need to reclaim some of the values of old. We need to remember that people rise no higher than what's expected of them. If we expect little or nothing from men, then we are likely to get just what we expect. If we expect more of them, we should express that, and look for it.

James and other men I have worked with give me great hope. They have shown that they are now involved in their children's lives. Even their wives have indicated dramatic changes in their husbands. Some are attempting to pay child support. All in all, they have begun to put away the sins of the past and to start a new future for themselves and their family and subsequent generations.

Twenty-five years from now it may not matter that our choir received the Best Choir Award. We may be judged not for our music, our preaching, or even our free worship style, but for how well we supported the African American family.

Notes

All Scripture quotations are taken from *God's Word* translation. Copyright 1995 by World Publishing, Grand Rapids, Mich.

1. Jawanza Kunjufu, "The Real Issue About the Male Academy," *Black Issues in Higher Education* 8, no. 16 (1991): 88; and Jawanza Kunjufu, "Need for African American Male Teachers Educating African American Males" (workshop presented to Second Annual African American Male National Conference, Milwaukee, Wisc., September 26, 1997).

2. E. Bernard Franklin, "As the World Turns: Developmental Issues Facing Today's College Man," parts 1 and 2, *Programming*, March and August 1997, Columbia, S.C.: National Association for Campus Activities.

3. See Kunjufu, "Real Issue" and Kunjufu, "Need for Male Teachers."

4. Bill Stephney, "The Welfare Rap: Why Black Men Hate It," *The New Republic*, 16 and 23 September, 1996.

5. Stephney, "Welfare Rap."

6. See Sarah McLanahan and Karen Booth, "Mother-Only Families: Problems, Prospects, and Politics," *Journal of Marriage and the Family* 51 (1989): 557-580; and Ken Canfield, *The Heart of a Father* (Chicago: Northfield Publishing, 1996).

7. See Ronald B. Mincy, *Nurturing Young Black Males: Challenges to Agencies, Programs, and Social Policy* (Washington, D.C.: Urban Institute Press, 1994).

8. See Franklin, "World Turns."

9. See Canfield, *Heart of a Father*.

10. Na'im Akbar, *Chains and Images of Psychological Slavery* (Jersey City, N.J.: New Mind Productions, 1984), 7.

11. Peter Paris, *The Spirituality of African Peoples: The Search for a Common Moral Discourse* (Minneapolis: Fortress Press, 1995).

12. John Mbiti, *African Religion and Philosophy* (Garden City, N.Y.: Doubleday, 1970), 2-3.

13. See Albert J. Raboteau, *Slave Religion: The "Invisible Institution" in the Antebellum South* (Oxford: Oxford University Press, 1978).

14. See Hugh Thomas, *The Slave Trade* (New York: Simon and Schuster, 1997).

15. See John Blassingame, *The Slave Community* (New York: Oxford University Press, 1972); Herbert Guttman, *The Black Family in Slavery and Freedom, 1750-1925* (New York: Pantheon, 1976); Andrew Billingsley, *Climbing Jacob's Ladder*; Robert Staples and Leanor Boulin Johnson, *Black Families at the Crossroads* (San Francisco: Jossey-Bass, 1993); and Paris, *Spirituality of African Peoples*.

16. See Eugene D. Genovese, *Roll, Jordan, Roll: The World the Slaves Made* (New York: Vintage, 1976); and Sister Souljah, *No Disrespect* (New York: Vintage, 1994).

17. See Genovese, *Roll, Jordan, Roll*.

18. See E. Franklin Frazier, *The Negro Church in America* (New York: Schocken, 1963).

19. See Billingsley, *Jacob's Ladder*.

20. See Frazier, *Negro Church*.

21. See Genovese, *Roll, Jordan, Roll* .

22. See Billingsley, *Jacob's Ladder*.

23. See Paul Glick, "Demographic Pictures of Black Families" in *Black Families*, second edition, ed. Harriet McAdoo (Newbury Park, Calif.: Sage, 1988), 111-132.

24. See William D. Allen and Michael Conner, "An African American Perspective on Generative Fathering" in *Generative Fathering*, ed. Alan J. Hawkins and David C. Dollahite (Thousands Oaks, Calif.: Sage, 1997).

25. See Billingsley, *Jacob's Ladder*.

26. See Allen and Conner, *Generative Fathering*.

27. Billingsley, *Jacob's Ladder*, 135.

28. Gordon Dalbey, *Healing the Masculine Soul* (Waco, Tex.: Word Books, 1988), 2.

29. Quoted in John Leland and Allison Samuels, "The New Generation Gap," *Newsweek*, 17 March 1997.

30. Akbar, *Chains and Images*, 3.

31. Quoted in Dalbey, *Masculine Soul*, 13.

32. See Theodore Rubin, *The Angry Book* (New York: Collier, 1989).

33. See Mario Bergner, *Setting Love in Order* (Grand Rapids, Mich.: Hamewith Books, 1995).

34. See John Sandford and Paula Sandford, *Healing the Wounded Spirit* (South Plainfield, N.J.: Bridge Publications, 1985).

35. See Sara H. Martin, *Shame on You!* (Nashville: Broadman Press, 1990).

36. See Charles R. Solomon, *The Ins and Outs of Rejection* (Littleton, Colo.: Heritage House, 1976).

37. Leanne Payne, *Crisis in Masculinity* (Grand Rapids, Mich.: Hamewith Books, 1985), 60.

38. See Martin, *Shame.*

39. Anastasios Yannoulatos, "Growing into Awareness of Primal WorldViews" in *Primal World-Views: Christian Involvement in Dialogue with Traditional Thought Forms*, ed. John B. Taylor (Ibadan, Nigeria: Daystar Press, 1976), 72-78.

40. See Martin, *Shame.*

41. Willie Richardson, *Reclaiming the Urban Family* (Grand Rapids, Mich.: Zondervan, 1996), 67-68.

42. Quoted in Dalbey, *Masculine Soul*, 13.

43. See Sandford and Sandford, *Wounded Spirit.*

44. See Sandford and Sandford, *Wounded Spirit.*

45. See Martin, *Shame.*

46. See Keith Phillips, *Out of Ashes* (Los Angeles: World Impact Press, 1996).

47. See Clarence Walker, *Breaking Strongholds in the African American Family* (Grand Rapids, Mich.: Zondervan, 1996).

48. See Dalbey, *Masculine Soul.*

Chapter 5

Fatherhood in the Roman Catholic Tradition

Most Reverend Anthony M. Pilla

Roman Catholics in the United States are eager to work with other churches and religious traditions and various community groups in order to raise awareness and to take action concerning the growing problem of men not being truly involved as fathers in their families. The crisis of "father absence" is both a societal and a religious challenge.

Religious and spiritual leaders have a duty to form the members of their own faith community according to a certain set of beliefs. In doing this, however, we collectively help to create a community of conscience within our society that will act as a leaven within the larger mass. Pope John Paul II has repeatedly urged the Catholic Church to undertake a "new evangelization" whereby the connection is made between personal conversion and faith and the transforming of social structures and cultural values.[1]

In my ministry as a bishop I am both a teacher and a pastor. Therefore, when I address a social and ethical issue such as fatherhood, I draw upon two resources present in our faith community. The first is a consistent set of *principles*, drawn from Catholic teaching and our biblically-based faith tradition, which provides a moral framework to guide choices. The second is our *experience* of serving those in need and of working on behalf of justice. Based on this day-to-day experience, we have some notions about what can work in a given situation and also how complex and systemic any problem is likely to be.

It is from those two vantage points that I offer my reflections about promoting involved fatherhood in two key areas. First, how the issue of fatherlessness is presented in the public arena, especially within faith communities, matters a great deal. Second, because of a rich faith tradition that celebrates the fatherhood of God, Catholic leaders are inspired to expend energy in support of fatherhood, particularly through the spheres of marriage and work.

Presenting the Issue

In calling attention to the causes, dimensions, and consequences of fatherlessness, I suggest we try to avoid three pitfalls. I say this not to point a finger in any direction, but to remind us of standards we should uphold, beginning in our own churches and synagogues. The case for fatherhood must be presented in terms that are not *simplistic*, *dualistic*, or *moralistic*.

First, we must not be tempted by a simplistic notion that reversing the trend toward fatherlessness will, in and of itself, become the solution to all that ails us socially and morally. The problem of physically and/or psychologically absent fathers should always be placed in a wider context which includes other reinforcing trends like the loss of a sense of the common good, the collapse of community structures, major upheavals in our economy, the flight of human and financial capital especially from our older cities, and so on. Fatherhood is part of a larger system known as the family, and this, in turn, is located within a larger social system. It is true, restoring the ideal and the experience of committed fatherhood may be an effective entry point into solving larger social problems. At the same time, however, we must seek to make fatherhood desirable and feasible within a contemporary family context.

Second, in framing the fatherhood issue we must avoid the dualism of false choices. The U.S. Catholic bishops have consistently taken a stand against the polarization that results when the desire for more exemplary personal values is pitted against the call for more effective social policies. These should not be mutually exclusive. Conversion and compassion are both gospel values. We bishops are on record for teaching that a renewed sense of personal responsibility must be coupled with new social policies if we are to strengthen our families and our nation. In the specific case of fatherhood, therefore, we need to hold in tension the solutions that, on the one hand, emphasize character building and the raising of moral standards and those that, on the other, advocate for economic change and political remedies.

Third, we should be on guard against moralism. This should not be confused with preaching and teaching morality. Rather, moralism is akin to the narrow-mindedness that Jesus condemned throughout his public ministry. It is the rigid adherence to one way of understanding or acting that, although rooted in a moral value, can never admit that this ideal will not be fully realized in each and every case. As regards the issue of fatherhood, we must be, on the one hand, as clear as possible that fatherhood should always occur within marriage and, on the other hand, realistic enough to acknowledge it does not in every instance. So we must ask: Does our concern for fathers extend even to those who might not be married, or who may have ended their marriages through divorce? Some of these men have not ceased to think of themselves as fathers. They, too, deserve our ministry.

Ministry on Behalf of Fatherhood

Two areas of ministry are considered by the Catholic Church to be very important for reversing the movement away from fatherhood. Both are related to the well-being of family life, for it is a stronger, more viable family—in which children are loved and provided for—that should be the goal of our effort to renew fatherhood. Both these focal points for ministry, also, are derived from our church's position that family life must be strengthened both from within—in terms of the behavior and relationships of family members, and from without—in terms of how social structures either help or hinder the family.

It is difficult to deal with fatherhood entirely in the abstract. Sooner or later I am drawn to thinking of my own father and the many men like him whom I have known. For them, being a father was entirely bound up with being a husband and being an economic provider. And although the conditions under which my father was married and earned a living for our family have changed, nonetheless it is still true that fatherhood must sink roots into two worlds—the world of marriage and the world of work—if it is to be a stable reality in the lives of children and in the community. Or to put it another way, take away a good marriage and/or a good job, and you make it much more likely that a man will become just another absent father.

The World of Marriage

Social research leads to conclusions such as David Blankenhorn draws in *Fatherless America* that "marriage constitutes an irreplaceable life support system for effective fatherhood."[2] In this instance, social research and church teaching reinforce one another. Catholic teaching holds that the family originates in marriage. "The family draws its proper character as a community, its traits of communion, from that fundamental communion of the spouses which is prolonged in their children."[3]

The obvious challenge for the church, then, is to help men and women see marriage as a worthy state and a holy vocation, to enter this union with the proper motivation and an adequate level of preparation, and to create over the years a marriage which gradually matures into lasting friendship, a deepening peace, and ultimately salvation.

Catholics believe that marriage is a sacrament—a living and effective sign of God's love in the world—and therefore we expend a lot of ministerial effort on behalf of marriages. Though far from perfect, our ministries run the entire gamut from marriage preparation to marriage enrichment to programs which help to reconcile failing marriages to support groups for the divorced to family counseling services to help for blended families and stepparents.[4] I invite you, my fellow religious leaders, to consider how we might share our resources in order to become churches that are truly marriage builders within our local communities.

There is a continuing question and challenge through all these ministries about how to draw men themselves into the project of building a stronger marriage. This is not easy. Marriage is relational work, and this is often considered a woman's domain. Thus we realize how necessary it is to present to men a compelling vision of marriage—one which can call forth the gifts of true masculinity and, at the same time, will fully respect the equal dignity of women in this relationship.

In a recent pastoral message, *Follow the Way of Love*, the U.S. Catholic bishops offered teaching and pastoral guidance on four virtues that make possible the kind of marriage that Pope John Paul II calls an intimate partnership of life and love. They are as follows: being faithful to commitments especially in the midst of change, giving life to children and being generative within the community, developing a relationship of mutuality between husband and wife, and devoting priority time and energy to marriage and family relationships. It is in teaching and preaching these virtues, I think, that we help couples to understand how marriage is possible—with human effort and God's grace—and therefore, also, how fatherhood can flourish when anchored in a healthy and holy marriage.[5]

The World of Work

The other anchor for fatherhood—a domain in which, like marriage, men participate in the creative power of God—is the world of work. In Catholic teaching, work is more than doing a job or making a living. It is an expression of our God-given personal dignity. It contributes to our humanization and to the common good.

Though increasingly mothers and fathers are sharing the role of economic provider in a family, we should not discount the critical difference that having a decent job (or fulfilling career) makes for a man's self-esteem. And this, in turn, is related positively to his ability to get married, stay married, and be involved with his children. There are empirical data that show a correlation between an increase in men's earnings and the increased likelihood of marrying along with the decreased likelihood of divorcing.[6]

The church has a vital role in ensuring that the world of work is supportive of fatherhood. In the Catholic community we do this by educating and providing moral guidance, as well as by advocating for public policy and legislation.

Our moral and educational task, which we attempt through preaching, bishops' pastoral letters, and other methods of teaching, deals with questions like reclaiming the proper balance between work and leisure (correctly understood as "Sabbath time"), setting priorities within a family when both spouses are involved in a job or career, putting the welfare of children first, adopting a simpler lifestyle that values "being" over "having," and so on.

Our responsibility as advocates for justice has led us over the years to support an increase in the minimum wage, the rights of workers to organize and bargain, an Earned Income Tax Credit for poor working families, reforming welfare in ways that encourage and reward work, providing job training, and in general introducing more family-friendly practices into the workplace.[7] As the world of work continues its rapid evolution, we support a discussion of such possibilities as job sharing, flextime, and reconsidering the practice of mandatory overtime.

Standing within the midst of a faith tradition that has always celebrated the fatherhood of God and drawn inspiration from the example of St. Joseph, we cannot now turn our backs on human fathers and let disappear all those qualities that sacramentalize God's love for us. There is much at stake for everyone when we examine the issue of fatherhood and then let it lead us into an ethical and social consideration of our communities of marriage, family, work, and civil society.

Notes

1. Pope John Paul II, *Apostolic Exhortation on the Vocation and Mission of the Lay Faithful in the Church and in the World* (Christifideles Laici). December 30,

1988. Washington, D.C.: United States Catholic Conference.

2. David Blankenhorn, *Fatherless America: Confronting Our Most Urgent Social Problem* (New York: HarperCollins, 1995), 223.

3. Pope John Paul II, *Letter to Families*. February 2, 1994. Washington, D.C.: United States Catholic Conference.

4. For a report of research on marriage preparation see Center for Marriage and Family, *Marriage Preparation in the Catholic Church: Getting It Right* (Omaha, Nebr.: Creighton University, 1995).

5. National Conference on Catholic Bishops. *Follow the Way of Love: A Pastoral Message of the U.S. Catholic Bishops to Families*. November 17, 1993. Washington, D.C.: United States Catholic Conference.

6. *1995 Kids Count Data Book* (Baltimore: Annie E. Casey Foundation, 1995), 5-16.

7. U.S. Catholic Conference Administrative Board. *Political Responsibility: Proclaiming the Gospel of Life, Protecting the Least Among Us, and Pursuing the Common Good*. September 1995. Washington, D.C.: United States Catholic Conference.

Chapter 6

Fatherhood in the Evangelical Tradition

Richard Land and Barrett Duke

Good Christian parenting is not a new topic for American evangelicals. As one looks at the written material that has been available to evangelicals over the past 30 years, it is obvious that quality resources have been developed to help parents raise their children. James Dobson, the evangelical equivalent of Dr. Spock, wrote *Dare to Discipline* in 1970 and *Love Must Be Tough* in 1983. Dozens of other books have been published by equally capable men and women to assist evangelicals with parenting.[1] Numerous study materials have been produced as well. For example, the Parenting By Grace curriculum is available through the Southern Baptist publishing house LifeWay Christian Resources, formerly the Baptist Sunday School Board. Parenting By Grace is an 11-week course that encourages couples to meet together, to study a detailed curriculum on various parenting issues, and to discuss them in a group setting. Since its publication in 1986, over 125,000 copies of the student guide have been sold.

In addition, most evangelical churches have some type of regular family emphasis. The Church Recreation Department at LifeWay Christian Resources estimates that 40 percent of Southern Baptist churches—about 15,000—sponsor a family activity time, during which families are encouraged to do things together. These activities include a sharing and discussion time so that there is genuine interaction among family members.

An increasing number of churches are building family life centers so that their church families have a safe and wholesome environment for recreation activities.

What Should Be Is Not What Is

Obviously, evangelicals understand the importance of strong families. Between the availability of the vast array of excellent written materials for individual and group study and numerous opportunities for families to do things together, the American evangelical family should be healthy. Yet the evangelical community, like the rest of America, struggles to keep its families from disintegrating. Evangelicals have struggled with the reality that even though much help is available, families are not getting better. Family activity times are poorly attended, and most family life centers are kept busier with age-graded activities or organized sports than with families actually doing things together.

As evangelicals have realized that many of their families are in serious trouble and that many of their converts are desperately in need of basic biblical foundations, including family training, they have taken a closer look at the problem and realized that the breakdown of the family is directly related to the absence of a man's involvement in his home, especially as a servant leader. There are numerous reasons for this lack of participation by men, but a primary reason is that evangelical churches have not taught their families sufficiently about core family issues, including fathering. While it may be true that the importance of fatherhood is something best learned in the home, it must also be admitted that evangelical churches should have been reinforcing this. However, what one finds when looking at the average American evangelical church is a surprisingly weak commitment to help men understand their responsibilities and very little support as these men attempt to fulfill their duties. Certainly, there are special emphases, like Father's Day and special father-daughter and father-son outings, but too often nothing is done between these times that provides any context for these events. They are merely times that show up on a calendar and are observed, then forgotten until they come around again. As a result, Father's Day is not effective long term, and father-child events are poorly attended.

Why a Fatherhood Emphasis Is Missing

There are numerous explanations for the failure of evangelical churches to provide men with an adequate emphasis on fatherhood. First, the churches assumed people knew their roles and were filling them. After all, it is a family matter. And as such, one expects a son to learn about fathering from his father and to learn about the honor of being a father from the honor that his father received in the home. Unfortunately, too often young boys have not learned these things in their homes.

Second, the churches focused as much energy and resources as they possibly could on their first priority—evangelism. If the average church had to choose between evangelism and strengthening families, and often they could not or simply were not interested in doing both, they chose evangelism.

A third probable cause for the loss of emphasis on fatherhood in evangelical churches can be traced to the feminist movement that has continued to grow over the past 30 years. This movement has developed through many different channels, ranging from arguments of male and female equality to the loss of role distinctions as women have continued to assume more of what were once considered male roles. The result of these various emphases has been the blurring of the lines of male and female distinctiveness. Evangelicals have struggled with defining just exactly what are the distinct contributions of men and women in the home, church, and society. This confusion coupled with a militant feminist mentality in certain public sectors, which has accused those who advocate male leadership models as the promoters of female inferiority or subservience, has, in some instances, silenced the evangelical churches' message to men. In order to avoid allegations of sexism, or out of sympathy or agreement with the feminist movement, some evangelical churches have chosen not to get involved in men's ministry.

It is likely that there are many other explanations. It is also true that all explanations do not apply to all evangelical churches, but the result is that many evangelical men have not received sufficient training or appreciation, in their homes or their churches, for the important part that fathers play in the life of the family. The result of the silence of evangelical churches on men's roles can be compared to handing a child a model and telling him to build it without the instructions. The child will produce something, but it will seldom resemble the model envisioned by the original designer. As one looks at what has become of fatherhood today, the analogy is clear. Men have been left to their own devices, and many of them have failed miserably. Consequently, fatherhood and the honor of fatherhood have been largely lost in the evangelical tradition.

The Need for a Sense of Unique Identity

Evangelical leaders have come to realize that men need to recapture a sense of their unique identity if the family is to be strengthened. They must be encouraged to fulfill their God-given responsibilities as men, in the home as husbands and fathers, in the church, and in the community. Evangelical laymen are becoming more aware of this as well, and they are looking for help to become the men and fathers that God designed them to be and that their wives and children need. The phenomenal growth of the Promise Keepers movement is testimony of the extent to which men are aware of their need for this kind of aid. Begun in 1990, this movement has become international in its influence and has seen more that 1.3 million men attend its events. The majority of these men have come from evangelical churches.

Clear evidence of evangelical men's interest in understanding and assuming their responsibilities is provided by the subject matter that they discuss when they gather for their meetings. A good example is the Promise Keepers group that started several years ago at Cornerstone Baptist Church in Littleton, Colorado. The men who gathered on Monday mornings decided to use the book *The Seven Promises of a Promise Keeper* to help them grow. The chapter titles of this book indicated what was important to these men: "A Man and His God," "A Man and His Mentors," "A Man and His Integrity," "A Man and His Family," "A Man and His Church," "A Man and His Brothers," "A Man and His Word." The chapter on the family was comprised of two sections: "Five Secrets of a Happy Marriage" by Gary Smalley and "The Priority of Fathering" by James Dobson.

The men who came together to talk about these issues were good Christian men who were looking for answers to problems that were affecting their own lives and roles. Each week they read a chapter, and at their Monday meetings one of the men led them in a discussion of it. The chapter on the family sparked the liveliest discussion. As a result of the Promise Keepers movement, men are meeting and talking to each other in public settings in ways and about issues that the church has seldom, if ever, experienced in the past. Today, Promise Keepers groups and various other men's ministries have sprung up in all evangelical groups in America. In this ground swell one can see the beginning of an answer to the dilemma of the American evangelical family—the fatherhood movement.

Print and Broadcast Initiatives

Currently, evangelicals are attempting to describe the influence of a father on his family, give guidance on how a father can accomplish this in his home, and encourage the father to accept the responsibility of guiding his family. Newspapers, books, and group studies have been produced within the past few years to help men understand the role and significance of fatherhood. Major publishers serving the evangelical community are producing books on men's issues in staggering numbers. These books either address fatherhood specifically or they include sections or specific emphases on fathering. The popular *Tender Warrior* by Stu Weber, published by Multnomah Books in 1993, includes three chapters on a man and his children. The book has so resonated with the hearts of evangelical men that in many circles men have begun giving it to other men as gifts. Broadman and Holman published *The Father Connection* by Josh McDowell in 1996. Zondervan released *Man to Man* by Charles Swindoll and *The Worth of a Man* by Dave Dravecky. Moody Press published *The Heart of a Godly Man* by E. Glenn Wagner, and Baker Book House offers *Dadship and Discipleship* by David Schroeder.

Focus on the Family, whose resources address numerous family issues, has recently published *Raising a Modern Day Knight: A Father's Role in Guiding His Son to Authentic Manhood* by Robert Lewis. And the ministry has recently revised James Dobson's extremely popular book *Straight Talk: What Men Need to Know, What Women Need to Understand*, which examines fatherhood.[2] Also, Focus on the Family continues to produce nationally syndicated broadcasts that speak to fathering issues.

In addition, there are family related magazines to help evangelicals develop an understanding of parenting issues. The *Focus on the Family* magazine regularly runs articles on fathering. The Southern Baptist publication *ParentLife*, which began in 1994, has a circulation of 117,000 each month. It is devoted solely to helping parents minister to their children. The magazine features a section entitled "Shaping the Next Generation" by David and Elaine Atchison. Each issue includes a brief article for fathers called "Dad's Workshop." Accompanying photographs throughout the magazine often depict the father in the center of family life. Another Southern Baptist publication, *HomeLife*, features a regular section entitled "Real Men." Each month this section addresses a different issue pertinent to men. Recent articles have included "Real Men Make a Difference" by pastor Ronnie Floyd and "Real Men Are Passionate" by Bill Peel. LifeWay also publishes a men's devotional guide. The guide is entitled *Stand Firm: God's Challenge for Today's Man*. It provides articles and daily devotional readings that speak specifically to men's needs and responsibilities. These are only a small part of what is available to the evangelical community. The National Fatherhood Initiative lists over 70 different secular and religious publications on fatherhood that are currently available from various publishers. Many of these publications are finding their way into more and more evangelical churches.

Programming Initiatives

Increasingly, evangelical churches are incorporating ministry to men into their regular programming through numerous approaches. In some churches parenting and family relationship issues are the key topics that pastors address on Sunday mornings. It is not unusual for churches to advertise their sermons to the public as practical, biblical direction for the family. While the specific topic of fatherhood is still usually addressed only on Father's Day, one will find frequent references to husbands and wives, fathers and mothers, and numerous other personal and family related topics in the course of an average sermon.

In addition, some evangelical churches are currently offering marriage and family classes during the traditional Bible study hour on Sunday morning. For example, Bellevue Baptist Church, a Southern Baptist church in Cordova, Tennessee, a suburb of Memphis, offers a parenting class for first-time parents during the Sunday school hour. Sometimes other Sunday school classes study material on parenting too. The Colorado Community Church, an Evangelical Presbyterian church in Denver, offers a parenting class on Sunday mornings, Wednesday evenings, and occasionally on Friday evenings. The First Church of the Nazarene in Denver, offers a home improvement class for newlyweds and young marrieds during the Sunday school hour.

Other evangelical churches are attempting to address marriage and family issues during regular or specially arranged times. For instance, the First Evangelical Free Church in Rockford, Illinois, offers men's accountability groups on Wednesday evenings from 6:30 to 8:00 and another program called Growing Kids God's Way, which is offered in homes at various times and at the church on Wednesday evenings. This church has also developed its own ministry to men called POPS. The ministry was developed in order to offer men something similar to women's MOPS (Mothers of Preschoolers) ministry. The group meets Thursday and Friday mornings. Its purpose is to assist men in implementing discipleship principles to help them become better fathers, husbands, and disciples of Christ.

Some evangelical churches are introducing symbolic activities that reinforce family emphases. At Cornerstone Baptist Church in Littleton, Colorado, a baby dedication service serves to point out the father's leadership role in his family and the responsibility of the family and the church to raise children in the nurture and admonition of the Lord. The evangelical tradition does not practice infant baptism as a grace-conferring event. However, most evangelical churches do offer their families some kind of mechanism for expressing their desire to raise their children in the Christian faith. This usually takes the form of a baby dedication activity where parents and congregation participate in a public statement of commitment to teach the child the things of Christ, to live a godly life before the child, and to ask God's blessings on the child and family.

In this service, usually performed before or after a regularly scheduled worship service, the parents stand before the congregation. The father holds the child, as a symbol of his spiritual leadership of the family. The pastor usually begins the service by speaking about the significance of the baby dedication service. The pastor then reads some pertinent Bible passages. After this, the parents, together and aloud, read their statement of commitment to raise their child in the Christian faith and pledge to live godly lives before their child. The father, as a participant in this public statement, commits himself to raising his child and providing for his child's spiritual and emotional, as well as material, needs. The congregation is then invited to respond with its own statement of commitment. Following this, the pastor voices a prayer calling on God to honor this commitment, to assist the family and the church to fulfill their obligations, and asking God's blessing on the child and the family.

Below is a sample baby dedication service conducted at Cornerstone Baptist Church:

The Dedication Service
of
Robert Allen Duke
June 14, 1992
Scriptures: Joshua 24:15; Psalm 139:13-18; Jeremiah 1:5

Statement of Commitment

Parents: Heavenly Father, we acknowledge that every good and perfect gift is from above and comes down from You, the Father of lights. Because Robert is Your gift to us and because we know that You love him even more than we do, we commit him into Your care and keeping. You are the Good Shepherd who carries the lambs in Your arms. So we place him in Your loving arms, Father. Guide us with Your Holy Spirit as we engage in training him. Make us patient. Give us tenderness, sincerity, and firmness that we may walk before him in a manner that is pleasing to You—with no hypocrisy or falsehood—that he may see the Lord Jesus in us. We commit ourselves to faithfully teach him the Holy Scriptures and to exert our influence and stewardship as Christians to lead him to a saving knowledge of God through Jesus Christ the Lord under the leadership of the Holy Spirit.

Congregation: We, the people of God, commit ourselves to join these parents in teaching and training Robert through the Holy Scriptures that he might, when coming to the age of accountability, receive Jesus Christ the Lord as Savior and Lord of his life and follow Him in obedience in baptism. We further commit ourselves to conduct our lives before him in a manner that honors Christ so that we may serve as an example to him of godly Christian character.

Prayer of Dedication: Blessed Father, You have heard the commitment of dedication by this father and mother and this congregation. We ask that you will grant to them the wisdom and grace to care for Robert and to teach him Your ways. We ask that You will help us to minister to this family in every way that they should need us. Help us to live godly, Christian lives before Robert in love and sincerity, without hypocrisy. Help us to teach him the things of God and to love him as You love him. Keep him safe from all harm. We ask that you would convict him of his sin at an early age that he might accept Jesus Christ as his savior. Finally, we ask that You would appoint a great purpose for him in Your kingdom. We join together this moment in the dedication of Robert and ourselves in service to You. We trust that You have heard us and will grant these requests in accordance with Your will. In the name of Jesus our Savior, Amen.

What one notices in the responses of evangelical churches to the current interest in men's issues is that the responses are individualistic. In fact, one could identify them as entrepreneurial. The reason for this individualistic approach is that there has not been such a plan in the church before. There is no currently existing program into which churches can plug these new emphases. As a result, churches are finding it necessary to create places for them. The more innovative the church and the more resources that are available to it, both in finances and workers, the more likely it is to have found a place for men's ministries within other ongoing ministries or to have created new organizations. However, it is likely that all evangelical churches will soon find it easier and more compelling to begin family ministries with an additional emphasis on fatherhood needs.

New Parental Materials

The development of new parental curriculum materials will also make it easier for churches to begin ongoing family ministries. These new curricula will enable churches to equip men for their unique role in the family by providing greater gender-specific training. These materials represent a significant movement beyond most previous parenting materials. First, though they will certainly approach parenting as a team, in which mother and father work together, they will also incorporate materials that address the unique contributions that men, and women, make to the family. Most earlier materials never addressed these differences. Second, the materials are perennial. They are intended as ongoing aid within the church, and they offer all the materials necessary to equip a church to maintain a permanent commitment to family training. Finally, these materials take a holistic approach. Parents and children are all trained in some way through the various components of the curricula.

Currently, several of these approaches are either available to evangelical churches or are in the final stages of development. The ministry known as Growing Families, International, which began eleven years ago and has experienced explosive growth in the last three years, is a parent-focused ministry with the stated objective of helping parents to raise godly children. The ministry, located in Simi Valley, California, produces six sets of curricula for evangelical churches to use in parent development and parenting training. The syllabus that accompanies the curriculum includes a chapter addressed specifically to fathers. Entitled "The Father's Mandate," the chapter encourages the father to "rightly reflect the truth of God and to develop a relationship of trust with his children based on God's truth."[3] Churches are encouraged to adopt this curriculum as a regular part of their plans. That this ministry is meeting a need in the evangelical community is evidenced by the more than 6,000 churches worldwide, most of which are evangelical, and the 600,000 people who use some part of the curricula.

Another significant contribution to the development in family ministry is a project currently under development in the Southern Baptist community. LifeWay Christian Resources is currently engaged in a major family initiative. This initiative is based on materials produced by Bill Mitchell entitled "Building Strong Families." Mitchell comes from a lifetime of experience in public school administration. He has seen, firsthand, the decline of the family and the devastating effects this decline is having on all segments of society. Mitchell's ministry is intended to provide the training and support that men, and anyone else interested in strengthening their families, will need. The church is seen as a key component in this training program. He views the pastor and the church as "the key to rebuilding the family unit in the community."

To introduce the ministry, citywide rallies are conducted, involving hundreds of churches and potentially thousands of people at a time. The purpose of these rallies is (1) to train people as trainers to work in the local churches; (2) to teach trainers to equip parents to raise their children, according to Proverbs 20:6; (3) to help each attendee to understand the mission of "Building Strong Families," which is to nurture strong, godly moral habits in the home; and (4) to create an awareness of the importance of building strong families.[4] The rallies are just the beginning. People will leave these gatherings and set up family training ministries in their local churches, where ongoing learning will take place.

This initiative is not a 12-week program. It is intended to be a continuing ministry of the church. It is envisioned as the key to helping churches reclaim their role in building strong families. Mitchell's material consists of a leader's guide, student workbook, videocassette, and several modules addressing different family issues. Currently, three modules are available: "Peace," "Kindness," and "Self-Control." Since this initiative is intended to become a perennial ministry of the local church, Mitchell and LifeWay Christian Resources will regularly produce new materials to assist in the training process. Through surveys of pastors, organizers have already identified many other areas of need. One of those needs is material to help men as fathers and husbands. Mitchell has noticed that men are returning from Promise Keepers meetings with a commitment to become the husbands and fathers they need to be, but they are not finding the support materials or resources that help them apply what they desire to do. At this time, gender specific material is being developed so that men can understand the importance of the role of fathers and husbands in the home.

Mitchell compares the necessary organizational structure of the home to that of an educational system. He says Christ should be seen as the superintendent, the father as the principal, and the mother as the helper. Mitchell does not intend any attitude of male superiority or female inferiority by this analogy. It is intended to communicate the chain of responsibility for the family. Mitchell recognizes that the father has some specific duties for the care and leadership of his family that are uniquely his. According to this analogy, the mother supports this leadership and exercises her own unique God-given responsibilities for her family. By continuing to stress the need for families to work together as units, Mitchell maintains the sense of partnership between husband and wife. But he intends to place more of the responsibility for training children on the shoulders of the husbands, which is the traditional evangelical model. This mentality is a significant development beyond the parents as partners materials produced to date. Since it is largely evangelical in its inception and promotion and it is built on biblical principles, I expect the evangelical community to support this movement with the same enthusiasm with which it greeted the previous family-oriented movements.

The Assemblies of God have recently entered into a partnership with an independent men's ministry in Little Rock, Arkansas. The ministry, called Dad: The Family Shepherd, will provide Assemblies of God churches with a broad range of ministries to men, including an emphasis on fatherhood. Part of the implementation process is the training of personnel for this ministry in the local churches. In order to facilitate this training, special workshops are being offered at district conventions. A good example of how this implementation process is being accomplished is the Dallas/Fort Worth district. The District Ministries Convention for the 553 churches in this district offers classes on men's ministries, which consists of four workshops. One of these workshops, called Daditude Adjustment, is intended specifically to train the leaders, teachers, and workers that the churches in that district will need to implement a men's ministry with a fatherhood emphasis.

Family University, headquartered in San Diego, has developed a program in this vein as well. The Family University is a university without walls. Churches, businesses, other organizations, and individuals can enroll in the various colleges of the university and begin receiving quarterly shipments of curriculum material. The university consists of six colleges: Fathering, Mothering, Child Development, Single Parenting, Stepparenting, and Grandparenting. Each college offers a variety of mixed-media materials, videocassettes, audiotapes, books, workbooks, and various other teaching and family development materials to help people gain the skills they need for successful family life. Currently, the university's emphasis has been focused on nonchurch groups. Zondervan will soon market the curriculum to over 350,000 churches and religious organizations in America.

Part of the strategy of the university is to encourage churches to establish themselves as an Extension Campus Church of Family University. Through this relationship with Family University, the church will receive the following benefits: (1) a half-day outreach-focused, family skills training event each year or a four-week plan that can be incorporated in the church's regular ministry calendar; (2) *Smart Families* magazines every quarter to distribute to families in the community; (3) a Family University Campus Pastor as a consultant; and (4) the availability of materials to establish a Family Resource Center Library.

The idea behind this approach is to equip the church to serve as a resource for families. Thom Black, vice president of Family University and former pastor at Willow Creek Community Church, believes that "families are responsible for themselves. The church should serve as a resource for them."[5] Black believes the key to strong families is to equip the entire family as a team, as well as to train each member. Their materials are designed to help accomplish this goal. Black encourages churches interested in making this ministry available to their families to sponsor a 30-day family ministry month. Family University will provide all the necessary materials for this month. Families will then enroll in one of the colleges of Family University. The materials will be sent to the churches and distributed by the churches. In this way the local church becomes the community resource for family strengthening ministry. Already, the university has a vast array of high quality materials available for all members of a family. Given their successful track record with the military and corporations, their materials should be well received by evangelicals as they become more aware of it.

This chapter has demonstrated that all of the necessary ingredients for a growing fatherhood movement currently exist in the evangelical community. There is tremendous need. A growing body of evangelical men are looking for help. There are numerous books, group study materials, and curricula available. Evangelical churches are beginning to respond to the call for help from their men and families. All that remains is for the majority of evangelical churches to respond and the fatherhood movement will find fertile soil.

What Churches Can Do

Churches must help fathers understand that in God's eyes they are accountable for the spiritual and emotional health of their families, and then they must offer fathers practical guidance on how to be godly husbands and fathers. There are several things evangelical churches can do to rectify the current weaknesses in ministry to fathers.

Focus on Accountability

Before all else, churches must help men understand that the success or failure of their families lies in large part with their involvement. At this time, most Promise Keepers groups that are active in local churches involve less than 10 percent of the men in the church. Though this statistic should not be construed to mean that the rest of the men in evangelical churches do not take an active role in the life of their families, it should serve as an indicator that most men in evangelical churches are not actively involved in improving their family skills. Until the church can get more than 10 percent of its men actively involved, nothing else that it does will make much difference.

The churches need to begin a men's movement within their own walls. They must make calling men to accountability one of their primary tasks. The churches can do this in the following ways: (1) by presenting more messages on the uniqueness of fatherhood, not just on parenting issues; (2) by bringing in special speakers who can teach men the importance of their place in the home; (3) by offering classes on the uniqueness of fatherhood, not only its responsibilities, and by encouraging men to attend them; (4) by developing activities that honor men and fatherhood. This last suggestion can be easily implemented. For instance, on Father's Day in 1997, the Harpeth Heights Baptist Church in Nashville honored fathers with a special recognition. The pastor asked all fathers to stand. He then shared with them the importance of their role as fathers, read some relevant Scripture, prayed for the fathers, and had the ushers hand each of them a copy of *God's Power for Fathers*, a book of topically arranged Bible passages that a man could turn to for biblical guidance or encouragement as he fulfills his responsibilities in all parts of daily life. Such demonstrations reveal the church's understanding of the importance of fatherhood and communicate a commitment to honor, support, and equip fathers for their place in the family. Variations of this could involve special presentations from wives or children.

Give Specific Guidance on Sunday Mornings

Once men become aware and committed to the importance of fulfilling their place in the home, the church must respond with some specific guidance. Churches could offer a "Biblical Parenting" class on Sunday mornings. This class could be offered as an elective alongside the traditional Sunday morning Bible teaching ministry of the church. The class would not supplant the important task of teaching the truths of the Bible for a Christian foundation, which is paramount. However, offering this class as an elective acknowledges that some Christians are not ready for in-depth truth materials yet, or they are just not interested in them. As a result, many of these people are not attending any Sunday morning Bible class. In other cases it is likely that some Christians have more immediate needs, like learning how to relate to their spouses or their children. Many good, well-meaning Christian couples are in desperate need of basic relationship and parenting skills. The church is the only place where many have an opportunity to receive this training from a spiritual perspective, without paying $50 to $75 an hour.

Furthermore, to reserve the offering of biblical parenting classes to

Sunday evening or Wednesday evening is to deny access to many of those most in need of this kind of ministry. Many families are too busy to attend Wednesday evening services, and they are often too tired to attempt any meaningful personal soul searching if they do attend on Wednesday evenings. Sunday evenings are becoming increasingly unpopular church times as families look for some kind of time to relax. The only time left is Sunday morning. Churches are going to have to offer more kinds of learning activities on Sunday mornings in order to provide for the variety of needs that exist in the Christian community. The only way they will be able to do this is by offering more variety during times that people are willing to come to church—Sunday mornings.

Offer Parenting Weekends

Churches should offer parenting weekends. These weekends could be one- or two-day seminars that offer separate classes for fathers and mothers. Perhaps several churches could join together to help defray the costs of bringing in some well-known, capable person to share during these seminars in order to provide their members the best possible ministry in this critical area.

Use Successful Fathers as Mentors

Churches should call upon the many successful fathers in their fellowships and use them as the foundation for a mentoring ministry. Mentoring would pair men to provide the kind of ongoing, practical support they need. Men who are looking to improve their parenting skills, or who are just trying to learn what it means to be a father, could spend time in fellowship, study, discussion, and prayer with someone who has demonstrated a successful commitment to fatherhood. In many instances this mentor would serve as the role model for fathering that many men have never had.

Develop Fatherhood Curriculum

A curriculum on fatherhood must be developed. Currently, the material that addresses fatherhood tends to be one lesson in a parenting or family relationship series. In other cases, fatherhood issues are merely addressed as part of parenting in general, with no real distinction between the different ways in which a man and woman contribute to the well-being of their family. Creating a distinction between the roles of fatherhood and motherhood should help men and women to understand better how their particular place in the family is uniquely important. Or course, there would certainly be overlap in the separate discussions, but there would also be an opportunity to develop material that is particularly geared toward helping men as fathers, as well as women as mothers.

Make the Ministry Perennial

Finally, it is important that today's evangelical churches recognize the need for a perennial ministry to its families and consider that ministry as one of the most important assignments. As society becomes more secular, the only place left where children will be able to learn about the biblical family is going to be the church, and the only place Christians will be able to turn for help will be the church. For this reason, churches will need to find ways to add a family ministries director to their church staffs. This person would be responsible for the ongoing ministry of the church to help its members develop biblical relationships and to fulfill their God-given responsibilities in their homes.

What Will Result

What will this emphasis on the importance of the father to his family produce? It will build stronger families. Wives will find genuine support in the home and will gain the sense of well-being that comes from knowing that they are not alone in the most important task given by God to men and women—to raise a generation that will love the Lord their God with all their hearts and minds and souls and strength. It will produce children who have a biblical concept of fatherhood and motherhood, not because someone taught it to them out of a book, but because their own parents modeled it before them. Children will become more confident about the future because they have been raised in an environment of care, genuine love, and protection that has built into their minds and souls a sense of security that will enable them to face the realities of a fallen world. This fatherhood emphasis will produce men who are proud of their families and who have a sense of accomplishment that enables them to see the meaningfulness of their lives. Ultimately, God will be wonderfully glorified as the world takes notice that his way is the best way.

Notes

1. Other books include *Magnificent Marriage* (1976) and *The Effective Father* (1977) by Gordon MacDonald; *The Best Dad Is a Good Lover* by Charlie Shedd in 1977; and *The Measure of a Man* by Gene Getz, first published in 1974 and still in print.

2. Other notable books include the following: *The Seven Seasons of a Man's Life* by Patrick Morley (Grand Rapids, Mich.: Zondervan, 1997); *The Hidden Value of a Man: The Incredible Impact of a Man on His Family* by Gary Smalley and John Trent (Colorado Springs, Colo.: Focus on the Family, 1992), with a study guide added in 1994; *The Silence of Adam: Becoming Men of Courage in a World of Chaos* by Larry Crabb (Grand Rapids, Mich.: Zondervan, 1995).

3. Garry Ezzo, *The Father's Mandate* (Simi Valley, Calif.: Growing Families, International, 1994).

4. Bill Mitchell, telephone interview by author, January 15, 1998.

5. Thom Black, telephone interview by author, January 21, 1998.

Chapter 7

Fatherhood in the Mainline Protestant Tradition

Diane Knippers

One spring afternoon, during the break at my parish retreat, I was in my room reading papers in preparation for speaking at a conference on fathering. My eight-year-old goddaughter bounced into my room to see if I was *finally* ready to walk down the lane for an ice cream, a practice that has become our tradition during the annual retreat.

"OK," I said. "But just let me finish this."

"What are you doing?" she asked.

"Reading about fathers," I answered. She looked puzzled. So I said, "I'm reading about why dads are important and what they do." Then it occurred to me that I had an opportunity to conduct some original research. "Colleen," I asked, "why do you think daddies are important? What do they do? What are they good for?"

"They take you on 'dates,'" she answered promptly and with a grin. She was talking about those regular occasions when she and her father do something special together. When I pressed her further, she continued, "They take care of you, make sure you have things you need. They make you safe. They make sure you know manners."

Then I asked, "What does your daddy do best of all?"

He's best at disciplining, she confessed. "He makes you go to time out."

"Why does he do that?" I wondered.

"So you can think about what you did and won't do it again."

Over the ice cream cones later, I shared this conversation with her father. Brian grimaced when I reported that he was "best" at disciplining. But I quickly consoled him. After all, according his daughter's own testimony, Brian was doing everything right. He was providing for her and giving her a sense of security. He was investing in a relationship that would help her establish a healthy sexual identity. And he was teaching her to self-regulate impulse gratification so she "would think about what she did" and not "do it again." In other words, Colleen's father provides what the experts recommend—both high warmth and moderately high control.

Sometimes the news out of the declining mainline Protestant churches isn't good. But there is something good to report. Part of the good news is that Brian is a member of a mainline church. And there are millions of husbands and fathers like him.

Why the Mainline Churches Must Be Enlisted

If one pays close attention to current religious news and events, one might be tempted to ask why bother trying to enlist the mainline churches in this effort to renew fathering. The mainline leadership is much more engaged in the debate over homosexuality than, say, parenting. One might look at the leadership of these churches, and so many of the formal policies and programs, and conclude that they are simply hostile to the values of the National Fatherhood Initiative. But that need not be the case—and it certainly is not the case with the people in the pews, people like my friend Brian.

As Don Eberly has made clear, we are facing a problem of civil society—of the "collapse of character-shaping institutions." American society will not be renewed—and will not be renewed as quickly as it must if it is to survive—without the historic Protestant denominations. The mainline denominations are influential, even beyond what their combined membership of over 50 million Americans would suggest. They have shaped the American experience for over 350 years, since Jamestown and Plymouth Rock. Our political, educational, social, and religious establishments are their creations, while America's decision makers and other leaders disproportionately belong to these denominations.

The historic Protestant traditions undergird and affirm the family. Martin Luther called the family a school of character. Luther also said, "There is no more lovely, friendly and charming relationship, communion or company than a good marriage." The Reformed tradition treated the family as a little congregation. A similar emphasis could be discerned in early versions of the Episcopal *Book of Common Prayer*, which included family prayers for morning and evening.

The nonseparatist and culture-shaping proclivities of the mainline churches enable them to encourage responsible fathering by making arguments that engage the broader culture. Another resource of the mainline is the basically healthy and responsible lifestyles and values of many of the people in the pews.

But there is a challenge in recruiting the mainline to help undergird fathering. The challenge is found in parts of the current leadership of these denominations, which has aided and abetted the deconstruction of our nation's formerly unquestioned Judeo-Christian consensus, including an agreement regarding habits and disciplines that support fathering. Because of the continued importance and influence of these denominations, the reformation of their leadership is necessary to maintaining civil society and to restoring the role and status of fatherhood in our culture.

What Hurdles Fatherhood Advocacy Faces

It is instructive to look at the hurdles we face in bringing our concern for fathers to the mainline churches. There is a case that must be made. Because the mainline is so close to the center of culture, often the biases and assumptions held by members in the mainline are the same biases and assumptions that exist in our secular culture. There are four areas of weakness in mainline churches which need to be understood and squarely addressed: a culture of radical feminism, misplaced and superficial ideas of compassion, the complete disassociation of sex and procreation, and a loss of moral authority and standards.

The Problem of Radical Feminism

First, there is the culture of radical feminism. By this I mean a culture that, in the name of justice for women, values autonomy, independence, choice, individual rights, absolute control over one's life and body, and equality often defined as sameness. Family life, of course, demands dependence, sacrifice, mutual responsibility, and compromise. A radical feminist view of equality that is essentially androgynous simply doesn't work for parents. It matters that a child has a mother and a father. Fathers are more than sperm banks and automatic teller machines.

The culture of radical feminism treats women as victims and men as oppressors. These victim/oppressor categories do not define merely individual behavior but are viewed as systemic, reflecting social structures. Therefore, there is a suspicion of male power, and even of male bonding and fellowship.

Make no mistake: There have been significant gains for women in terms of opportunity—gains that have benefited me and my generation, and which are not necessarily destructive of family life. Yet even this positive emphasis on new roles and opportunities for women may have contributed to marginalizing men's ministries and neglecting the consideration of men's responsibilities and roles. Men's leaders in several denominations have identified this vacuum and are committed to strengthening attention to men and their concerns, without undermining legitimate gains for women.

David J. McCracken of the Disciples of Christ says plainly, "Men have been neglected." He explains that in the two decades prior to the 1990s, "the church was heavily involved with opening opportunities for full participation in the life of the church to all persons. Men had always had the opportunity for full participation but as it opened to all, some men no longer felt needed."

Dale Vandiver, a leader in men's ministries in the Presbyterian Church (U.S.A.) notes that the trend toward gender neutrality has created an environment where there is no distinctive message for men or their responsibilities and roles. He states bluntly, "Over the past 10 to 15 years, the denomination has moved away from use of male terms, emphasizing gender neutrality. Women have become the driving force in the denomination, while men have left." While he sees some resurgence of interest in men's ministry, it still "does not strengthen fathering to any degree."

Joseph Harris, who heads the United Methodist Men's organization, notes a similar problem: "the lack of male leadership in the local church." He says that this "produces few models of strong Christian male leadership. Males in the church are too often on the periphery." There is "little emphasis on the role of strong Christian fathers." He states that it is crucial to help "women understand that strong fathers need not be a threat to the freedom of women."

The reaction of the mainline churches to the Promise Keepers movement illustrates the ideological conflicts within the denominations. Many outspoken church leaders were hostile to Promise Keepers—and especially to the October 1997 "Sacred Assembly" in Washington, D.C. The United Methodist Building in Washington was the site of two press conferences sponsored by the National Organization for Women to denounce Promise Keepers. (Local United Methodist men, seeking some balance, later persuaded officials to open the building for Promise Keepers attendees in October.) Several mainline leaders helped organize "Equal Partners in Faith," a religious front to attack Promise Keepers. In May 1997, the executive board of the National Council of Churches (NCC) viewed a video exposé of Promise Keepers, produced by the Center for Democracy Studies, a project of the leftist *Nation* magazine. The video charged that "our constitutional rights will be challenged on Saturday, October 4." The Promise Keepers rally would represent a "dry run for a more ambitious holy war, and further national-scale assaults on the positions of women, gays and lesbians, the future of government action for social programs and the legal separation of church and state."

While the NCC leadership was clearly in sympathy with the views of the film, some denominational leaders demurred. An official of the Reformed Church in America, himself a professed pro-feminist, told his fellow NCC board members that his own initial hostility to Promise Keepers was dispelled when men from his denomination were energized by Promise Keepers. "My own denomination is now only 35 percent male," he said. "I think we need to ask why Promise Keepers is effective in reaching men when our mainline denominations are not."

Clearly, leaders of denominational men's ministries are increasingly asking that same question. McCracken of the Disciples of Christ notes that "the men's movement of the last decade has heightened the church's awareness of a need to reach out to men who are spiritually hungry and searching for deep meaning in their lives."

Whether or not these leaders can respond successfully to these new opportunities to minister to men, without being squashed by radical feminist forces that are threatened by the idea of men meeting and organizing on their own, remains an open question. It is difficult to overestimate the influence of radical forms of feminism in the mainline. Radical feminism is the dominant ideology that controls mainline seminaries; indeed, our theological schools are in the grips of a kind of feminist fundamentalism that brooks no dissent or opposition. The leadership of most of our women's organizations has abandoned the missionary emphasis of an earlier era in favor of a highly politicized gospel. To the more radical form of feminism, those of us who care about fathers, and mothers, need to say "no."

The Problem of Misplaced Compassion

Second, there is an often sentimental, superficial, and misplaced compassion. It is difficult to make a case for fathers these days without someone assuming you are demeaning single mothers or bashing divorced people.

A couple of years ago, I spoke in a chapel service at my alma mater for political awareness week. I made the argument to the audience of primarily

18-to 22-year-olds that one of the major contributions they could make to our society—a crucial social and political witness if you will—was to enter into marriage commitments that they would keep. I explained that while I enjoyed a very happy and secure marriage, I nevertheless felt that the failed marriages of others chipped away at mine. My point was that, in marriage as in so many other parts of life, no man (or woman) is an island. Or, as I've heard William Mattox put it, "It takes a village to support a marriage."

When I was finished, a tearful woman approached me. She told me she was in her early forties as I was, but had been divorced. She let me know in no uncertain terms that she had suffered enough and didn't need the extra hurt of my telling her that her divorce harmed me and my marriage. I told her that of course my purpose was not to cause her further heartache, reminding her that most of my audience wasn't yet married. But I didn't back down on my basic point. To have shown excessive "sensitivity" to individuals in her situation would have betrayed the many more young people who desperately need to be encouraged to marital faithfulness. The message of God's compassion and redemptive holiness does not negate a call to holiness.

As more and more citizens and church members become divorced or single parents, it becomes more difficult to speak the truth in these matters without offending someone. Our silence is misplaced, short-term compassion. We need to develop the longer view. Our compassion needs to be aimed at our children and our children's children. Stable marriages and strong, engaged fathers are essential to the health and well-being of children. This is real compassion.

The Problem of Delinking Sex from Procreation

The mainline Protestant churches have gone a long way in delinking sexual activity from procreation. The procreative function of marriage and sexuality is clearly expressed in the creation story with the command to the first couple to be fruitful and multiply. While there is other good accomplished by sexual intercourse, one of the most important elements is that it is intended as a means of bringing other human beings into existence, to perpetuate the human race. We are given the extraordinary privilege of being co-creators with God. The Christian view of love is that it reaches out and reproduces itself; Christian love takes joy in its fruit.

In recent decades, the procreative function of sexuality and marriage has been increasingly marginalized. Birth control and abortion technology, increased acceptance of extramarital sexual pleasure as an end in itself, and a social order less and less child-friendly are trends that have contributed to the delinking of sexual intercourse and childbearing. For men especially, sexual activity is easily reduced to personal pleasure and divorced from any notion of responsibility to one's partner or to potential new life.

No, I am not suggesting that mainline Protestants accept Catholic doctrine on this point. But I am suggesting that even we would do well to reexamine the unintended consequences of these social trends. We must rediscover a link between love, expressed in intimate self-giving in sexual intercourse and, growing out of that love, an openness to the creation of human life.

The Problem of Loss of Moral Authority

Finally, there is a general loss of moral authority in the mainline Protestant church, with an emphasis on both "moral" and "authority." There is a basic suspicion of authority in general. Authority, whether held by men or women, is often viewed as inherently patriarchal, and even servant leadership is unacceptable. Furthermore, the mainline churches maintain a keen sense of moral outrage against structural and societal evils, but they evidence a growing reticence about making judgments against those ancient, garden-variety personal sins of lust, greed, and selfishness. In our society, a call to personal holiness is counter-cultural indeed. But it is precisely these classic characteristics of godliness such as fidelity, self-restraint, and self-sacrifice that the best fathers exhibit.

The Protestant tradition looks first to Scripture, but also to reason, experience, and tradition as sources of moral authority. Our churches must reclaim and embrace these sources in order to preach and teach disciplined and holy living. Ironically, the more vigorous and demanding this call—witness the Million Man March or the Promise Keepers "Stand in the Gap" assembly—the more likely it is to inspire and challenge men. Mainline Protestantism's tepid and compromised personal ethics are easy for men to ignore.

The Unifying Potential of Fatherhood Advocacy

The Mainline Protestant churches are deeply divided, reflecting the culture wars in our larger society. The differences between elements within the various denominations are much greater than the differences between the denominations as a whole. The central, flash-point issue over which the current division is played out is homosexuality. No mainline church is immune from court cases, legislative maneuvering, and ferocious arguments regarding the acceptance of homosexual activity.

As important as the issue is, both in itself and as a symbol for deeper theological divisions, the battles are often fought in narrow and defensive manners. Homosexual advocates focus on a tiny minority of individuals, casting them as victims of the church and society. Traditional Christians too often similarly respond with a narrow focus on homosexual behavior, neglecting the larger teaching of Scripture regarding marriage and sexuality.

Homosexuality is, relatively speaking, a side issue. It's important to the minority who struggle with homosexual temptation and to those who care about and for them. We owe these persons both compassion and candor. But the bigger challenges for the church and for our society relate to the marriages and families of the heterosexual majority. The Bible passages dealing explicitly with homosexuality are few, but the passages dealing with marriage and family are many and rich. From the Ten Commandments to the exhortations of the apostle Paul, marriage and family are portrayed as crucial areas in which God is to be obeyed.

A strong focus on family life and on strengthening the roles and responsibilities of fathers and mothers has the potential to unify large segments of the mainline churches—clergy and laity who turn from the homosexual battles with distaste or weariness.

The real victims of moral neglect in our society are our children. The demographic evidence is clear and irrefutable. Both the religious left and the religious right package their agendas in defense of children. Few church members would question the key importance of healthy family life in rearing children, and mainline centrists could be attracted to programs seeking to build up family life.

The church has so much to say regarding the family. Marriage is the central biblical symbol for the relationship between God and his people. Father is the name that our Lord Jesus gave us to call God himself. Many Christian couples work hard on their marriages because they are called intentionally to model the enduring and loving relationship between Christ and the church. Many men and women have good images of a loving Heavenly Father because their earthly fathers gave them strong, principled discipline and unconditional love.

These are the things our society so desperately needs to hear. This is the kind of social and political witness our churches should be fostering. And these messages could unify large portions of our fractured, dwindling, and demoralized mainline churches.

In our parishes, presbyteries, dioceses, and national conferences, we need to preach and teach and argue for these values. We need to offer programs that will make a difference. We need to be unapologetic, bold, and assertive. This is a strategy for strengthening fatherhood and family life, for renewing our civil society, and for rejuvenating a unified witness in our churches.

What Churches Can Do

There are so many creative ways in which our churches can mobilize to strengthen fathering. Among the major challenges before us are lowering the high rates of divorce, lessening the rates of out-of-wedlock births, and giving men—especially young men—strong male models including models for fathering. Mainline Protestants are willing to be activists and are comfortable with committees and agencies focused on key tasks. Below, I offer several ideas for local and national church leaders and laity to consider.

Strengthen Marriages

Imagine an automobile industry that constantly manufactured new cars, but entirely neglected repair and maintenance. Too many of our congregations are wedding factories, with no programs to sustain the marriages they've helped create. Every local congregation should have a copy of the book *Marriage Savers* by Michael McManus and should be working to implement his ideas. Strategies such as community marriage policies, rigorous premarital counseling, interventions to save troubled marriages, couple mentoring, divorce reform, and abstinence promotion are all a part of his handbook for saving marriage and are discussed in a chapter in this volume. Congregations should carefully examine their programs and ministries. Ask whether or not weekly meeting schedules allow your clergy and lay leaders adequate time with their families. When was the last time there was a sermon, teaching series, or class on sexual fidelity or family life?

Many churches find ways for families to serve together. In my parish, families usher together and sing in the choir together (children too young to sing are still welcome to sit with their parents in the choir loft). Our children-friendly home group finds service projects we can all do together, from Christmas caroling at a retirement home to scrubbing the pews in our sanctuary.

Expand Men's Ministries

Where men's ministries do exist, they need to be expanded. Where they do not exist, they should be started, both locally and nationally. Laymen, in particular, are an underused and underchallenged resource in mainline churches. One of the most encouraging signs within the mainline churches is the renewed interest in men's ministries. Leaders in the Presbyterian Church (U.S.A.) report an increase in men's prayer, Bible study, and fellowship groups in local congregations, with some taking the initiative to affiliate with Presbyterian Men. United Methodist Men has recently been established as an independent agency within the denomination, with the goal of strengthening its ability to grow effectively. Hugh Magers of the Episcopal Church Center reports that there is a move to launch a program, with staff and funding, for men.

Allen Abbott of American Baptist Men (AB Men) reports that his organization has "experienced phenomenal growth and renewal. This has a direct impact on our men and boys." Throughout American Baptist Men's materials one finds an emphasis on boys and on joint activities with men and boys. AB Men appears to have one of the most extensive collections of materials available, reflecting Abbott's conviction that what is necessary in a congregation is not simply one men's group, but several different men's ministries that will attract men and boys. "Some may enjoy work projects, others one-on-one mentoring, others sports, cookouts, prayer breakfasts, camps/retreats, etc. It's far better to have six ministries for men and boys of various interests and abilities rather than a one-size-fits-all 'men's group.'"

Men's ministries must be challenged to develop explicit programs to acknowledge and develop fathering, and they must be encouraged to include boys in many activities. Such ministries have enormous potential to be among the most theologically sound and life-transforming agencies of our denominations.

Counter the Divorce Culture

We must find ways to address the problem of divorce and particularly the influence of divorced leaders—clergy and otherwise. Over 20 years ago, with all the certainty of youth, I wrote an article for an evangelical magazine arguing that divorced clergy should leave the ministry. A couple of years ago, I sat on the personnel committee of my church and voted to hire a divorced priest—a man I admire enormously and who is a wonderful influence in our parish. But I am not easy with my changed views. Nor am I comfortable with the high number of divorced lay people in leadership in my parish.

One step I would advocate is to lay out formal accountability procedures, with ongoing accountability groups. Not only would such procedures offer protection and support for divorced persons, it would send a message to the entire community that divorce matters and is not simply overlooked. We need to put the brakes on the growing, easy acceptance of divorce. We need an admission, from the divorced persons and from the church, that divorce is failure, is wrong. We need publicly stated and agreed-upon criteria for behavior toward former spouses and children, for dating, for remarriage. We need public repentance. Yes, there are times when we even need a revival of shame. Most of all, the whole congregation needs to know that divorce among its leaders isn't to be taken lightly.

Develop Role Models

We need to seek out and support positive models. The single most important relationship in my local church may well be that of my rector and his wife. If anything went awry with that marriage, it would do irrevocable harm to our church—for generations. It is in the interest of our entire congregation to protect and support that marriage. The same is true for any congregation. We need to nurture and support the marriages of our leaders.

We need to seek out lay leaders with strong marriages as well, including youth ministers and Sunday school teachers. And we need more men working with children. A United Methodist church that I once attended had a policy that every Sunday school class that had boys and girls in it must have at least one male and one female teacher. Sex-segregated classes, in the elementary grades, could have either male or female teachers. My husband recently finished a six-year stint teaching a second grade Sunday school class. The boys not only loved him, they thought Sunday school was great!

When I was discussing this point with a single mother I know, she told me about a male Sunday school teacher who taught her son how to tie a necktie. Even such small services can become rites of passage for boys when men they admire confer upon them symbols of the status of manhood. We don't need men on our church budget committees nearly as much as we need them in the church school.

Offer Mentoring Programs

We also need to institutionalize mentoring. Most denominational leaders point to Boy Scouts as the primary means for relating men and boys. The Presbyterian Association of Scouters is seeking to expand church sponsorship of scout troops. The Presbyterian Men's Organization has a mission emphasis for men mentoring boys and young men, but the leadership reports that the program's scope is limited at this time. United Methodist Men is also developing a mentoring program.

The American Baptists place a strong emphasis on scouting as well. But when constituents requested a "more spiritual and American Baptist-oriented ministry," ABBoys and ABYoungMen was developed. ABBoys is for grades six and under; ABYoungMen is for grades seven through twelve. Both include a curriculum with 18 sessions available in English and Spanish. The material includes a church coordinator's kit and kits for mentors (of both age groups). ABBoys and ABYoungMen are unapologetically aimed at gathering young men in "a male, gender-specific environment." Three areas of focus are personal faith, personal values, and Christian discipleship. There are even caps and t-shirts for the program, plus my personal favorite—free dog tags with the ABBoys and ABYoungMen logo. (A sample packet of this material is available for $9.99 plus $2.75 postage and handling from AB Men USA, P.O. Box 851, Valley Forge, PA 19482-0851.)

It isn't necessary to wait for sophisticated denominational material to be developed. Every child in a congregation who doesn't live with his or her father ought to have a man from the church assigned to him or her. One option is to refurbish the whole tradition of godparents, with real job descriptions and accountability and help. My husband and I have godchildren who are blessed with a wonderful mother and father. But we still take our job seriously. Each year, my husband takes our godson and I take our goddaughter out for breakfast near the anniversary of their baptism. These meals are becoming a tradition, and the children are learning that they can expect an opportunity to talk about their spiritual growth and to tell us things we should pray for them.

Eventually, men in our congregations could reach out to local schools and communities and "adopt" fatherless children. This could become an enormous commitment of time. But I'm convinced that nothing is more important to the well-being of the next generation and the preservation of our civilization. If we can recruit, and if necessary, draft young men to fight the enemies of democracy abroad, we need to find a way to recruit men of all ages to fight the difficult and urgent battles to save civil society at home.

Honor Fathers

There are various ways to call attention to fathering, and especially, to honor fathers in our churches. I have helped sponsor resolutions at national church conventions to raise the issue of the problem of father absence. Below is a sample text of a resolution considered by the 1997 General Convention of the Episcopal Church, which was adopted in a slightly modified form:

> Resolved, that this 72nd General Convention recognizes the importance
> of fathers in the life of their families, particularly in the life of their

children; and be it further

Resolved, that this convention urges all Episcopal parishes to encourage the spiritual development of men, to preach and teach on the responsibilities and rewards of fatherhood, to encourage men to teach Sunday School, and to challenge all fathers to explore the implications and demonstrate the importance of full equality with mothers in their parenting roles; and be it further

Resolved, that the Washington Office be directed and the dioceses in various states be encouraged to support public policies that encourage family unity and provide incentives for fathers to care for their children.

EXPLANATION

American culture is witnessing a breakdown in the institutions of civilized society. High divorce rates and steadily increasing rates of out-of-wedlock births have meant an increase in the number of children growing up without a father. According to a Pennsylvania State University study, more than half of the increase in child poverty in the 1980s was attributable to changes in family structure. Children in single-parent families are six times as likely to be poor than those growing up with both parents. These children are also 2 to 3 times as likely to have emotional or behavioral problems, says the National Survey of Children. The National Center for Health Statistics found in 1988 that children from single-parent families are more likely to drop out of high school, abuse drugs, be sexually promiscuous and get into trouble with the law. As study after study and our own common sense tells us, children are better off with fathers. The fact is, God has given men unique gifts to be used in raising children. The Church must seek to understand and support men in their roles as fathers, husbands, providers and teachers to their families. By encouraging men to fully participate in fatherhood, we will be ensuring the care of the youngest members of our society for generations to come.

While I'm hesitant to treat Mother's Day as a high holy day in the liturgical year, I'm convinced that whatever is done to honor mothers should be matched by honoring fathers. Ironically, in a well-intentioned effort to minimize grief for childless men and women or for fatherless or motherless children, some churches have abandoned opportunities to honor parents. In the Presbyterian Church (U.S.A.), for example, Father's Day is observed as "Men's Emphasis Sunday," with a particular emphasis on men in mission and an intentional effort to involve single men. Perhaps it's time to emphasize fathers again. Father's Day would be a good opportunity for testimonies from individuals with a strong story to tell. In one United Church of Christ congregation, fathers are invited to stand and pray over their families on Father's Day. A variation on those ideas would be to offer special prayers for fathers, on Father's Day and throughout the year.

Events such as father-son dinners or father-daughter dances have likewise fallen into disuse, but ought to be reconsidered. These are often great occasions to involve fathers who no longer live with their children. In short, it is wrong always to deny the majority important relationship-building events for fear of leaving some out. Instead, find a way to include children whose fathers are absent, either permanently or temporarily, by recruiting godfathers, uncles, and others.

Explore Rituals and Other Special Occasions

Baptisms, weddings, and confirmations are all occasions in which fathers may be given special roles or acknowledged. Traditions often develop their staying power for very good reasons. Many a bride and her father have cherished the walk down the aisle preceding her wedding.

But creative new rituals and traditions may also be developed. My parish offers communion at each service on Sunday. Just prior to the celebration of the Eucharist, toward the end of the service, a number of fathers slip out of the sanctuary, go to the nursery and bring their infants back with them. When the family goes forward to receive the elements, the priest prays for each baby, often held in his or her father's arms.

Develop a Theological Basis for Fathering

Not a single denominational official I contacted was able to point to a church teaching document that defined or discussed a theological understanding of fatherhood. The mainline churches have repudiated family models that are seen as excessively authoritarian or hierarchical. What is left is a great vacuum. The question that must be asked is this: Does Scripture or other authoritative Christian teaching have anything to say about the role and responsibility of fathers as we enter the twenty-first century?

United Methodist Men has a new emphasis on "servant leadership," which may be a glimmer of a response. Hugh Magers of the Episcopal Church took a different, but also intriguing, tack when he urged helping "men to deepen their conversions." He continued,

> It seems to me that men who claim Jesus as Savior, submit to his Lordship, are much more likely to be good fathers. My observation as a pastor is that converted men are much less likely to be adulterous (always hard on

marriage and family), addicted (always hard on family), or casual about loving or being engaged. They are also less driven by greed, so they work to provide; [they don't] work to find meaning.

Some of the denominational officials I talked to noted a decline in Trinitarian language and in referring to the first person of the Trinity as Father. While I would be the first to affirm that God, who created sexuality, is neither male nor female, I also consider it a privilege to emulate Christ by addressing God as Father. Our understanding of God suffers when we abandon this personal and intimate form of address for impersonal substitutes. Nor must we allow the pathologies of failed fathers to undermine this powerful image for God. We must boldly call God our Heavenly Father, and call on earthly fathers to aspire to that standard of love.

My Own Father

When I was asked to address the subject of fatherhood in the mainline churches, my first reaction was to decline. After all, I'm not a father and never could be. But then it occurred to me that I have one really splendid qualification to discuss fatherhood. I was reared by a truly wonderful father. I can give personal, first-hand testimony to what outstanding fathering is all about.

At one General Convention of the Episcopal Church, I testified on behalf of a resolution that, in part, urged the church to give higher priority to strengthening fathers. In my testimony, I said something about my parents and my strong and good upbringing. I'll never forget a woman who came up to me later. She was weeping as she told me that most of the testimony she had heard in the committee was about brokenness and sin and human frailty. She told me how blessed she was to hear a story of a Christian family that did it right. "We need more of these positive stories," she told me.

I've got such a story. It was my father who paddled me when I was young, and grounded me when I got older, but who I know was always more deeply grieved by the punishment than I was. I learned from him that even the times of correction were reflections of his unconditional love, and that lesson has made it easy for me to understand God's love for me.

From my father I learned that while those gangly boys in junior high might not ask me to dance, someday the right man would find me attractive for who I was. I learned that I didn't have to give up my virginity to gain the attention of or love from a man.

It was from my father I learned that we make sacrifices for moral principles. It was my father who gradually let go, taking the risk of letting me make my own moral decisions in order to develop my own character. And even today, when my husband and I face a serious problem or have a serious need, I know we can call my father for wise advice or help.

When it's all said and done, the reason I so urgently want to enlist mainline churches in this campaign for fatherhood is because I believe that every man and woman and every boy and girl deserve a father like mine.

Part Three

Fatherhood and Faith in the American Public Debate

Chapter 8

The Rise of an American Fatherhood Movement

Wade F. Horn

For much of the past 30 years, fatherhood has been in a state of collapse. Propelled by the twin engines of divorce and illegitimacy, the percentage of children growing up in a home without their father nearly tripled between 1960 and the early 1990s. By 1994, 24 *million* American children were living absent their biological fathers. But not to worry, we were increasingly told, all families were relative and the one relative children could do without was their father. Put simply, the modern family might need a village, but it no longer needed a dad.

Then something remarkable happened. Rather suddenly, and quite unpredictably, fatherlessness began to be cited as the most disturbing and consequential social trend of our time. Soon, football stadiums were filling with Promise Keepers, bus loads of African American men were arriving in the nation's capital for a Million Man March, and news stories began to regularly highlight the connection between absent fathers and such social ills as crime, educational failure, and welfare dependency. Some social observers were even talking of the birth of a new social movement: a fatherhood movement.

The collapse of fatherhood and its recent rediscovery is one of the most important, and under-chronicled, cultural stories of the last 30 years. How did this all happen? How did we go, in just three short decades, from a nation of fathers to a fatherless nation? Even more importantly, what accounts for the recent resurgence of the fatherhood idea and the emergence of a fatherhood movement?

The Collapse of Fatherhood

The retreat from fatherhood began in the 1960s, gained momentum in the 1970s, and hit full stride in the 1980s. Driving this collapse of fatherhood were three ideas about parenting, fathers, and children. Ideas do have consequences, and the cultural and social consequences of these three ideas were profound.

The Myth of the Androgyny Ideal

For much of the history of Western civilization, differences between men and women were widely recognized and even celebrated. As late as the 1950s, social scientists largely accepted that men and women had different biologies that translated into differences in behavior. This was seen not just as natural, but good. The widely accepted view was that men and women formed a natural complementary wherein each strengthen and extended the other. So ingrained was this idea that for much of this century educators routinely endeavored to reinforce male and female distinctiveness and sex role behavior.

But beginning in the 1960s, recognition of gender distinctiveness gave way to the ideal of androgyny. Growing out of concern for achieving greater social equity between men and women, androgyny advocates preached that men and women not only ought to be treated exactly the same, but ought to behave exactly the same as well. Social psychologist Sandra Bem was particularly influential in spreading the gospel of androgyny, arguing that persons freed from traditional sex-role behavior would be better adjusted, more adaptive, and psychologically healthier. By 1980, 72 percent of mental health professionals described a "healthy, mature, social competent" adult as androgynous.

The ideal of androgyny found fertile soil in parenting experts. With extraordinary rapidity, expert parenting advice changed from discussing the virtues of parental complementary to exhorting mothers and fathers to parent exactly the same way. According to many parenting experts of the 1970s and 1980s, mothers and fathers should parent such that their children would not know whether it was their mom or dad in the room, nor would they care.

To achieve the ideal of androgynous parenting it was the men who had to be retrained. As James Garbarino, the president of the Erikson Institute for Advanced Study in Child Development, has written: "To develop a new kind of father, we must encourage a new kind of man. In *My Fair Lady*, Professor Higgins asks, 'Why can't a woman be more like a man?' It's time to ask the opposite question. . . . 'Why can't a man be more like a woman?'"

Androgyny became the basis of the New Nurturing Father ideal, in which a good father was defined as a man who shares equally in all childrearing activities from the moment of birth. The New Nurturing Father was expected not only to cry at movies, but to change precisely one-half of all diapers and to be as adept at fixing his baby's formula as he is at fixing a flat tire.

This view is now deeply ingrained in the American psyche, and especially among social service providers. Indeed, at a recent workshop I conducted on restoring fatherhood, I was lectured by a social worker that it was not just incorrect, but *dangerous*, to use the word "father." "Parent" was the required lexicon.

The degree to which it has become politically correct to glorify androgyny as an ideal has reached such absurd lengths that many find it difficult even to define "father" as a male. Recently, two agencies of the federal government reportedly nonconcurred on a proposed HUD regulation because it defined a father as a male. Better, these agencies said, to define father as "father figure," who, of course, could be a male or a female. Whether or not the father figure could be an animal or a plant was not discussed.

The androgynous father has proven to be an awfully uninspiring model for most men. And no wonder. Essentially, the androgynous message says, "Fathers, you are doing it wrong. To be a good father, you must be more like mother." The result is the feminization of fatherhood and the increasing disappearance of the father from the home.

The Myth of the Superfluous Father

Once androgyny advocates had established that most fathers were "doing it wrong," it became relatively easy to argue fathers were not really necessary to the "modern" family. Social scientists began to assert that there was a "nuclear family bias" in past research, and exhorted fellow researchers and practitioners to stop extolling the importance of a father—even a New Nurturing Father—to the well-being of children. By 1982, psychologist Charlotte Patterson of the University of Virginia felt assured enough to state flatly, "Children don't need a father to develop normally."

Spurred on by such radical feminist rhetoric as Gloria Steinham's retort that "a woman needs a man like a fish needs a bicycle," some even began to assert that children actually did *better* without fathers. In a study of father-absent households published in 1982 in the *Journal of Marital and Family Therapy*, Barbara Cashion stated that girls growing up without fathers are more independent, have higher IQs, and enjoy greater self-esteem than girls growing up with fathers. This, according to Barbara Cashion, is because

> [t]he two-parent family is hierarchical with mother and father playing powerful roles and children playing subordinate roles. In the female-headed family there is no such division. Women and children forgo much of the hierarchy and share more in their relationships. . . . There is a general lack of conflict, and decisions are made more easily and quickly, provided resources are adequate.

Advocacy on behalf of the superfluous father idea had its intended effect. By 1994, 35 percent of men ages 18-29, and an astonishing 62 percent of women in the same age group, agreed with the statement "one parent can bring up a child as well as two parents." Indeed, by telling men that they are at best superfluous and at worst detrimental to the well-being of children, men could now claim they were doing their children a *favor* by leaving them solely in the hands of the mother.

The Myth of Resilient Children

A final idea that contributed to the decline of fatherhood in America was that children are resilient. For much of human history, children have been seen as requiring tenderness, affection, and protection from the adult world. Although the definition of childhood may have lengthened over the years, and specific childrearing practices certainly have changed, the historical record is replete with references to parental love and affection, and the need to protect children from stress. For example, the Old Testament of the Bible is filled with admonitions for parents to protect, teach, and love their children.

This view of childhood as a time of innocence and vulnerability led to the prevailing cultural virtue that parents in troubled marriages ought to stay together "for the sake of the kids." This does not mean that divorce is a recent invention; indeed, divorce has been a part of mankind's experience throughout human history. But it did place a natural braking mechanism on impulses to leave one's spouse, which helped to keep divorce rates relatively low.

As pointed out by Barbara Dafoe Whitehead in her recent book *The Divorce Culture*, this view of childhood posed a problem for the divorce advocates in the 1970s. If children were vulnerable to stress and disruption, how does one divorce without feeling guilty? The answer: Children are really more resilient than we think. Divorce, and its consequent father absence, may be painful at first, but the children will get over it. They are, after all, just children.

Some even went further to suggest that divorce can be a self-actualizing experience for children. In their 1974 book, *The Courage to Divorce*, authors Susan Gettleman and Janet Markowitz argued that "divorce can liberate children" and can lead to "greater insight and freedom as adults in deciding whether and when to marry" and to "break away from excessive dependency on their biological parents." Similarly, therapist Mel Krantzler in his 1973 book, *Creative Divorce: A New Opportunity for Personal Growth*, stated that divorce provides "an ambiguous, expanded experience that moves kids to better adjustment in a society that is highly ambiguous and expanded."

Propagation of the resilient child myth was extraordinarily successful. By 1977, 80 percent of respondents to a national survey disagreed with the statement, "when there are children in the family, parents should stay together even if they don't get along." Thus, freed from guilt about walking away from marriages adults found dissatisfying, divorce rates nearly tripled between 1960 and the early 1980s. By 1990, nearly a million children annually were experiencing the "liberating effects" of divorce.

Turning the Tide

Given that during the 1970s and 1980s so many influential social scientists were advocating androgyny, family relativism, and child resiliency, it is surprising that it was social science that also provided the seedbed for fatherhood's rescue. Beginning in the early 1980s, evidence began accumulating in social science literature that would fundamentally challenge these three myths about parenting, fathers, and children.

First, developmental psychologists discovered that mothers and fathers do, in fact, approach parenting somewhat differently and that these differences may, in fact, be beneficial to a child's development. Rather than finding support for the notion that androgynous parenting was the ideal way to raise children, researchers increasingly found that some degree of parenting specialization was helpful in the rearing of children.

For example, one consistent finding that emerged was that mothers tend to be more verbal in their interactions with their children and fathers more physical. That is, mothers like to talk to their babies, whereas fathers like to play with them. During the height of the androgyny craze, childrearing experts often asserted that the physical play of fathers—so-called rough and tumble play—was superfluous to childrearing. Consequently, many parenting experts of the time exhorted fathers to stop playing with the kids and do more housework. Some even asserted that the rough and tumble play of fathers taught children aggression.

But research increasingly found that the physical play of fathers gives children practice in self-regulating behavior and aids in the development of the capacity to recognize the emotional cues of others, two hallmarks of a properly socialized child. At the same time, research was demonstrating that for the language centers of the brain to develop properly, young children need lots of verbal stimulation. Thus, dads' physical play helps children develop self-regulation and moms' verbal stimulation helps children develop language.

Another consistent finding that emerged is that mothers tend to be stronger comforting figures and fathers stronger disciplinarians. Given that research has consistently shown that children do best when reared with a combination of high warmth and moderately high control, the combination of mothers' nurturance and fathers' discipline was found to have beneficial effects on the well-being of children. Despite the protestations of androgyny worshipers, parental complementary was making a comeback.

At the same time that developmental psychologists were rediscovering the uniqueness of fathers, social demographers and family policy analysts were rediscovering their importance. Over the past decade an astonishingly voluminous body of data has accumulated documenting the ill-effects on a child of growing up without a father. Children without fathers were, for example, found to be three times more likely to fail at school, two to three times more likely to experience emotional or behavioral problems requiring psychiatric treatment, three times more likely to commit suicide as adolescents, and up to forty times more likely to experience child abuse compared to children growing up with both a mom and a dad. Fatherless children were also five times more likely to be poor. But poverty alone was not found to be an adequate explanation for the increased risk of poor outcomes associated with growing up fatherless; for even after controlling for income, children growing up without their fathers were found to do worse compared to those who grew up with both a mom and a dad.

As fathers were found to be more unique and irreplaceable than previously thought, children were also discovered to be more vulnerable. Beginning with the groundbreaking work of psychologist Judith Wallerstein, clinical researchers began to document that children experience not temporary strain from divorce or abandonment, but long-term negative emotional and behavioral consequences. Far from being resilient, children were found to suffer forever when they don't live in forever families.

By the early 1990s, these research findings worked their way into the conclusions and recommendations of several widely disseminated and influential family policy reports. One of the earliest of these was entitled "Putting Children First: A Progressive Family Policy for the 1990s" published in 1990 by the Progressive Policy Institute, the official think tank of the Democratic Leadership Council. Authored by Elaine C. Kamarck and William A. Galston, both of whom would later go on to high-ranking positions within the Clinton Administration, the report argued that the most consequential social trend contributing to declining child well-being was the collapse of the American family. In particular, the report identified father absence as a primary culprit in declining child well-being and recommended ways to bolster the two-parent family by strengthening marriage and making divorce less common.

The next year, the National Commission on Children released its final report entitled "Beyond Rhetoric: A New American Agenda for Children and Families." Borrowing heavily from Kamarck and Galston, this report asserted that "[c]hildren do best when they have the personal involvement and material support of a father and a mother and when both parents fulfill their responsibility to be loving providers." Even more remarkably, the report concluded:

> There can be little doubt that having both parents living and working together in a stable marriage can shield children from a variety of risk. Rising rates of divorce, out-of-wedlock childbearing, and absent parents are not just manifestations of alternative lifestyles, they are patterns of adult behavior that increase children's risk of negative consequences.

The Birth of a Movement

Despite accumulating evidence of the uniqueness and importance of fathers, and assertions by prestigious reports that two-parent families and marriage were important to child well-being, nothing remotely resembling a fatherhood movement, or even a fatherhood consciousness for that matter, had yet to appear. This changed dramatically as a result of 39 words delivered by a public figure widely perceived at the time as an intellectual lightweight—Vice President Dan Quayle.

While campaigning for re-election, Dan Quayle made a speech on May 19, 1992, at the Commonwealth Club of California in San Francisco, during which he asserted: "It doesn't help matters, when prime time TV has Murphy Brown—a character who supposedly epitomizes today's intelligent, highly paid, professional woman—mocking the importance of fathers, by bearing a child alone, and calling it just another 'lifestyle choice.'

The importance of this event was not that Dan Quayle himself went on to lead, or even propose the formation of, a fatherhood movement. Rather, its import is that it galvanized others to come to the defense, if not of him, at least of the larger point he was trying to make—that fathers matter to the well-being of children and that society experiments with father absence at its peril.

The first of these spirited defenses was the appearance in the *Atlantic Monthly* magazine of an extraordinarily influential article by Barbara Dafoe Whitehead of the Institute for American Values entitled "Dan Quayle Was Right." In this article, Whitehead laments that "every time the issue of family structure has been raised, the response has been first controversy, then retreat, and finally silence." Undaunted, she continues:

> The debate . . . is not simply about the social-scientific evidence, although that is surely an important part of the discussion. It is also a debate over deeply held and often conflicting values. How do we begin to reconcile our long-standing belief in equality and diversity with an impressive body of evidence that suggests that not all family structures produce equal outcomes for children? . . . How do we uphold the freedom of adults to pursue individual happiness in their private relationships and at the same time respond to the needs of children for stability, security, and permanence in their family lives?

The themes laid out in Whitehead's article were further refined and expanded in a series of compelling articles and books, including *Life Without Father* by David Popenoe, *New Expectations: Community Strategies for Responsible Fatherhood* by James Levine and Edward Pitt, *FatherLove* by Richard Louv, and especially *Fatherless America* by David Blankenhorn. Particularly influential was an article by Charles Murray entitled "The Coming White Underclass." Appearing in the *Wall Street Journal*, Murray dramatically and compellingly broadened the perception of father absence from a "black family problem" to one that was quickly encompassing all of American society.

These writings, in turn, spawned a renewed interest in programmatic activity on the fatherhood issue, including skill-building programs, outreach programs for unwed fathers, and public advocacy. Among the most important of these efforts is the National Institute for Responsible Fatherhood and Family Development, headed by Charles Ballard. Toiling for over a decade in inner city Cleveland, this program utilizes men from the local community to work with young unwed fathers, many of whom have either dropped out of school, are unemployed, or have substance abuse problems. Using a combination of parenting skills, education, and faith, this program has been extraordinarily effective in encouraging young, mostly unwed, fathers to become and stay involved in the lives of their children and to support the mother of their children. So successful has been this program become that it is now operating in half a dozen cities across the country.

Another innovative fatherhood program that was soon garnering national attention was MADDADS. Headquartered in Omaha, Nebraska, this program began one spring evening in 1989 when the 20-year-old son of John L. Foster, a 45-year-old African American, staggered home, badly beaten, blood streaming down his face. When Foster found out his son had been beaten by a gang of teenagers, he loaded his .357 magnum and took to the streets looking for the culprits. Fortunately, he didn't find the gang of kids that had beaten his son, but that night he did have an epiphany: "I was literally a *mad dad*, and I knew I wanted to organize strong black men who were willing to stand up and fight this thing." The first man he recruited was Eddie Staton, and the two of them decided that they had had enough of drug dealers, crack addicts, and prostitutes in their neighborhood. Soon they had organized a group of nearly 100 black men who began father street patrols to remove graffiti and rid their neighborhood of drug dealers, pimps, and addicts. Today, MADDADS claims 30,000 members in 49 chapters in 14 states, and their mission has been expanded to include outreach to young fathers and mentoring of fatherless children.

A third, and by far the largest, fatherhood promotion effort is Promise Keepers. Begun in 1990 by former University of Colorado football coach Bill McCartney, Promise Keepers seeks to inspire men to be faithful husbands and responsible fathers within a servant-leader model. The message is clearly striking a responsive chord. The first gathering in 1991 drew 4,000 men; the next year 22,000 attended. By 1996 nearly 1.1 million men were attending Promise Keepers events at 22 stadiums around the country. Promise Keepers headquarters now has a full-time staff of over 400, and an annual budget of nearly $100 million.

A similar mass gathering of fathers, known as the Million Man March, was hosted in October of 1995 by Nation of Islam's leader Louis Farrakhan. Although nearly three-quarters of a million African American men did attend the event, there are few signs that the Million Man March has enjoyed anything near the staying power of Promise Keepers, undoubtedly due to the controversial personality of Louis Farrakhan and the political nature of many of the speeches at the march itself.

In addition to these individual efforts to reinvigorate fatherhood, fatherhood advocates, researchers, analysts, and programmers began to show increasing interest in coming together to seek common cause. The earliest manifestation of this desire to come together under a single fatherhood banner was the convening of a National Summit on Fatherhood in Dallas, Texas, in October of 1994. Hosted by the newly formed National Fatherhood Initiative, this gathering attracted over 200 fatherhood advocates, researchers, and public policy analysts, along with fathers' rights advocates, fathering-education and skill-building experts, advocates for low-income fathers, and religious leaders involved in fatherhood promotion. Other gatherings followed, including an Interfaith Summit on Fatherhood, several state-wide, governor-sponsored fatherhood conferences, and a meeting in October of 1996 in Minneapolis at which a statement of principle for the fatherhood movement, entitled *A Call To Fatherhood*, was negotiated and endorsed.

Today, there are literally dozens of national groups advocating on behalf of fatherhood and hundreds more providing local support, encouragement, and skill-building programs targeted at fathers. The National Fatherhood Initiative, for example, conducts national and state-wide public education programs building awareness of the unique and irreplaceable contributions that fathers make to the well-being of children, organizes local fatherhood forums, and operates a National Clearinghouse and Resource Center, which provides training and technical assistance to local organizations that desire to implement a fatherhood program. The National Center for Fathering, headquartered in Kansas City, conducts seminars for men on how to be more effective dads and provides training to help social service agencies meet the needs of fathers. The National Center on Fathers and Families, based at the University of Pennsylvania, conducts research on ways programs can facilitate the effective involvement of fathers. And the Fatherhood Project of the Families and Work Institute, located in New York City, provides information to employers on how they can make their workplaces more father-friendly.

There are signs that this new "fatherhood movement" is starting to have an impact. Surveys indicate that increasing numbers of Americans are getting the fatherhood message. A 1996 Gallup Poll found that 79 percent of Americans believe "the most significant family or social problem facing America is the physical absence of the father from the home," up from 69 percent in 1992. Another recent survey found that 84 percent of men in their 30s and 40s agree that the definition of success is being a good father.

There is even evidence that this shift in attitudes is beginning to translate into behavioral change. Since the mid-1980s, the divorce rate has been decreasing. And last year, for the first time in two decades, the percentage of children born out of wedlock actually declined by half a percentage point. Increasingly, families are, once again, making room for daddy.

Challenges Ahead

Still, challenges remain. Tonight, nearly 40 percent of all children in America will go to bed in a home without their father available to read them a bedtime story, bring them a glass of water, and give them a goodnight kiss. Many millions more live with disconnected, neglectful, and sometimes even abusive fathers.

Furthermore, there is no guarantee that, even after accepting the importance of fathers, we will head in the right direction. Many, while agreeing that fathers are important, say that we must accept the realities of out-of-wedlock childbearing and divorce, and work instead to ensure that children benefit from the financial support of their nonresident fathers. Their solution is to become more efficient at establishing paternity and to help nonresident fathers become employed so that they can pay their child support obligations.

Paternity establishment and child support enforcement are, of course, not without merit. And a just and good society ought to do all it can to increase job opportunities in low-income communities. But an over-focus on child support ignores the many noneconomic contributions that fathers make to the well-being of their children. Indeed, emphasizing fatherhood in largely economic terms has helped to contribute to its demise. After all, if a father is little more than a paycheck to his children, he can easily be replaced by a welfare payment.

If we want fathers to be more than just money machines, we will need a culture that supports their work as nurturers, disciplinarians, mentors, moral instructors, and skill coaches, and not just as economic providers. To do otherwise is to effectively downgrade fathers to, in the words of Barbara Dafoe Whitehead, "paper dads."

Others suggest cohabitation as the solution to fatherlessness. In part driven by the younger generation's simultaneous desire for intimacy and fear of divorce, cohabitation as a form of "trial marriage" is one of the fastest growing family forms. Among adults ages 25-34, the percentage of cohabiting couples in which children are present increased from 34 percent in 1980 to 47 percent in 1993. Overall, 2.2 million children (roughly one in seven) currently reside in cohabiting families.

But cohabitation before marriage actually makes subsequent marriages *less* stable, not more. In fact, divorce rates are higher for couples who cohabit before marriage compared to those that did not. Thus, the very solution that many in the younger generation have gravitated toward to solidify long-term relationships is, in reality, likely to weaken them.

Cohabitation is also unlikely to produce lifetime dads for children.

Although a quarter of nonmarital births occur to cohabiting couples, six out of ten cohabiting couples never go on to marry, and those that do are more likely to eventually divorce than those couples who bear children within the context of marriage. For far too many children of cohabiting couples, their dads are likely to become—at best—only occasional visitors.

Fatherhood and Marriage

While it is becoming increasingly popular to speak of the importance of fathers to the well-being of children, it is still out of fashion to speak of the importance of marriage to the well-being of fatherhood. Yet, research has consistently found that unmarried fathers, whether through divorce or out-of-wedlock fathering, tend over time to become disconnected, both financially and psychologically, from their children. About 40 percent of children in father-absent homes have not seen their father in at least a year. Of the remaining 60 percent, only one in five sleeps even one night per month in the father's home. Overall, only one in six sees their father an average of once or more per week. More than half of all children who don't live with their fathers have never even been in their father's home.

Unwed fathers are particularly unlikely to stay connected to their children over time. Whereas 57 percent of unwed fathers are visiting their child at least once per week during the first two years of their child's life, by the time their child reaches seven and one-half years of age, that percentage drops to less than 25 percent. Approximately 75 percent of men who are not living with their children at the time of their birth never subsequently live with them.

Consequently, there is a growing chorus of voices within the fatherhood movement singing the praises of marriage as the solution to the fatherhood problem. The National Fatherhood Initiative in particular is increasingly advocating the need to promote marriage as an important means of promoting fatherhood. For example, in a recent report jointly published with the Hudson Institute on fathers and welfare reform, it is argued that low-income men are unlikely to be responsible fathers unless state reforms make low-income men more attractive marital partners by including them in job placement programs and provide explicit preferences for married couples in the distribution of certain, limited-supply welfare benefits, such as slots in public housing and Head Start. As a follow-up to this report, the National Fatherhood Initiative will be implementing a national monitoring project to determine what, if anything, states and local communities are doing to promote marriage and fatherhood within the context of welfare reform.

This does not mean that all marriages are made in heaven; it does not even mean that nonresident fathers cannot be good dads. But based on the evidence, the inescapable conclusion is this: If we want to increase the number of children growing up with involved and committed fathers, we will have to convince men to delay fathering children until after they have established a committed and enduring marriage.

The Beginning of the End . . . Perhaps

The good news is our culture is re-awakening to the idea that fathers are important to the well-being of their children. Men are increasingly likely to aspire to be loving, committed, and responsible fathers. And there does seem to be a fatherhood movement emerging in America. But, at the same time, millions of children still live absent their fathers or with dads who might as well be. And many persist in a cultural illusion that marriage and involved fatherhood have little to do with each other.

The battle for fatherhood, while encouraging, is far from over. In 1942 after the allies had won the battle of North Africa, Winston Churchill cautioned his countrymen, "Now this is not the end. It is not even the beginning of the end. But it is, perhaps, the end of the beginning." So it may be with fatherhood in America.

Chapter 9

The Role of Marriage in Strengthening Fatherhood

Michael J. McManus

The most visible sign of the growing fatherhood movement could be seen on the mall in Washington, D.C., in October 1997, when a million men—roughly one percent of all men in the United States—gathered at a Promise Keepers "Stand in the Gap" rally. More important than the numbers was its purpose. A poll by the *Washington Post* found that the single biggest reason men came was to "confess their sins."

American men have a lot to confess. Two-fifths of children (43 percent) live in homes where their father does not live. No civilization in the history of the world has seen such a massive abandonment by fathers of their responsibilities to their children. The number of children living only with their mother has soared from 5.1 million in 1960 to 16.5 million in 1995.[1]

Sexual irresponsibility lies behind America's fatherlessness. As noted below in more detail, cohabitation has soared seven-fold just since 1970, and since 1960 illegitimacy jumped five-fold, and divorces tripled. Of course, women were as involved in sexual sin as men. But the abandonment of children has largely been by fathers, not mothers.[2]

Fortunately, the fatherhood movement in America is working to reverse these trends. And there are early signs of success.

Promise Keepers is the most visible catalyst of the movement. It attracted 2.6 million men to stadium rallies through 1997 in addition to the million men attending "Stand in the Gap." Of course, many men have been to more than one event, but perhaps two million different men made new vows to keep the promises they have made to their wives and children. That's two percent of the nation's one hundred million men.

A less visible leader of the fatherhood movement is the National Fatherhood Initiative (NFI) chaired by David Blankenhorn. Working with the Ad Council, in which advertising executives donate their time to create ads, NFI's executive director, Wade Horn, convinced ABC-TV to run public service ads narrated by James Earl Jones. One showed a male emperor penguin sheltering its chicks in the folds of its skin, noting that if the father did not do so, the chicks would die. Jones adds, "Just a reminder of how important it is for fathers to spend time with their children." More than $100 million worth of airtime and space was donated by media for the ads. NFI's publication "Father Facts" has helped educate journalists about the issue, resulting in at least 700 articles in newspapers with 70 million readers.

NFI has had a measurable impact. A survey of America's 25 largest newspapers by David Brenner of the Institute for American Values revealed there were five times as many articles about father absence on Father's Day in 1995 (40 articles) as in 1990 (8 articles).

More important, the illegitimacy rate has stopped increasing. Out-of-wedlock births, which have been growing by one percent a year for a generation, declined for the first time ever in 1995, and in 1996 are still slightly below that of 1994.

And divorces fell in 1996 to their lowest level in a generation.

While cause and effect can't be proven, I believe the fatherhood movement is beginning to have an impact. This development is urgently needed.

However, the movement needs to be deepened and broadened by a conscious strategy led by the nation's churches to strengthen marriages, resulting in an effort that will look quite different from the current fatherhood movement. For one thing, marriages cannot be strengthened by simply having men talk to men, the current Promise Keepers pattern. Women must be involved with men in a marriage movement—husbands and wives in strong marriages, reaching out to help other couples prepare for a lifelong marriage, strengthen existing marriages, and save troubled ones.

Central Domestic Problem Is Family Disintegration

The central domestic problem of our time is the disintegration of the traditional family of married husband and wife with children. Consider these facts:

1. Half of all new marriages are failing, as are 60 percent of second marriages.
2. Cohabitation has soared seven-fold, rising from 523,000 couples living together in 1970 to 3.7 million in 1994.[3]
3. The marriage rate has fallen 41 percent since 1960.[4]
4. The number of divorced, un-remarried people has skyrocketed from 4.3 million divorced, un-remarried people in 1970 to 17.4 million in 1994.
5. Only 55 percent of American adults are married—the lowest percentage ever.
6. A million kids a year see parents divorce, and 1.3 million more are born out of wedlock. Compared to kids with intact families, these kids are *six times* more at risk to be in poverty, *five times* more inclined to commit suicide, three times more prone to have an illegitimate baby, and twice as likely to drop out of school.

Sky-High Divorce Rate

Divorces in the United States fell by 41,000 between 1994 and 1996, to the lowest number in 18 years. However, before looking at the drop, consider the massive increase in divorces that came between 1960 and 1980. Divorces tripled from 393,000 to 1,189,000. Then the numbers fluttered for 15 years, with minimal changes in number of divorces from 1980 to 1995. In 1992, the year of the first big Promise Keeper rallies, there were 1,215,000 divorces, 1,191,000 in 1994, and then the numbers fell to only 1,169,000 in 1995 and 1,150,000 in 1996.[5] That's the lowest number of divorces since 1978. It is also the lowest divorce rate since 1970. In 1996, there were 4.2 divorces per 1,000 people, down from 4.6 per 1,000 in 1994 and a peak of 5.3 per 1,000 in 1981.[6]

Table 9.1
Divorce Rate

Year	Number of Divorces	Divorces/1,000
1960	393,000	2.2
1978	1,130,000	5.1
1980	1,189,000	5.2
1986	1,178,000	4.9
1990	1,182,000	4.7

1991	1,187,000	4.7
1992	1,215,000	4.8
1993	1,187,000	4.6
1994	1,191,000	4.6
1995	1,169,000	4.4
1996	1,150,000	4.2

The more common way of discussing the divorce rate is to project the number of expected divorces over time, compared to the number of marriages. Since 1975, there has been one divorce for every two marriages in the United States. In 1996, for example, there were 2,344,000 marriages and 1,150,000 divorces. By extending that 21-year trend, demographers project that more than half of America's marriages will end in divorce or permanent separation.[7] America's divorce rate is nearly the world's highest. It is twice that of France or Germany, and triple that of Japan, and 10 times that of Italy.[8] Further, some studies show that 80 percent of divorces are unilateral—forced by one person on a spouse who wants to reconcile.[9]

Declining Marriage Rate

One reason the divorce rate is down is that the marriage rate has plunged even more. In 1982, there were 2,495,000 marriages and only 2,344,000 in 1996. Of course, with 150,000 fewer marriages, there will be fewer divorces! In fact, the marriage rate is at its lowest rate in 30 years (8.8 per 1,000 in 1996, down from 10.6 in 1982).

Measured differently, the marriage rate in the United States has fallen 41 percent since 1960.[10] It is shocking that only 55 percent of U.S. adults are married and living together today—the lowest figure in history.

Why are so few getting married and so many getting divorced? One cause has been largely ignored—cohabitation.

Soaring Cohabitation Rate

America's cohabitation rate has soared seven-fold in one generation. It is replacing marriage for millions of couples. In March 1970, only a half million couples were living together, according to the U.S. Census, which interviews 50,000 households. By 1994, the figure had shot up to 3.7 million couples. About one million cohabiting couples in 1994 have children. Thus, it is also a major cause of illegitimacy.

Table 9.2
Cohabiting Couples

Year	Number of Cohabiting Couples
1970	523,000
1980	1,589,000
1986	2,220,000
1990	2,856,000
1994	3,661,000

Cohabitation is a double cancer of marriage. Couples who live together often say they are in a "trial marriage," testing their compatibility. But cohabitation should be called a "trial divorce" because the key ingredient to making a marriage work—commitment—is missing. The University of Wisconsin interviewed 13,000 people in 100-minute personal interviews for its National Survey of Families and Households.[11] Its stark conclusion was this: "Marriages that are preceded by living together have 50 percent higher disruption rates than marriages without premarital cohabitation" (emphasis added). Thus cohabitation is a cancer at the center of marriage.

And it is a cancer at the front end too. Living together has become a substitute for getting married at all. Forty percent of those whose unions begin with cohabitation, break up short of marriage. Result? The number of never-married Americans doubled from 1970 to 1994 from 21 million to 44.6 million in 1994 largely due to cohabitation.[12] America's population only grew 28 percent while the number who shack up soared four times faster.

Stable Illegitimacy Rates

There is some good news. Out-of-wedlock births, which have risen every year for a generation, fell in 1995 for the first time. They fell from 32.6 percent of all births in 1994 to 32.2 percent in 1995, according to the National Center for Health Statistics.[13] However, they edged back to 32.4 percent in 1996. While that is lamentable, what's encouraging is that illegitimacy in 1996 is slightly below that of 1994.

More important, the rate of out-of-wedlock births, which had been increasing by one percent a year for a generation, has been halted.

Table 9.3
Out-of-Wedlock Births

Year	Out-of-Wedlock Births	Illegitimacy Percent
1960	224,000	5.2
1970	399,000	10.7
1980	666,000	18.4
1990	1,165,000	28.0
1991	1,214,000	29.5
1992	1,225,000	30.1
1993	1,240,000	31.0
1994	1,290,000	32.6
1995	1,254,000	32.2
1996	1,287,000	32.4

As heartening as the new stability is, nearly a third of American babies continue to be born out of wedlock. And the small decline of 1995 was somewhat reversed in 1996. The 1996 illegitimacy rate is still a full percent higher than in 1993, and six times that of 1960. Each year 1.3 million children are born out of wedlock. And illegitimacy increased somewhat in 1996 among whites to 25.7 percent, while decreasing slightly among blacks to 68.8 percent. In fact, by 1994, 40 percent of never-married American women in their thirties have had a child, reports Maggie Gallagher in her important book, *The Abolition of Marriage*.[14]

Part of the decline was due to a 4 percent drop in births to teenagers. "More teens are choosing abstinence," said Grace Hsu with the Family Research Council.

If there was a connection in the slight decline to the fatherhood movement, no one made such a claim. But I see a connection. Promise Keepers has made male commitment to biblical principles of chastity and fidelity, if not cool, at least no longer snickered at by the mainstream press. As men keep their promises to their wives and girlfriends, there will be less illegitimacy and fewer divorces.

Yet *two-fifths* of American children still go to bed in homes where their father does not live. *Bold new initiatives are needed—especially by pastors.*

I have spoken to groups of clergy in about 70 American cities. I often recount the data about how cohabitation is not a trial marriage but a double cancer of marriage and thus a trial divorce and a cause of out-of-wedlock births. Then I ask this question: "How many of you have ever preached a sermon on cohabitation." At most one pastor in 50 will raise a hand.

So I say, "You are part of the problem. Sociological data backs up Scripture. Paul said to 'Flee fornication.' And the University of Wisconsin's National Survey of Families and Households proves the wisdom of this position. Of 100 cohabiting couples, 40 break up short of marriage, and of the 60 who marry, there will be 45 divorces (50 percent above the national average of half of marriages failing). So of the original 100 trial marriages, only 15 couples are still together after a decade. You need to preach with this secular evidence of Scripture and say, 'Some of you have children who are living with someone. You have anguished about it, but not known what to say. Now you do. You can tell your adult children to move apart since there is only a 15 percent chance of success.'"

Research also shows that virgins at the time of marriage have much lower divorce rates than those who are sexually active. Whether couples married in the 1960s, 1970s, or 1980s, sexually active couples are two-thirds more likely to divorce than those who marry as virgins.[15]

Churches as Wedding Factories

It is time to acknowledge that organized religion is partly responsible for the soaring divorce rate. Three-fourths of all first marriages are blessed by priests, pastors, or rabbis, according to the National Center for Health Statistics. Gallup Polls indicate two-thirds (69 percent) of all adults are members of a church or synagogue and 43 percent attended religious services in an average week of 1995.[16] Yet nearly half of those marrying in the late 1960s and early 1970s are already divorced.[17]

Since U.S. churches have access to the vast majority of American marriages, the conclusion is inescapable that most churches are only "blessing machines" or "wedding factories" when it comes to marriage. They grind out weddings on Saturdays with no clear strategy to help couples prepare for a lifelong marriage. Most churches do nothing to strengthen marriage at the midterm, or to save them when they are headed for divorce, other than to send the couple to largely ineffectual counselors.

Churches as Marriage Savers

However, there is some good news at the heart of these dismal trends. A successful movement of "marriage saving" programs is springing up across the continent, created largely by churches. Thousands of churches are what I call "Marriage Savers," places which have pioneered important reforms to save marriages. This chapter and *Marriage Savers: Helping Your Friends and Family Avoid Divorce* present evidence that some churches are helping couples achieve six great goals:

- *Avoid a bad marriage before it begins.* Some 50,000 churches administer a premarital inventory that can predict with 80 percent accuracy which marriages will end in divorce. In fact, a tenth of couples using one inventory, PREPARE, break their engagements when they see the results. Their scores are equal to those who marry and later divorce. So they are avoiding a bad marriage before it begins.

- *Give the engaged "marriage insurance."* During the first four years that my wife and I led marriage preparation at our church, 25 couples out of 135 couples decided not to marry, but in five years there have been only three separations that we know of, of 110 couples who did marry—not a perfect record, but close to "marriage insurance."

- *Strengthen existing marriage.* Sixty academic studies of a weekend retreat called Marriage Encounter provide evidence that 80 to 90 percent of attendees fall back in love with a spouse, and learn skills permanently improving their marriage.

- *Save 80 to 90 percent of deeply troubled marriages.* One national program called "Retrouvaille" has saved 80 percent of nearly 50,000 marriages headed for divorce, and two church interventions reported in Marriage Savers save 92 to 95 percent of them.

- *Help more than half of separated couples to reconcile.* Between 20 percent and 40 percent of Retrouvaille attendees are already living apart, yet four-fifths of the marriages are saved.

- *Push down the divorce rate for an entire metro area.* When clergy from 19 denominations in Peoria signed a "Community Marriage Policy" that jump-started these reforms, divorces plunged 21 percent in the first year. In ten years they plunged a big 40 percent in Modesto, California, and divorces are down in seven other cities.

Modesto's Community Marriage Policy

Twelve years ago in January 1986, I made a speech to the clergy of Modesto, California, at the invitation of First Baptist Church and several other pastors who had read my column. "It should mean more to get married in a church than before a Justice of the Peace," I argued,

> but the divorce rate of those getting married in the church is nearly the same as those in civil weddings. We have four times the weekly church attendance of Europe (40 percent versus 10 percent) and yet our divorce rate is double that of Europe. Clearly, something is profoundly wrong with what U.S. churches are doing.
>
> However, one denomination is pioneering answers—Roman Catholicism. Catholics have a "Common Marriage Policy," in which they agree to require six months of marriage preparation for any couple who wants a Catholic wedding, whether it is in St. Mary's or St. John's Catholic Church. If Catholics can require a six month minimum, could Protestants consider a four month minimum? (The largely Protestant audience laughed uneasily.)
>
> Catholics often require couples to take a "premarital inventory" to give the couple an objective view of their strengths and weaknesses as a couple. Doesn't that make sense for Protestants, too? And they have turned marriage preparation over to couples with solid marriages. Apostle Paul said the job of the pastor is "to equip the saints for ministry" or to "train God's people for service" (Ephesians 4:12). What more important ministry or service is there than saving marriages? Yet what church has even a solid premarital program?
>
> Marriage Encounter moves 80 percent to 90 percent of couples to fall back in love. Why not encourage all married couples in your church to attend? Why not cooperate across denominational lines and create a Modesto Community Marriage Policy with a conscious aim to radically reduce the divorce rate? If the churches cooperated with a goal of pushing down the divorce rate, it should be possible to cut Modesto's divorce rate in half—to that of Europe, in five to ten years.

Led by First Baptist's associate pastor, Jim Talley, 95 pastors did sign the nation's first Community Marriage Policy, which noted that three-quarters of marriages "are performed by pastors, and we are troubled by the nearly 50 percent divorce rate." As Dave Seifert, pastor of Big Valley Grace Community Church, put it, "We were grieved by statistics of divorce among Christians. We were in a state of confession and repentance over our part in failing to properly equip couples for the challenge of marriage." Clergy signed a document in which they set an extraordinary goal:

[T]o radically reduce the divorce rate among those married in area churches. It is the responsibility of pastors to set minimal requirements to raise the quality of the commitment in those we marry. We believe that couples who seriously participate in premarital testing and counseling will have a better understanding of what the marriage commitment involves.

Specifically, they decided that if a couple wanted to get married in any local churches of 19 denominations, the pair would have to undergo four months of marriage preparation that included taking a premarital inventory "to help couples evaluate the maturity of their relationship" and meeting with "a mature married couple" to help the engaged couple bond for life.

Plunging Divorce Rates in Nine Cities

The result of Modesto's Community Marriage Policy has attracted national attention. The city's divorce rate has plunged 40 percent in a decade, falling from 6.3 divorces per 1,000 population in 1986 to 3.8 per 1,000 in 1995. The city is saving more than 1,000 marriages a year!

This success has inspired 72 cities to create a Community Marriage Policy or Community Marriage Covenant, as it is sometimes known. By calling up the clerks of the court in the counties where some cities with a Community Marriage Policy are located, I have found that divorce rates have fallen in nine metropolitan areas in six different states. Four cities in Illinois—plus one each in Alabama and Georgia—have had their divorces drop 8 to 18.6 percent in only two to four years. They are Peoria, Moline, Rock Island, and Quincy, Illinois; plus Montgomery, Alabama; and Albany, Georgia. Thus, these cities are in three distinct parts of the United States. And these few small cities account for one-fifth of America's decline of 9,000 divorces from 1986-1995. In addition, the rates have dropped modestly in Austin, Texas, and Woodbridge, Virginia, after one year.

Significance of These Trends for the Fatherhood Movement

Millions of dollars are being spent annually by such organizations as Promise Keepers and the National Fatherhood Initiative—with only a small discernible impact upon either the divorce rate or illegitimacy. The Promise Keepers budget alone in 1996 was an astonishing $97 million.

By contrast, my wife, Harriet, and I, working on a part-time basis, without even a secretary, have helped hundreds of pastors in 72 cities to adopt proven, Marriage Savers strategies that are pushing down the divorce rate in a number of them. Each of those strategies was created by others. All that we have done is to call attention to what works in articles, books, speeches, and interviews in the media. In Minneapolis-St. Paul alone, nearly 300 pastors, priests, and rabbis signed what they called a "Twin Cities Community Marriage Agreement" on April 3, 1997.

Based on this experience, I suggest that the fatherhood movement could do more to restore fatherhood by taking an explicit marriage-saving strategy. America will not restore marriage simply by having men talk and pray with one another. The women must be involved! Just as marriages die one couple at a time, they can also be saved one marriage at a time if there are mentoring couples with strong marriages, trained by the church, to help. What's been lacking is a vision and practical help for pastors who'd like to have a Marriage Savers church.

The Importance of Marriage Mentors

At the core of the best Marriage Savers is a simple idea: In every church there are couples with vibrant marriages, who really could be of help to other couples—but have never been asked, inspired, or trained to come alongside other couples and help them at key stages of the marital life cycle. These mentoring couples or "Marriage Mentors" can transform a church from being a wedding factory or blessing machine, grinding out weddings on Saturday, into being a Marriage Saver church, saving even 90 percent of the most troubled marriages.

In other words, the key to creating a movement that will push down the divorce rate is to see the absolute necessity of church reform in dealing with marriage: equipping local churches with the vision and skills to adopt proven, marriage-saving strategies, such as requiring engaged couples to take a premarital inventory and training solidly married couples to be "Marriage Mentors" to discuss the issues that surface.

The good news is that thousands of churches already are "marriage savers." What they are doing right is not well known. That's why I wrote *Marriage Savers*, which puts a spotlight on ten major reforms that have been pioneered by scattered churches. One strategy can be seen in more than 50,000 churches—the use of a premarital inventory.[18] Another, Marriage Encounter, has helped renew nearly two million marriages. Other solutions have emerged from a single church and have been transplanted, thus far, in only a few other congregations.

The central idea behind most of these reforms is very simple. Every church has a marriage-saving resource in its pews—couples who have built rewarding, lifelong marriages. They can come alongside other couples, and help them to be successful. However, in 95 percent of churches, they have never been asked, inspired, or equipped to become Marriage Mentors.

There is one major exception to this generalization. For 20 to 25 years, Catholic churches have turned marriage preparation over to older couples with solid marriages. Since priests are celibate, they asked married couples to do marriage preparation.

Another couple-led movement that came out of Catholicism is called Marriage Encounter, though it is now in a dozen Protestant denominations. Finally, Catholic couples whose marriages nearly ended in divorce tell others how they recovered in a weekend retreat for currently troubled marriages. They call the weekend *Retrouvaille*, which is French for "rediscovery."

These couple-pioneered reforms—and even better ones that have grown out of a few Protestant churches—are explored below in more detail. What's common to each innovation is volunteer "mentoring couples" who give days to help other couples make it. This movement is analogous to other successful self-help groups, such as Alcoholics Anonymous, but it is led by couples, not individuals. Marriage Mentors are a ray of hope.

The Premarital Inventory

"A dating relationship is designed to conceal information, not reveal it," wrote Dr. James Dobson in *Love for a Lifetime*. "Each partner puts his or her best foot forward, hiding embarrassing facts, habits, flaws, and temperaments. Consequently . . . the stage is then set for arguments and hurt feelings [after the wedding] that never occurred during the courtship experience."[19]

Romance is deceptive. Therefore, churches and synagogues—who marry 74 percent of all those in first marriages[20]—have an obligation to help couples accomplish two important goals. First, churches should help those before marriage begins. Second, churches should equip couples with conflict resolution skills, which can almost give them "marriage insurance."

How? To begin with, couples approaching marriage desperately need an objective view of their strengths and weaknesses as a pair. There is no better way to do this than by asking engaged couples to take what is called a "premarital inventory." One of the best is called PREPARE (Premarital Personal and Relationship Evaluation) developed by Dr. David Olson, a family psychologist at the University of Minnesota. He recommends that PREPARE be taken at an earlier stage, by seriously dating couples as part of their decision-making process about whether to become engaged. It is an infinitely more constructive way to consider a possible partner for life than a "trial marriage," where the odds are only one in six that one will still be with that partner after a decade.[21]

PREPARE frames 165 statements that both the man and woman agree or disagree with on a questionnaire taken separately. Many of the items cleverly ask about one's partner—a subject about which people are more honest than they are about themselves:

- Sometimes I am concerned about my partner's temper.
- When we are having a problem, my partner often refuses to talk about it.
- Sometimes I wish my partner were more careful in spending money.

The inventory is mailed to PREPARE/ENRICH, Inc.[22] with a check for $30, and the results are mailed back in an easy-to-read, computer-scored report to one of 30,000 pastors or counselors now using it. All of them have attended a six-hour training session to learn how to use the instrument. The inventory cannot be bought off the shelf. One has to be trained by a certified trainer. More than one million couples have taken PREPARE, and half as many have taken its sister inventory, ENRICH, which measures satisfaction among the already married.

Remarkably, PREPARE predicts with 80 percent accuracy which couples will divorce, and with 79 percent accuracy who will have a good marriage.[23] More important, 10-15 percent of those who take it break their engagements. Several studies show that their scores are the same as those who marry but later divorce. Thus, those who break their engagements are avoiding a bad marriage before it begins. Others are helped to build a more successful marriage because they are helped to talk through issues while the relationship is young and both people are more willing to change because they are deeply in love.

Taking a premarital inventory is a vastly better way to decide whether to marry someone than living with one's partner. In fact, a study of 17,024 couples taking PREPARE found that cohabiting couples had

> significantly lower premarital satisfaction compared to couples where the two people still lived alone. . . . Almost two-thirds (64 percent) of the cohabiting couples fell into the low satisfaction group, whereas almost two-thirds (64 percent) of the couples where both partners lived alone, fell into the very satisfied group.[24]

Another premarital inventory used by Catholics is called FOCCUS (Facilitating Open Couple Communication Understanding and Study). It was written by the Family Life Office of the Diocese of Omaha, 3214 North 60th St., Omaha, NE 68104. It is used widely as PREPARE, but is less predictive of which marriages will fail (70 percent versus 80 percent for PREPARE).[25]

Involving Mentoring Couples in Marriage Preparation

Usually, PREPARE is administered by clergy. However, it can be a bridge between a young couple and one whose marriage has worked for decades. The inventory is simple enough for a "Marriage Mentoring Couple" to administer. PREPARE/ENRICH provides a kit for $10 that a pastor can use to train a solidly married couple to undertake marriage preparation with the engaged couple. In fact, my wife, Harriet, and I have trained 42 couples in our church (Fourth Presbyterian in Bethesda, Maryland) to give the inventory and go over its results with young couples.

One part of the training involves having the potential mentor couple take ENRICH. This has a double value. It gives the mentors a sense of what it is like to take PREPARE. And it helps the pastor to be sure a couple has a strong marriage before asking them to serve. No pastor wants to send "unguided missiles" out to work with engaged couples.

Four couples we trained had such poor scores we told them we did not think this was an appropriate ministry for them "at this time." (We then told them how Marriage Encounter strengthened our marriage and urged them to go.)

My wife, Harriet, who runs our church's mentoring program, and now accompanies me in speaking around the country about our marriage-saving work, tells pastors:

> This is the most rewarding ministry we have ever been involved in. I have taught Sunday school, and Mike has also taught. But that divided us as a couple at church. This is a ministry you can do in the comfort of your own home, as a couple. It has strengthened our own relationship. We have rediscovered what Jesus meant when he said, 'Give, and you shall receive.'

She adds,

> A mentor couple can do a better job than a pastor. First, both sexes are involved. I usually understand the woman's concerns, and Mike, the young man's. We can be vulnerable, and admit where we made mistakes, which is inappropriate for a pastor. Also, we have the time to go over 125 issues with each couple, since our kids are grown. In four years, we've given PREPARE to 110 couples. A number broke engagements, but there are no divorces.

Last winter a physician in her thirties called to say she and her male friend were considering marriage, but were concerned about communication problems they were having. "Can you help us?"

"Yes," I replied. "Come to our marriage prep classes which we're running right now, and my wife and I will mentor you."

My heart sank when I looked at their inventory. They scored 0 on Communication and 20 percent on Conflict Resolution. Both said their partner was giving them the silent treatment. Andrew said Gloria made comments that put him down. She wished he was more willing to share his feelings with her. And the young man, an engineer, said, Gloria "does not understand how I feel."

"Andrew," I asked, "if you don't share your feelings with Gloria, how can you expect her to understand you? If she calls you at the end of the day, and asks, 'How was your day?' what do you say in response?"

"Great or terrible," he replied.

"Bad answer. What she wants is detail. Even though you're an engineer, you can push yourself to say, 'I had a great day because I finished my project much earlier than expected, and my boss complimented me.' Or, 'It was terrible. I lost two days of work on my computer by pushing the wrong button.' What she wants is detail."

Both Harriet and Gloria nodded in agreement.

Three weeks later, they came to our home for another session with big smiles on their faces. "How is it going?" I asked. "Gloria, is he sharing his feelings with you?"

"He really is," she replied.

"Andrew, do you now feel understood?"

"Yes, and she's not nagging any more."

"How about the silent treatment?" Harriet asked.

"We don't do that any more. You told us that what we were doing was childish, and you were right."

I was so astonished I took out the inventory and went over the 10 items in Communication and 10 more in Conflict Resolution. They scored 100 percent! I asked, "What happened to turn things around?"

"You were right that I was not sharing my feelings with Gloria. When I did so, it solved other problems."[26]

Rarely does a couple's learning come so swiftly and completely. However, the case illustrates the value of using the inventory as an X ray of a couple's relationship, and of having a mature man and woman sit down with a younger man and woman, and talk through the results. Their previous scores had predicted a future divorce.

But the inventory is only predictive—not determinative. A couple who wants to solve its problems can do so. We simply used a common sense that comes with a three decade marriage to suggest how they could improve their communication. Both Gloria and Andrew had more degrees than did Harriet or I. But they lacked our 30 years of experience as a married couple. And their inner-city African American church had not trained any mentor couples. So they were willing to cross over the racial and cultural barrier, and drive 12 miles to our home. The case also illustrates that a mentoring couple can ask probing questions to give a young couple the perspective they need to grow toward one another.

Interestingly, the couple's experience was so profound, that they convinced their pastor at Shiloh Baptist Church and other couples to be trained by Harriet and me in using the inventory.

At present, about 250,000 to 300,000 of the 2.4 million couples who marry every year take a premarital inventory.[27] However, not one percent of churches has trained mentor couples to do this exciting work. Frankly, the training is easy to do—the same six-hour seminar attended by clergy. And the inventory provides an X ray of the relationship an older couple needs to be helpful in talking through their particular issues.

Apostle Paul, in writing to the Ephesians, said the job of the pastor is to "equip the saints for ministry" or "train God's people for service." My question for pastors is, what more important ministry or service is there than saving marriages?

Marriage Encounter: The Best Marriage Saver

I know first-hand the difference a church-based intervention can make. Twenty years ago, a project I was working on required me to commute weekly from Connecticut to Washington, D.C. I would board the train at 2 a.m. on Mondays and try to sleep on the train and shave in Union Station. I'd work all week in Washington and arrive home late Friday night. Harriet graciously put up with this for months, and even had a candle-lit dinner waiting for me at 11 p.m. on Fridays.

At that time some couples at church encouraged us "to go on Marriage Encounter." I asked, "What is it?"

They replied, "It's a way to strengthen your marriage."

My first reaction was resentment: "I've got a good marriage, thanks."

"No. This is a way to make a good marriage better," they asserted. It sounded like a PR line to this reporter. But I kept hearing rave reviews from otherwise sensible people. So I asked Harriet if she wanted to go.

"No!" she snapped.

"Why not? We have been apart for months. This will be good for us."

"We can't afford it," she said.

I sensed that her real reason not to go ran deeper, but did not know what it was. Later, couples told us our way was already paid.

"By whom?" I asked.

"By people who love you." That impressed me, since we had only been in this church a year or so. Harriet had no more excuses, so we went to a motel 70 miles away. Our first surprise was that the couples who had urged us to go had all gotten there ahead of us and fixed a wonderful dinner and decorated with balloons. We had never experienced such unmerited compassion.

The weekend itself consisted of a series of talks by the lead couples. After each one, they gave attendees an assignment to write for ten minutes on a given question. We then met for ten minutes with our spouse in private to discuss what each had written. The first assignment was easy: "What is it that I admire about you and about our marriage, and how does it make me feel?" I wrote pages about how wonderful Harriet and our marriage were to me. We exchanged notebooks back in our motel room, and I noticed Harriet was much less enthusiastic.

Later, the writing assignment was, "What is it that I have not told you that I should have shared?" Harriet wrote, "When you went to Washington, you abandoned me. You love your work more than me." I felt like I had been punched in the stomach, and asked her to tell me more. "Well, you're not a husband and not a father! You're never home, except weekends. And even then you're always working. I asked you to take the kids for a 15 minute swim and you said, 'I don't have time. I have to work.'"

I was so caught up in personal difficulties that I had not realized the impact I was having on Harriet. I wept and held her and said, "I do not love my work more than you. In fact, I've hated much of it, because I was failing. Please forgive me."

We did fall back in love that weekend. For me, it was like being on a second honeymoon—only better, because we had shared ten years together and rediscovered how much we loved one another.

I asked Harriet recently for her assessment of the importance of that weekend 20 years ago. She replied, "Marriage Encounter was a unique weekend, an opportunity to focus on each other on two different levels. One was to learn lifetime tools to equip us for intimate communication, the kind of communication every husband and wife needs to nourish or sustain a marriage. Second, we have attended two different Marriage Encounters, one ten years after we were married and another 29 years afterwards. In the process of sharing feelings deeply, one overriding issue that had laid dormant in our relationship, yet needed to be dealt with, floated to the top and was addressed."

Nor was our experience unique. About two million couples have attended a Marriage Encounter weekend. And 61 academic studies, which interviewed couples before attending Marriage Encounter and afterwards, reveal a "vastly preponderant positive impact," according to a Doctor of Ministry thesis by Dr. George McIlrath.[28] He writes, "Marriage Encounter programs have often received affirmations of 80 percent to 90 percent in post-weekend surveys, and the program demonstrates clear effectiveness when its participants are involved in rigorous and controlled pre- and post-weekend research." To put it more simply, 80 to 90 percent fall back in love!

An important study, cited by McIlrath and mentioned in chapter 9 of *Marriage Savers*, was conducted by the National Institute on the Family to commemorate Marriage Encounter's 25th anniversary in the United States.[29] Questionnaires were sent to 4,000 couples who had attended over a 25-year period, 325 of whom responded. Only 55 percent said their marriages were good or excellent before attending, and 45 percent said their marriages were "average" or "poor." In terms of improving their communication, 83 percent said the immediate impact of the weekend was high. Years later, 200 of the 325 respondents said the long-term impact on "intimacy and closeness" was high or very good, and the same number rated their current couple communication as "excellent"—nearly two-thirds of respondents.[30]

Why does Marriage Encounter have such a long-term impact? Couples learn the absolute necessity of taking time on a daily basis to listen to one another, to talk, and to pray together. Some ME couples continue the discipline of writing for ten minutes and talking for ten minutes on a daily basis. Asked why, one man told me: "I'm a salesman and very verbal. My wife told me that I was always interrupting her. When she writes, she can say what she wants, and I owe it to her to pay attention." For 20 years Harriet and I have gotten up a little earlier than necessary—not to do "ten and tens"—but to have coffee in bed as we talk informally, read some Scripture and some commentary from books such as *Quiet Times for Couples* by H. Norman Wright.

The result? No longer does Harriet bottle up her feelings as she once did. And I have become a better listener. We conclude with a prayer for each other, seeking to make the Lord a third partner of our marriage. It is a great way to start the day. I would never have looked for other examples of how to strengthen marriage—or written *Marriage Savers*—had not Marriage Encounter's impact upon our marriage been so profound.

Further, while Marriage Encounter began among Catholics, there are a dozen denominations involved now.[31] But it is a lay couple movement, which gets relatively little official church support from any denomination. Attendance at ME weekends has fallen from more than 100,000 couples a year in the late 1970s to only 20,000 couples in 1995. But the trend is reversible. In some areas with new leadership, Marriage Encounter is growing.

Retrouvaille: Saving 80 Percent of Troubled Marriages

Catholic leaders of Marriage Encounter in Quebec noticed that a few couples who attended the weekends ended up getting divorced. Asked why, some of them said, "You were talking about powder-puff problems like poor communication. Our problems were much more serious—like ten years of adultery, an issue that no one mentioned at Marriage Encounter."

In response, Quebec Marriage Encounter couples created a more intensive weekend called Retrouvaille to help save marriages headed for divorce. They asked "back-from-the-brink" couples who had rebuilt marriages after adultery, alcoholism, or abuse to lead the weekends. These veteran survivors share openly about how they overcame those problems, and thus serve as role models or mentors to attending couples on Retrouvaille weekends. But the technique of writing ten minutes and then talking in private about what each has written is the same as Marriage Encounter. Retrouvaille has swept across the border and is now in 100 metropolitan areas in the United States and has been attended by nearly 50,000 couples.[32]

Its results are spectacular. In Northern Virginia, a fifth of the 400 couples who attended were already separated, yet 79 percent of the couples rebuilt their marriages. In Michigan, a third of the 600 attendees had already filed divorce papers, yet 80 percent restored their marriages. Two-fifths of 817 couples in Fort Worth had already separated or divorced, yet 70 percent are still together.[33]

What makes Marriage Encounter and Retrouvaille work are couples I would call "Marriage Mentors."

Marriage Ministry: A Congregation-Based Retrouvaille

Marriage Ministry is a similar proven way to save couples headed for divorce courts—but it is based in a local church. It began when Father Dick McGinnis of St. David's Episcopal Church in Jacksonville said one Sunday, "I would like to meet with any couples whose marriages were once on the rocks, but are now in a state of healing. Meet me in the chapel after the service."

He did not know if any couples would come forward. But ten couples did so, out of a congregation of 180 people. McGinnis was thrilled. He told them, "I am overwhelmed trying to counsel all the tough marriages in this church. I went to the Lord in prayer, and what came to me was the way Alcoholics Anonymous works. Someone who has successfully overcome the addiction tells how he did it. We need similar couples who can tell how they turned around a bad marriage."

Of the ten couples, seven agreed to work with him. Their stories were wildly diverse. One woman had been in an adulterous affair for eight years. One man was a bisexual, who once had homosexual affairs on the side. Another man was a former alcoholic.

However, those seven couples developed 17 Marriage Ministry action steps (analogous to AA's 12 Steps) on how to save a bad marriage. These steps, found on page 204 of *Marriage Savers*, can be transplanted into any of America's 350,000 churches. And they are potentially more important than AA's 12 Steps because only a tenth of Americans are alcoholics, while more than half of marriages are failing. Here are examples of the "M and Ms":

- Through other Christian's testimony and example, we/I found hope for our marriage.
- I made a decision to love: Christ, mate, self.
- We made a decision to stay together.
- I accepted my mate as he/she is.
- I realized the problem was with myself.
- I became aware I needed to change, became willing to change, learned what and how to change, and began to change.[34]

For example, one woman said her husband was an alcoholic who lost his job, and was out of work two years. "He would not discipline the children. He threw his clothes all around. All he did in this marriage was football and the garbage." But then she realized that part of the problem was that she had a "sharp tongue." So she prayed to God to send angels down "to hold my tongue." Her husband noticed right away that she was no longer griping. So he picked up his clothes one day. That night, she was more amorous than she had been. He thought that was great. She could not change him. But she could change herself, and as she did so, she inspired change on his part.[35]

Those seven Marriage Mentors couples have now worked with 40 currently troubled marriages, and they saved 38 of them. That's a 95 percent success rate with the most troubled marriages![36]

Father McGinnis and his wife, who are now retired, have planted "Marriage Ministry" in churches in six states. For example, after Sioux Falls, South Dakota, created a "Sioux Empire Community Marriage Covenant" in May 1997, the organizers invited the McGinnises to train seven couples from two churches to create a Marriage Ministry there. It has gone so well, Sioux Falls invited the McGinnises to return in January 1998 to train ten additional couples over a weekend. (To reach Father McGinnis, call 904-514-4255 or 904-724-2563.)

Stepfamily Support Groups: Another Marriage Saver

Some 46 percent of all marriages today involve at least one person who was previously married. Those with stepchildren are the most explosive in America—breaking up at an estimated 65 percent rate.[37] Stepchildren resent their new "parent" and know how to drive them out: "You are not my mother! You are the wicked stepmother who never lets me do anything."

Roswell United Methodist Church near Atlanta has created a major answer—a "Stepfamily Support Group" led by those who have learned to make a blended family work. They mentor couples new to the problem, and have helped 230 out of 250 couples to be successful.[38] That is a 92 percent success rate.

Thus, a church that creates a Marriage Ministry and a Stepfamily Support Group can reasonably expect to save 90 percent of its worst marriages! Over the past year, Harriet and I have created a group to help stepfamilies be successful, with five stepfamily couples who have truly created "blended families" in our congregation that we are calling Stepfamilies Offering Support—SOS. It was launched in 1997. We used an excellent kit of materials written by Rev. Dick Dunn in creating the Roswell Stepfamilies Support Group. (To learn more, call him at 770-993-6218.)

Community Marriage Policies and Mentoring Reforms

There really are proven ways any church can be a Marriage Saver. All of the reforms described up to this point were created by others. Only one reform is original with me. In my meetings with local clergy groups over a decade, I have challenged pastors to jump-start all of these reforms in many churches at one time in what I call a "Community Marriage Policy" (CMP) or "Community Marriage Covenant."[39] Earlier in this chapter I described the Modesto Policy. Later policies were similar in their commitment to strengthen marriage preparation by requiring four months of marriage counseling during which a couple would take a premarital inventory and be mentored in at least four sessions by an older couple trained "to work as role models and counselors with engaged couples," as the 1991 Peoria policy put it. Pastors also agreed that they or mentors should meet with newlyweds twice in their first year of marriage.

However, CMPs beginning with Peoria also took steps to strengthen existing marriages and save troubled ones. They encouraged "all married couples to attend a couples retreat such as Marriage Encounter," and said the married clergy "should be the first to attend." Finally, they pledged an important additional step to create a "Marriage Ministry of mentoring couples whose marriages once nearly failed to work with troubled marriages." Subsequent CMPs look similar.

Pastors from 17 denominations in Muncie, Indiana, adopted a similar policy in February 1996, but added this paragraph to their Preamble: "We also believe that the church has an ongoing responsibility to help strengthen existing marriages and save the troubled ones. 'For I hate divorce, says the Lord God of Israel' (Malachi 2:16). What God has joined together, let the church help hold together."

The Greater Grand Rapids Community Marriage Policy

On June 17, 1997, the Greater Grand Rapids Community Marriage Policy was adopted, representing a new generation of American marriage covenants. It was the first created by a mayor and the first to involve university presidents and corporate CEOs on a steering committee with clergy. It is also the first to be based on the founding principle of the need "to improve the well-being of children" and the first to be signed by 2,000 community leaders only 175 of whom are pastors. Credit must be given to Bill Hardiman of the suburb Kentwood, who spearheaded the effort, convincing business, political, civic, and therapy leaders to join with clergy. All previous CMPs put the full burden of saving marriages on organized religion.

In Grand Rapids, primary responsibility for rebuilding marriage is given to "houses of worship," because "the clergy potentially play a critical role." But the leaders of all community institutions—such as businesses, universities, public schools, and government—are also asked to examine how "our current policies may unwittingly undermine marriage formation," and are asked to "implement changes" to "promote marriages and stable families." For example, some companies may require so much overtime that marriages are undermined. One lumber company executive told me, "Perhaps we should pay for marital counseling as a corporate benefit. Certainly when a worker gets divorced, he or she is an ineffectual worker for months."

"Yes," I replied, "or pay for a Marriage Encounter or Retrouvaille weekend!"

Due to its breadth of community support, the Preamble of the Grand

Rapids CMP is quite different, and has already inspired similar versions in Denver, and Newport News, Virginia. An excerpt is below:

> There is an emerging consensus among spiritual, academic, civic and political leaders across the spectrum that increasing the proportion of children born and reared in healthy, married two-parent families would constitute one of the most positive social changes we could undertake to improve the well-being of our children. Some hold this view because of their religious belief that marriage and family are institutions ordained by God. Others base their support on evidence that children of such families have significantly lower rates of poverty, teenage pregnancy, school dropout, delinquency and substance abuse. Moreover, when these children are supported by a permanent two-parent union, they have the best chance of optimal life adjustment as measured by successful completion of education, employment and families of their own . . . .

Results of Community Marriage Policies

The results of Community Marriage Policies have been extraordinary. Modesto clergy did not simply achieve their own goal to "radically reduce the divorce rate of those married in area churches," but did so on a countywide basis. *The divorce rate of metropolitan Modesto is down 40 percent in a decade!*

Modesto is in fast-growing Stanislaus County. Between 1986 and 1996, the county's population soared from 303,000 to 420,000, a 39 percent hike in population. Yet the number of divorces fell from 1,923 in 1986 to only 1,606 in 1995. Had the Modesto area's divorces simply grown with the population, there would have been *2,672 divorces—not 1,606.* Thus, Modesto is now *saving more than 1,000 marriages a year.* The divorce rate of Stanislaus County was 6.3 divorces per 1,000 population in 1986. It fell to 3.8 divorces per 1,000. That is a 40 percent drop in the divorce rate!

Table 9.4
Modesto (Stanislaus County) Divorce Rate

Year	Population	Divorces	Divorce Rate/1000
1986	303,000	1,923	6.3
1995	420,000	1,606	3.8
Percentage Change	39 percent increase	16.5 percent increase	40 percent decrease

By comparison, U.S. divorces were virtually unchanged over that same decade. They fell from 1,178,000 in 1986 to 1,169,000 in 1995. That's a national drop of only 9,000 divorces. Modesto is thus responsible for more than a tenth of the nation's fewer divorces.

Divorces Cut in Four Illinois Cities

Modesto's Community Marriage Policy is not unique in pushing down the divorce rate. Four Illinois cities adopted Community Marriage Policies in 1991. All have had significant drops in the divorce rate in subsequent years, ranging from 8 percent in Moline and Rock Island (140,000 population in 1990); a 12.1 percent drop in Quincy (51,000 population); and a remarkable 18.6 percent plunge in Peoria (220,000 population). A fifth Illinois city, Rockford, which adopted its policy in 1993, has had a slight increase in divorces of 3 percent. But as Rock Island and Quincy (and Montgomery, Alabama, below) illustrate, it sometimes takes more than a year or two to push down the divorce rate, as churches train mentoring couples.

Table 9.5
Peoria, Illinois: 18.6 percent drop in divorces from 1991-1995

1991	1,210 divorces
1992	947 (21.8 percent drop in one year)
1993	997
1994	984
1995	985

Table 9.6
Quincy, Illinois: 12.1 percent decrease 1991-1995

1991	482 divorces
1992	477
1993	418
1994	494
1995	424

Table 9.7
Rock Island County: 8 percent drop 1991-1995
(Moline and Rock Island, Illinois)

1991	1,027 divorces
1992	1,023
1993	944
1994	968
1995	945

Table 9.8
Rockford, Illinois: 3 percent increase 1993-1995

1993	1,492 divorces
1994	1,541
1995	1,535

Divorce Rates Drop in Montgomery and Albany

In both Alabama and Georgia cities, there have been comparable drops in the number of divorces—in only two years! They fell 8.6 percent in two years in Albany, Georgia, and 11 percent in Montgomery, Alabama.

Table 9.9
Albany, Georgia (Dougherty County): 8.6 percent drop, 1993-1995

1993	738
1994	670
1995	675

Table 9.10
Montgomery, Alabama: 11 percent drop

1993	1,539
1994	1,568
1995	1,378

Thus, there are 1,688 fewer divorces in seven cities that adopted Community Marriage Policies in four quite different states: California, Alabama, Georgia, and Illinois. As noted earlier, the total drop of divorces in the nation between 1986 and 1995 was only 9,000 divorces. This handful of cities is thus responsible for nearly a fifth of the entire country's reduced number of divorces.[40]

Some 252 Austin, Texas, clergy signed a CMP in January 1996. They made the premarital inventory and couple mentoring optional, and relatively few pastors (35) became trained to administer it in the first 18 months. The result was that divorces fell, but only slightly, from 4,204 in 1995, the year before the CMP was adopted, and 4,136 in 1996—a 1.6 percent drop. In Woodbridge, Virginia, 24 pastors signed a policy in 1994. Though they are only a small percentage of the Prince William County's clergy (perhaps a tenth), they had an impact on saving marriages. Divorces had been growing countywide by 50 per year, in line with a rapidly growing population. But divorces were almost exactly the same number in 1995 and 1996, though the population grew 6 percent from 243,600 in 1994 to 257,600 in 1996. In effect, that is a 6 percent drop in the divorce rate.

Thus, there are nine cities with a Community Marriage Policy with a documented drop in the divorce rate.

Can the Divorce Climate Be Changed?

While most cities took at least a year or two to experience a drop in the divorce rate, Peoria is clearly an exception. Its divorces fell 21.8 percent in one year. Why did Peoria have such a big initial impact, while others did not? The newspapers in all of these cities publish my column and all paid my honorarium to speak to local clergy, but there was a substantial difference in coverage.

Only the *Peoria Journal Star* put the story of pastors signing the policy on the front page. It also made the TV evening news in Peoria only. Media coverage of the adoption of a CMP appears to be as important as the work of the clergy. That there would be any first-year drops in divorce is illogical.

It takes time for pastors to be trained in PREPARE, and then to train mentoring couples in it. What appears to have happened in Peoria due to better coverage of the event is that couples who were in tough marriages decided to work at them rather than give up! As the earlier table shows, Peoria County's divorces have remained below 1,000 every year since 1992: 985 in 1995, for example, compared to 1,210 in 1991.

That's evidence we can affect the divorce climate, changing couples belief that the answer to a bad marriage is to work at it, rather than to give up and divorce.

In other words, pastors cooperating across denominational lines to cut the divorce rate is news. And as Community Marriage Policies push down the divorce rate of cities, it sparks more good news. As that good news is reported, it helps spread the Marriage Savers movement. It interests more clergy and counselors in creating Community Marriage Covenants in more communities. I personally spend hours each day talking either to reporters or to pastors and counselors who want to spread this movement. The net result is that individuals shift from despair about a difficult marriage to tangible hope that area churches can help couples save their marriages.

Why Are Most Churches Failing Marriages?

One final question might be asked: Why are churches generally doing so little to strengthen marriage at the present time? In covering the religious denominations as writer of "Ethics & Religion," a nationally syndicated column, for 16 years,[41] I have heard the issues of marriage and divorce discussed only twice in state or national denominational meetings. (Mainline denominations expend their energy in debating homosexuality and political questions while evangelical denominations focus on abortion, evangelization, and political questions.) Though divorce is considered a sin by all denominations, and the nation creates two million single parent families every year, marriage has been surprisingly largely ignored. Why?

First, there is a pervasive sense of hopelessness about marriage among the nation's clergy—a sense that there are immutable forces assaulting the institution of marriage over which they have no control. Clearly, movies and television have not only endorsed sex with anyone at anytime, but portray it with explicitness that is designed to be sexually arousing. In the face of so many hours of television every week about the joys of fornication and adultery, pastors wonder what an occasional sermon on chastity might be able to accomplish. Second, so many of their church members are getting divorced despite the best efforts clergy give in counseling that a grim sense of resignation has set in.

On the other hand, clergy seem blind to their own complicity. Organized religion fails at four levels.

First, too many churches and synagogues are simply "ecclesiastical vending machines," which rent their sanctuaries and organs for weddings. Pay $300, get a lovely church on Saturday, $100 for the pastor and $50 for the organist—and out pops an instant church wedding. Most clergy today say they require premarital counseling. But when a 1989 Gallup Poll asked how many of once-married people had received premarital counseling, less than a fifth said they had. Gallup also found that those who divorced and those still together "are equally likely (15 percent and 18 percent, respectively) to have had advance preparation or counseling for marriage." [42]

A 1997 poll by the Family Research Council found that 81 percent of married couples in Colorado got married in a church, but 60 percent said they had received no premarital counseling. And 40 percent who said they did have some reported meeting with the pastor an average of 1.6 times. This is evidence most churches are "wedding factories" or "blessing machines."

Thus, whatever marriage preparation exists in 90 percent of churches is mostly worthless, as far as preparing couples for a lifelong marriage.[43] What clergy call "premarital counseling" is often little more than getting acquainted and planning a wedding service. My wife and I were married by a bishop who spent 15 minutes in a "counseling session." He asked Harriet, "How are your parents?" To me, he said, "What kind of work do you do?" With those questions easily answered, we were out of there.

Second, virtually no churches have programs in place consciously designed to strengthen existing marriages. Church weekend retreats to enrich marriages, like Marriage Encounter, are only held by one church in 1,000. They ought to be held annually. Third, most churches have no strategy to save marriages headed toward divorce. True, many churches do offer "counseling" for troubled marriages. But there is not a single study proving that church counseling of marriages headed for divorce is effective, according to Dr. David Larson, a research psychiatrist who is president of the privately funded, National Institute for Healthcare Research in Bethesda, Maryland.[44]

Finally, clergy largely avoid preaching on issues relating to marriage or divorce. As the writer of "Ethics & Religion," a syndicated column, I have had the opportunity to speak with cross-sections of clergy in 70 cities. As noted earlier, I routinely ask pastors: "How many of you have ever preached on cohabitation?" Rarely does anyone raise a hand. I then ask how many have preached a full sermon on divorce. Only a few hands go up.

I have been very encouraged that as pastors hear about the Marriage Savers outlined in this chapter, they want to see them implemented in their churches. The answers outlined here are not taught in seminary, nor are most denominations telling their clergy about them. Clergy are so delighted to hear that most marriages can be saved that they are willing to join a Community Marriage Policy upon first hearing about it. Furthermore, the interest is as keen in liberal as in conservative churches.

The major problem is simply getting the message out to clergy that churches *can be* marriage savers. And that every church has couples with good marriages who really could be of help to other couples—but have never been asked, inspired, or trained to come alongside a couple and help them to be successful.

The Marriage Savers Resource Collection

This is a nation of 300,000 churches that involve two-thirds of all Americans. What's needed is a conscious strategy to help thousands of those churches learn about the most effective ways to prepare couples for a lifelong marriage, to strengthen all existing marriages, and to save the ones headed for divorce courts.

Toward that end, I have created a *Marriage Savers Resource Collection* that includes three books and six videos that communicate these answers at different levels of sophistication. Some 2,500 churches are already using the materials to recruit potential mentoring couples and teach them proven marriage-saving answers. The package includes the following:

> 1. *Marriage Savers: Helping Your Friends and Family Avoid Divorce*, an expanded 1995 edition of my original book, published by Zondervan, with new chapters on "Helping The Separated, Divorced and Stepfamilies" and on "Couple Mentoring." It is 346 pages long, and includes an index and an appendix listing the names, addresses, and phone numbers of 25 "Marriage Saver" ministries.

> 2. *Insuring Marriage: 25 Proven Ways to Prevent Divorce* is a little book, only 112 pages long, published in 1996 by Zondervan. It is designed for pastors to give to couples who want quick answers on how to choose a mate for life, deepen a flat marriage, save one headed toward the rocks.

> 3. *Leader's Guide to Marriage Savers* is a 96 page outline of a 13 week course that any church could offer to recruit mentor couples which utilizes the videos and gives participants a choice of reading either *Marriage Savers* or *Insuring Marriage*.

4. Six half-hour videos. Video 1 is an overview of the answers, as stated by couples who have experienced them.[45] It has excerpts of three network shows featuring Marriage Savers: *NBC Nightly News with Tom Brokaw, ABC World News Tonight with Peter Jennings*, CBS' *48 Hours with Dan Rather*. My wife and I describe and illustrate what couple mentoring looks like and we are seen training mentors in our church. Other videos look at answers at each stage of life. Video 2 is to help seriously dating couples see an alternative to cohabitation for choosing a mate. Video 3 shows how to give an engaged couple "marriage insurance." Video 4 spotlights couples whose marriages have been deepened through Marriage Encounter. Video 5 shows three ways to save marriages from destruction by such proven steps as Retrouvaille and Marriage Ministry. Video 6 illustrates how to help the separated or divorced and those in stepfamilies.

Resource Collections are being distributed by the publishing arms of such conservative denominations as the Southern Baptist Convention and such mainline ones as the Episcopal Church and the Evangelical Lutheran Church of America. They can also be ordered from Marriage Savers, Inc., 9500 Michael's Court, Bethesda, MD 20817 for $150 plus $8 postage.

Fatherhood and Marriage

About two million men have made pledges at Promise Keeper events that they will honor the promises they have made to their wives and children. As noted earlier in this chapter, there is some evidence that more men are doing so. Divorces fell to a 20-year low in 1996 though that may be due to a 41 percent drop in the marriage rate since 1960. Out-of-wedlock births in 1996 were slightly lower than in 1994, but were still a third of all births.

However, the potential for dramatic reductions in the divorce rate can only be seen in the Marriage Savers movement. Divorces are down in 9 of 72 cities in which clergy have adopted a Community Marriage Policy or Covenant, by as much as 20 to 40 percent. At the heart of this movement is a partnership of men and women with good marriages—helping other men and women prepare for lifelong marriage, strengthen an existing one, or save a troubled one. Jesus sent his disciples out "two by two."

Could that not be teams of husband and wife, husband and wife?

One thing is certain. The institution of marriage cannot be saved by men talking with men. The women must be involved. And so should the church—which marries three-fourths of those who get married.

What God has joined together, churches should hold together.

Notes

1. In 1990, 36.3 percent of all children under age 18 lived in homes where their biological father did not live, according to a Russell Sage Foundation study published in 1993 by Donald J. Hernandez, "America's Children: Resources from Family, Government and the Economy." Since 1990, the percentage has grown to more than 40 percent. For example, according to *The Green Book* of the Ways and Means Committee, the percentage of children living with the mother only increased from 18 percent to 23.4 percent in 1995—a 5.4 percent growth. And the percentage of kids living with neither parent increased from 2.8 percent to 4.2 percent, another 1.4 percent increase. By adding this 6.8 percent increase to the 36.3 percent fatherless figure, data suggests that 43.1 percent of children do not live with their own dad.

2. However, the number of motherless children, who are living only with their fathers is also up sharply, form 724,000 in 1960 to 2,461,000 in 1995.

3. "Marital Status and Living Arrangements," by Arlene Saluter, March 1995, Table A-5, The Census Bureau.

4. *Advance Report of Final Marriage Statistics 1989-1990*, by S. C. Clarke, July 1995, Monthly Vital Statistics, National Center for Health Statistics.

5. "Births, Marriages, Divorces and Deaths for 1996," the July 17, 1997 *Monthly Vital Statistics Report*, written by the National Center for Health Statistics.

6. This data is from annual reports published in the "Monthly Vital Statistics Report" of the National Center for Health Statistics, a division of the Centers for Disease Control of the U.S. Department of Health and Human Services.

7. Of the 108,500,000 individuals who are married in America, 6,730,000 are separated from their spouse, according to the Census Bureau's report, "Marital Status and Living Arrangements: March 1994," published in February 1996, and written by Arlene F. Saluter. If these separated individuals are added to those who divorce, the "marriage dissolution" rate is "closer to 60 percent" said Dr. Larry Bumpass of the University of Wisconsin in his 1990 Presidential Address to the Population Association of America, published in *Demography*, no. 27 (November 1990).

8. In 1991, the latest year of complete data, the U.N. Demographic Yearbook of 1995 reports the divorce rate for the United Kingdom was 2.96 per 1,000 population, 1.89 for France, 1.67 for Germany and only 1.44 for Japan—in the same year it was 4.7 per 1,000 in the United States. More recently, Europe's numbers are moving closer to the United States. In Great Britain, the number was 3.3 in 1996, and 2.7 in Sweden and Norway when the U.S. rate was 4.3 per 1,000. At the opposite extreme, however, Italy is only 0.4 per 1,000—one tenth of America and the rate of Spain, Poland, and Greece is 1 per 1,000, a fourth of the U.S. Divorce rates soared behind the former Iron Curtain since 1991, where some nations, such as Russia, have rates higher than America.

9. Maggie Gallagher, *The Abolition of Marriage: How We Destroy Lasting Love* (Washington D.C.: Regnery Publishing, Inc., 1996).

10. The marriage rate has fallen 41 percent since 1960, from 148 marriages per 1,000 women to 87 per 1,000 in 1990, according to S. C. Clarke, *Advance Report of Final Marriage Statistics 1989-90* (July, 1995), Monthly Vital Statistics, National Center for Health Statistics.

11. This estimate is also from the *National Survey of Families and Households*, conducted by Larry Bumpass and James Sweet at the University of Wisconsin. Estimates are based on 100-minute interviews with 13,017 respondents in 1987 and 1988. See "The Role of Cohabitation in Declining Rates of Marriage," working paper 5.

12. Saluter, "Marital Status and Living Arrangements: March 1994."

13. "Monthly Vital Statistics Report," vol. 44, no. 11, June 24, 1996, of the National Center for Health Statistics of HHS.

14. Gallagher, *Abolition of Marriage*, 5.

15. Michael J. McManus, *Marriage Savers: Helping Your Friends and Family Avoid Divorce* (Grand Rapids, Mich.: Zondervan, 1995), 92-93.

16. "Emerging Trends," Princeton Religion Research Center, February 1996.

17. Dennis A. Ahlburg and Carol J. DeVita, "New Realities of the American Family," *Population Bulletin* 47, no. 2 (August 1992): 15.

18. This figure is my estimate on the fact that more than 30,000 pastors and counselors have been trained to do PREPARE, mostly in Protestant churches. FOCCUS, an inventory developed by the Diocese of Omaha, is used in most of the nation's nearly 20,000 Catholic churches, and there are other inventories, such as PMI, in thousands of churches.

19. James C. Dobson, *Love for a Lifetime* (Portland, Ore.: Multnomah, 1987), 22-23.

20. National Center for Health Statistics: Vital Statistics of the United States, 1987, vol. 3, iii, Marriage and Divorce. DHHS, Pub. No. (PHS) 91-1103. Public Health Service, Washington, D.C., 1991.

21. Forty out of 100 couples who begin a "trial marriage" break up short of the wedding, according to the University of Wisconsin. Of the 60 who marry, the divorce rate is 50 percent above that of those who don't live together. So instead of half of the marriages failing (30 of the 60), 75 percent will fail—45 out of the 60 by the ten-year mark. That leaves 15 still together. Crummy odds. By contrast, 10 percent of those who take PREPARE break up short of the wedding, and another 5 percent postpone the wedding date—with much less grief.

22. PREPARE/ENRICH, Inc. Box 190, Minneapolis, MN 55440-0190.

23. Blaine J. Fowers and David H. Olson, "Predicting Marital Success with PREPARE, A Predictive Validity Study," *Journal of Marital and Family Therapy* 12, no. 4 (October 1986).

24. PREPARE/ENRICH Newsletter, vol. 2, no. 2 (fall 1998).

25. "Marriage Preparation in the Catholic Church: Getting It Right," November 1995, a report by Creighton University.

26. The couple is now engaged, and as I write this, mail arrived this morning with a wedding invitation!

27. This is my estimate, based on several facts. PREPARE is given to more than

100,000 couples a year. Exact numbers of those who take FOCCUS are unknown, because they are not processed centrally like PREPARE. But at least a significant minority of the 350,000 Catholics who get married each year take the inventory. In the Archdiocese of Washington, for example, 60 of 140 parishes use the inventory. Therefore, I have estimated that 150,000 Catholic couples are probably using FOCCUS. There are other inventories, such as PMI, reaching at least 50,000. So the 250,000 estimate is conservative.

28. See chapter 3 of his thesis, "Assessing Marriage Encounter," written for a D. Min. thesis for the University of Dubuque Theological Seminary. The chapter cites 61 studies on the impact of Marriage Encounter, two of which are briefly quoted here.

29. "Worldwide Marriage Encounter National Survey" was conducted in 1990 by the National Institute for the Family, 3019 Fourth Street, NE, Washington, DC 20017.

30. For more detail on this 25 year retrospective, see pages 172-174 of *Marriage Savers*.

31. For a list of those denominations and contact persons, see the *Marriage Savers Study Guide*, a 96-page discussion manual for a 13-week Sunday School course, which is part of the *Marriage Savers Resource Collection*. The collection includes six videos, and two other books, *Marriage Savers* and *Insuring Marriage: 25 Proven Ways to Prevent Divorce*, a slim 112-page book for nonreaders.

32. For a complete list of local Retrouvaille leaders, phone numbers in each city and dates of upcoming weekends, see the "Retrouvaille Communique," a quarterly newsletter edited by Norm and Mary Moore, 2156 Lakeview Drive, #258, Ypsilanti, MI 48198.

33. These estimates are from couples who lead Retrouvaille in the mentioned cities: Alicia and Bob Waning in Northern Virginia (703-351-7211); Mark and Betty Squier in Detroit (810-296-9589); and John and Lorriane Luna (817-267-9391). The number of Fort Worth attendees was as of 1993, and has grown since.

34. For a list of the Marriage Ministry steps, see p. 204 of *Marriage Savers* or write for "Marriage Ministry: Crossing Our Divorce" by the Rev. and Mrs. Richard McGinnis, Marriage Ministry, 6999-2 Merrill Road #283, Jacksonville, FL 32277, (904-724-2563).

35. These principles for turning around a bad marriage are exactly the same as those identified by a nonreligious therapist named Michele Weiner-Davis who says she can heal 85 percent of bad marriages in four or fewer counseling sessions. See her book, *Divorce Busting*, (Summit Books, 1992). One chapter title sums it up: "It Takes One to Tango: Change Your Marriage by Changing Yourself."

36. Interview with Rev. Richard McGinnis, January 1996.

37. This is my estimate. Second marriages fail at a 60 percent rate according to Arthur J. Norton and Paul Glick's article in *Family Relations*, January 1986. "One Parent Families: A Social and Economic Profile." Marriages involving stepchildren must fail at a higher rate because such children complicate a second marriage. I have seen no studies, but make the estimate that at least 65 percent will fail.

38. This is an estimate by the program's director, Rev. Dick Dunn, made in

January 1996.

39. For more information about the Community Marriage Policy (CMP) movement, including a full list of participating cities, sample Marriage Policies, memos on how to create a CMP, write me at Marriage Savers, Inc., 9500 Michael's Court, Bethesda, MD 20817, or call 301-459-5870.

40. The 1,688 fewer divorces in seven Community Marriage Policy cities are 18.8 percent of the nation's drop of 9,000 divorces.

41. My column "Ethics & Religion" is published by about 90 papers weekly. It is distributed by the New York Times Syndicate.

42. These findings are based on telephone interviews with 1,037 adults, 18 and older, who are married, widowed, or unmarried and involved in a romantic relationship. The Gallup survey was conducted between September 24 and October 9, 1988. Possible error: plus or minus four points.

43. As noted below, a tenth of the nation's churches do have a more rigorous approach involving giving of a premarital inventory, with counseling based on an objective measure of a couple's needs.

44. The National Institute for Healthcare Research is not part of NIH, despite the similarity of its name. But it is run by Dr. David Larson, a research psychiatrist at NIMH for a decade. Its particular focus is on the impact of faith or religion on health and marriage. It routinely reads the scholarly literature and promotes scholarly research, and is funded by the John Templeton Foundation. (For more information, call 301-984-7162.)

45. Video 1 is often used to interest a group of local clergy in considering the creation of a Community Marriage Policy. It can be ordered separately for $25 plus $2 for postage.

Chapter 10

Beyond Government to Faith-Based Community Strategies

Senator Dan Coats

A young teaching assistant in a Midwestern city recently saw the sad, disturbing evidence of an American generation raised without fathers. One day, a second-grader climbed onto the volunteer's lap and touched his fingers against the teacher's five o'clock shadow. "What are those?" the boy asked. The child was mystified by the little stubs growing out of the teacher's cheek. "Do they hurt?" the boy asked. The teacher was shocked. This student and many of his classmates had never been close enough to an adult male to see him shave.

A generation of Americans is being raised without fathers. The ill-effects are exacerbated when not only individuals but entire communities lack fathers. A responsible, adult male in a neighborhood is often an example and source of discipline for children who are not his own. Yet some neighborhoods and public housing projects are almost completely devoid of males who are more than visitors. Without the restraining influence of fathers and male role models, these communities often become "juvenilocracies," in which power is exercised by immature, violent adolescents. Charles Ballard of the Institute for Responsible Fatherhood and Family Revitalization tells of meeting young adults in these areas who have attended several funerals of their friends, but not one wedding.

Liberal ideology dictates that our society should be neutral to these trends. A preference for intact families is dismissed as nostalgia, or even oppression. But as Alan Ehrenhalt notes, "Too many of the things we do in our lives, large and small, have come to resemble channel surfing, marked by a numbing and seemingly endless progression from one option to the next, all without the benefit of a chart, logistical or moral."[1]

In the context of caring for children, channel surfing will not suffice. The abandonment of children, particularly by fathers, is not simply a "lifestyle choice." It is a form of adult behavior with profoundly destructive consequences for children and for society. The "liberation" of adults from traditional family commitments is the most direct cause of suffering for children—more than hunger, lead paint, or failed schools. In reality, then, an emphasis on intact families is a particularly practical form of compassion.

Not long ago, the importance of fathers was a matter of debate. Now, however, the suffering of children caused by absent and irresponsible fathers is so obvious and so overwhelming that the debate has advanced to a point of widespread agreement. Senator Daniel Patrick Moynihan has said that a society of unattached males "asks for and gets chaos." The converse also is true. When the role of fathers is respected and restored, a neighborhood and a society become better places to live.

This does not, in any way, diminish the importance or minimize the contribution of millions of single mothers who raise their children in hard circumstances. They often are examples of both sacrifice and commitment—models of what a parent should be.

So what can we do? What can the government do, through effective and responsive public policy, to address the critical void the absence of fathers has created in hearts, homes, and neighborhoods across the county?

Government has a definite role, but this role often is misunderstood. Government prescriptions often focus on economic solutions to absentee fatherhood, striving to reduce the financial strain on single-parent families. Economics, however, is not enough. Despite the booming economy, in the 1980s the number of single-parent households increased by 40 percent. We have found that economic indicators cannot measure the values held by our children, or the suffering felt by broken families. Our growing gross national product is accompanied by massive prison construction to house a lost generation, drug counseling in elementary schools, suicide hotlines, teen pregnancy centers, and clinics for battered children. The government also attempts to help by trying to enforce child support. This, too, is an important goal, but the financial role of fathers is just one role among many, and it clearly is not as important to children as the emotional support, love, and discipline fathers provide.

Ultimately, our problem is not a failure of political will or imagination, but a failure of love and commitment. Our worst crisis is not the budget deficit, but a deficit of time and attention given by fathers to their children. Even in families where Dad is present, children often see less of their fathers than if they had grown up in an earlier era. Parents today spend roughly 40 percent less time with their children than parents did a generation ago, and fewer than 25 percent of all children experience an average of at least one hour a day of individualized contact with their fathers.[2]

Our greatest challenge is not a lack of resources but a lack of conscience and character and integrity. These problems persist, no matter who has a temporary hold on political power—Right or Left, Republican or Democrat. We have discovered that no amount of political tinkering will restore our social order while there is moral disorder in our souls.

Cultural problems demand cultural solutions. Responsible fathers are essential to the health and survival of civil society. Government must encourage the private, religious, and nonprofit organizations that deliver and enforce this cultural message of the importance of fatherhood.

Public Policy and the American Family

Of all the institutions that comprise civil society, the institution of the family is the most essential and the most endangered. Here we need to be specific: The most serious problem is absent, irresponsible fathers. It should not be controversial, though it often is, to say that fathers are not expendable and families are not optional.

In the words of Edmund Burke, the family is the origin of "the little platoon we belong to in society" and it is "the germ of public affections."[3] Families are the seedbed of our skills and attitudes. They teach us the principles of economics, the value of relationships, and the importance of moral truths. They define our view of work, responsibility, and authority. They teach us the meaning of trust, the value of honesty. They are the wellspring of every individual's strength against alienation, failure, and despair.

Families are the source not only of our personal values and security, but of our political, economic, and social order, as well. Any nation whose families are weak will eventually find itself without strong institutions of any kind.

There was a time in our country when we believed in the axiom "What strengthens the family, strengthens society." This was also true about local neighborhoods and communities. Michael Joyce and William Schambra state it this way:

Before the modern age, American life had been organized around what historian Robert Wiebe described as "island communities." As this phrase suggests, civic life was characterized by both its self-containment and its cohesiveness. Individuals were closely bound one to another by strong families, tightly knit neighborhoods, and active voluntary and fraternal groups. Through these small, local, "human-scale" associations, Americans not only achieved a sense of belonging and connectedness but also tackled the full range of social and human problems that today have largely become the province of government. [4]

The government gained this province, according to Joyce and Schambra, when the Progressive elites of the early twentieth century decided to replace local institutions with the paradigm of a "national community." Progressive leader Herbert Croly stated that the desire of the individual would be subordinate "to the demand of a dominant and constructive national purpose," as each citizen would "think first of the State and next of himself."

Families, churches, and community groups no longer would be needed to solve social problems. In fact, as Joyce and Schambra write, they were the enemy, "actively hostile to such intermediate associations." In the end, "the triumph of progressive structural reform would mean, in essence, that citizen involvement in public affairs was reduced from active, intense, face-to-face problem solving on a daily basis to passively casting a lonely, solitary ballot once in a great while for a handful of offices." [5]

As a result, where the family was once the dominant force—in educating our children, in caring for the aged, in providing for the infirm and the needy—its role has been significantly weakened and often subordinated to that of the state. In fact, the family has been under withering attack, often by government policy. Yet, by every measurable standard, the state has failed to assume adequately the role of the family. Nowhere is this more apparent than in the policies that govern welfare and poverty.

In a special message to Congress on public welfare programs in 1962, President John F. Kennedy laid down the first principle of a sound welfare policy:

> The goals of public welfare programs must be positive and constructive.
> . . . It must stress the integrity and preservation of the family unit. It must contribute to the attack on dependency, juvenile delinquency, family breakdown, illegitimacy, ill health, and disability. It must replace the incidence of these problems, prevent their occurrence and recurrence, and strengthen and protect the vulnerable in a highly competitive world. [6]

The *New York Times* described Kennedy's message as a recognition that no lasting solution to the problem of welfare could be bought with a government check and that, while the initial financial cost would be higher than the continuation of handouts, the dividends would come in the restoration of individual dignity and the long-term reduction in the need for government help.

President Kennedy and the *New York Times* were right. Welfare subsidies alone are never enough to lift individuals and families out of poverty. They can, and often do, subsidize habits and pathologies that lead to self-destructive behavior.

Our nation's welfare programs have served to make unmarried women dependent upon the state. While well-intentioned, they destroy the incentive young men might have for taking responsibility for their own offspring. As George Gilder once observed, we have persuaded poor fathers that they are dispensable. They believe it, and so do the mothers of their children.

For six decades, men and women who wanted to improve their world came to Washington, D.C., to affirm their faith in government. Faith in the government's ability to raise the poor. Faith in its power to drain an ocean of human misery. But that faith is dying before our eyes. Violence fills graveyards with fatherless boys not old enough to shave. The decay of sexual standards leaves countless women and children exploited and abused. Poverty grows wild among the ruins of single parent families.

The welfare reform bill passed by the 104th Congress sought to reverse some of these debilitating and pernicious incentives by emphasizing work and imposing time limits. Requiring work for welfare and setting time limits for benefits make entry-level jobs more attractive and discourage many from entering the welfare system in the first place. Work is one of our nation's highest values. No child should be without the moral example of parents, especially fathers, who work.

The recent welfare reform legislation also has removed government-imposed incentives to fail. Government has been gravely mistaken in paying cash to teenage girls on the condition that they have children out of wedlock and never marry the father. Public policies that penalize marriage and promote illegitimacy can never be justified. Government violates its most fundamental responsibilities when it tempts people into self-destructive behavior, especially behaviors that devalue the importance of fatherhood.

Beyond Government

While these lifesaving welfare reforms are long overdue, the destructive incentives that have existed in our nation's welfare system are only part of the problem. The decline of marriage, the rise of illegitimacy, and the destructive growth of fatherlessness in America are rooted clearly in broader cultural trends that affect everyone, rich and poor. Without a welfare system, these trends would still exist and still threaten our society.

James Q. Wilson accepts the figure that less than 15 percent of rising illegitimacy between 1960 and 1974 was due to increased government benefits. "Some significant part of what is popularly called the 'underclass problem'" he argues, "exists not simply because members of this group face perverse incentives but because they have been habituated in ways that weaken their self-control and their concerns for others."[7]

In other words, Wilson believes the basic problem lies in the realm of values and character, and those values are shaped, particularly in early childhood, by certain cultural standards. "I do not wish," Wilson adds, "to deny the importance of incentives, such as jobs, penalties, or opportunities, but I do wish to call attention to the fact that people facing the same incentives often behave in characteristically different ways because they have been habituated to do so."[8]

People are not purely economic beings, analyzing costs and benefits. We are moral beings. We make choices that reflect our values. Incentives are not irrelevant, but it is ultimately our beliefs and habits that determine our future. The social problems confronted by our nation, including the crisis of irresponsible fatherhood, are rooted in the breakdown in public trust in the institutions that direct and have humanized our lives throughout history—institutions of family, neighborhood, community associations, charities, and religious-based groups.

Sociologists talk about "mediating structures." They say that these institutions build "social capital" and "positive externalities." These academic phrases can be presented in simple terms. A child will never find an adequate substitute for a father who loves him or her. The mantle of government, the assistance of government, will never replace the warm hand of a loving parent. The impersonal directions of a government bureaucrat can never replace the wise counsel of a dedicated dad.

This is precisely the reason Nathan Glazer warns of the unintended consequences of social policy:

> Aside from these problems of expectations, cost, competency and limitations of knowledge, there is the simple reality that every piece of social policy substitutes for some traditional arrangement, a new arrangement in which public authorities take over, at least in part, the role of the family, of the ethnic and neighborhood group, of voluntary associations. In doing so, social policy weakens the position of these traditional agents and further encourages needy people to depend on the

government for help rather than on the traditional structures.[9]

This concern is real and ought to reorient our thinking and our efforts. Public policy ought to be centered on a respect and reinvigoration of these traditional structures—families, schools, neighborhoods, and voluntary associations—that provide training in citizenship and pass on morality and civility to future generations. Only then will government policy truly encourage responsible fatherhood.

Wilson agrees. Since government programs tend not to produce self-reliance, "then our policy ought to be to identify, evaluate, and encourage those local private efforts that seem to do the best job at reducing drug abuse, inducing people to marry, persuading parents, especially fathers, to take responsibility for their children, and exercising informal social control over neighborhood streets."[10]

Many of our worst social problems, including irresponsible fatherhood, will never be solved until the hearts of parents are turned toward their children, until respect is restored for human life and property, until a commitment is renewed to care about our neighbor. Government cannot reach this deep into human character. But there are people and institutions—families, churches and synagogues, private charities, grassroots community organizations—able to communicate these ideals and restore individual hope. Armed with tough love, individual responsibility, and spiritual values, they often are vehicles of life-changing miracles of renewal.

Robert Woodson, a community activist, makes the point that every social problem, including irresponsible fatherhood, is currently being defeated somewhere, by some religious or community group. This is one of America's great, untold stories. No alternative approach to our cultural crisis holds such promise, because these institutions have resources denied to government at every level—love, spiritual vitality, and true compassion. It is time to take their side—publicly, creatively, and actively—in the struggle to recivilize American society.

This reduces, though it does not necessarily eliminate, the direct role of government programs, but it also points to an active public mission: to transfer government roles and resources to the value-building institutions of our society without burdening them with intrusive regulations. Centralized, bureaucratic government control has failed, but the institutions of family, neighborhood, schools, church, charitable organizations, and voluntary associations offer hope and promise. They do not just feed and house the body; they touch the soul. They have the power to transform individuals and the power to renew our society. And as Amitai Etzioni argues, the more we rely on these private efforts the fewer demands we will make upon government. "The anchoring of individuals," Etzioni writes, "in viable families, webs of friendships, communities of faith, and neighborhoods—in short, in communities—best sustains their ability to resist the pressure of the state."[11]

While we realize that the role of government must be reduced and reoriented, we must also acknowledge that our nation will still be left with unacceptable suffering. Too many children will still grow up without a family's stability and a father's love. Too many will still enter schools through metal detectors. Too many communities will still be imprisoned by violence and fear. The fact that government programs have not worked is no excuse for those in government not to act.

Therefore, we ought to ask one question of every social policy considered by every level of government, and that question is: Does it work through these mediating, traditional, historical institutions; does it work through families, neighborhoods, or religious or community organizations; or does it simply try to replace them?

Accepting this priority would focus our attention on three areas: emphasizing the role of family, particularly the role of fathers and mentors where fathers are not present in the lives of children; rebuilding community institutions that support families; and promoting private charities and religious institutions in the work of compassion.

Private, religious, and nonprofit organizations are demonstrating how fathers can renew their commitments to their children and how mentors can transform the lives of the fatherless. In the absence of fathers and families, children need more than funding and programs; they need mentors and examples. These efforts are proving that broken trust and attachment within families can be restored.

Mentors also are needed for young fathers who are learning how to raise their families. Other young dads who have simply shirked their responsibilities and abandoned their families need mentors to reconnect them with their children. Precisely because we have a crisis in fatherhood, we need to be creative in providing models of responsible male behavior.

Private organizations, such as Promise Keepers and Big Brothers-Big Sisters, are bringing the message of responsible fatherhood and the importance of adult male role models to a broad audience, reminding fathers of their moral duties of paternity. The success and extraordinary growth of these groups are hopeful signs that many Americans sense that our nation has indeed arrived at a moment of crisis. Efforts like these show that broken trust and attachments within families can be restored. Government offers no comparable hope.

Public policy also must reestablish a preference for marriage, which does more than any other institution to encourage responsible fatherhood. Wilson observes: "Of all the institutions through which people may pass—schools, employers, the military—marriage has the largest effect. For every race and at every age, married men live longer than unmarried men and have lower rates of homicide, suicide, accidents, and mental illness. Crime rates are lower for married men and incomes are higher."[12] As a nation, our policies ought to promote, instead of serve as a disincentive to, strong, healthy marriages.

Government policy should communicate a clear, public preference for marriage and family on matters such as public housing, the tax code, family planning, and divorce law. Rewarding intact families is not, as some argue, a form of discrimination. It is a form of self-preservation. We must be more creative in this effort.

Government also can encourage the business community that is becoming more aware of creating father-friendly workplaces. A good example is the automobile factory in Springhill, Tennessee, where assembly line workers are employed on alternative schedules. Once a month, these schedules give workers five straight days at home with their families.

Turning Our Hearts Toward Home

Families used to work together; extended families lived together; families were much less mobile; family size was larger; schools were smaller and located nearby; and technological and informational overload were terms not yet coined. Family members were more directly dependent upon each other—for income, for care for both younger and older family members—and conveniences to ease household chores were minimal, which meant that all family members derived significant self-worth from being critical to the functioning of their families.

With the decline of extended families, with fewer brothers and sisters, with frequent changes in schools, neighborhoods, and churches, children thus became more dependent upon interactions with their parents. At the same time, parents became caught up in the striving for material progress and the symbols of success, without stopping to treasure the more valuable things in life and without giving their children the quantity or quality of time they needed.

In his best-selling book *The Road Less Travelled*, M. Scott Peck writes that children know by both the quantity and quality of time given them how much they are valued by their parents. They want "to believe that they are loved but unconsciously they know that their parents' words do not match up to their deeds."[13] Peck says that children are not deceived by "hollow words" and "mechanical actions."

As the current fatherhood movement shows, many Americans have realized this and are now turning their hearts toward home, looking for the lasting principles upon which strong homes are founded. This has led to a re-examination of values in a search for enduring truths, including spiritual truths.

Many seem to look upon this rediscovery of fatherhood and the family as a wonderful political opportunity. Children, however, do not exist so that political parties can control power by pretending to be able to solve the problems facing families. Children are not an opportunity to repackage an economic and social agenda so people can be persuaded into supporting what they have heretofore rejected. Children are human beings to be loved, nurtured, and developed.

What America needs most at this moment is not a new political leader. Our nation needs parents, especially fathers, who will bend to hear a child's voice and care for a child's soul. What America needs most is not a set of new programs or policies. Our country needs people of conviction and tenacity who will say, "This is my family, this is my home, this is my community. I must do what I can to reclaim it, rebuild it, restore it."

When the NBA's Philadelphia 76ers won the top choice in the NBA's 1996 draft lottery, something more significant occurred than Philadelphia's simple luck of the draw. The team's general manager, Brad Greenberg, decided not to attend the league's draft lottery, missing a chance to talk about his team's success on national television. Instead, Brad Greenberg decided to stay home with his son Cory and celebrate Cory's tenth birthday—a decision encouraged by team owner Pat Croce. The rest of America will forget this story almost immediately. Cory, however, will remember it for his entire life, and it may even shape the kind of father that he becomes.

It has been said, "Character is what you are in the dark."[14] Almost all of the decisions necessary to be a good father are made in the dark, out of the control of government. Uncle Sam cannot fabricate fatherhood. But government can and, indeed, should actively take the side of private, religious, and nonprofit organizations that themselves are shining light on the indispensable role of fathers. This is the positive, hopeful, and limited role government can play.

Notes

1. Alan Ehrenhalt, *The Lost City* (New York: Basic Books, 1995), 272.

2. William Mattox, "Parent Trap: So Many Bills, So Little Time," *Policy Review* 55 (winter 1991): 6-13.

3. Edmund Burke, *Reflections on the French Revolution*, Everyman Edition (London: J. M. Dent and Sons, Ltd., 1955), 44.

4. Michael Joyce and William Schambra, "A New Civic Life," in Peter L. Berger and Richard John Neuhaus, *To Empower People: From State to Civil Society*, ed. Michael Novak (Washington, D.C.: AEI Press, 1996), 11-12.

5. Joyce and Schambra, "New Civic Life" 16.

6. John F. Kennedy, Public Papers of the Presidents of the United States, 1962 (Washington, D.C.: U.S. Government Printing Office, 1963), 102-3.

7. Henry J. Aaron, Thomas E. Mann, and Timothy Taylor, eds., *Values and Public Policy* (Washington, D.C.: Brookings Institution, 1994), 55.

8. Aaron, Mann, Taylor, *Values*, 55-56.

9. Nathan Glazer, *The Limits of Social Policy* (Cambridge, Mass.: Harvard University Press, 1988), 7.

10. Aaron, Mann, Taylor, *Values*, 7.

11. Amitai Etzioni, "Robbing Our Moral Voice," *The Public Interest* 116 (summer 1994): 112.

12. Aaron, Mann, Taylor, *Values*, 74.

13. M. Scott Peck, *The Road Less Travelled* (New York: Simon and Schuster, 1978), 23-24.

14. Attributed to D. L. Moody by his son in William R. Moody, *D. L. Moody* (New York: Macmillan, 1930), 503.

Chapter 11

Fatherhood as a Point of Convergence Beyond Old Categories

Don S. Browning

In examining fatherhood from the perspectives of the liberal academy and the liberal religious denominations, I make five fundamental assumptions that are well elaborated in the other articles in this collection or are self-evident. A short listing here will suffice.

First, father absence is an unprecedented reality in our society. It is not a manufactured issue. The problem of vast numbers of children being raised without resident fathers has not been fabricated by political conservatives, alarmist social scientists, or the media. Furthermore, the phenomenon is unprecedented; it has never happened in this fashion and to this degree before.

Second, father absence has consequences. We know for certain that it has unhealthy effects on children. But father absence has negative consequences as well for the well-being of adult women, adult men, and the institutions within which they work and play.

Third, father absence is a problem created primarily at the cultural level of society; it is first of all a crisis in our cultural values and symbols. There are social-system causes for why fathers are increasingly disconnected from their children. For instance, there are economic pressures, which drive fathers away from their children or make it difficult for them to marry or stay married. More important still, however, are historical and cultural factors which create fatherlessness, such as the increasing individualism of modern cultures, the spread of market values or cost-benefit logic into family life, and the decline in our commitment to the institution of marriage. It is important to keep focused on the cultural aspects of the fatherhood problem, especially if one is to conceive adequately the central role of religion in addressing this crisis.

This leads to the fourth assumption: Religion is one of the primary shapers of culture. Therefore, if the problem of absent fathers is to be addressed at its most basic level, the religious institutions of our society must play a central role.

Finally, father absence is still not widely understood as a problem in our society. This is confirmed by a conversation I had with a very bright taxi driver when I was on my way to a conference on fatherhood. This woman driver surprised me by her intelligence and wide-ranging capacity to articulate her thoughts on a variety of issues. She was so clever that, although she had never attended college, she coached other people on how to write a term paper. Since I had the fatherhood issue on my mind, I asked her, "Do you believe it is a problem for our society that so many fathers are residentially absent from their children while they are growing up?"

"Well, you know, I never thought about it. But it might be," she replied. "My father left my mother, and that may be one reason why I never went to college." Clearly, the fatherhood issue had not been uppermost in her mind even though the course of her life and the underdevelopment of her obvious abilities were doubtless attributable in part to this social reality. This is an example of how people, even though profoundly affected by the phenomenon of absent fathers, are also so embedded in it that they are largely unaware of the issue.

This observation was further confirmed by a recent conversation I had with a priest who teaches at the Catholic University of East Africa in Nairobi, Kenya. Fatherlessness, he told me, is rampant in the urban centers of central Africa, and children and single mothers are deeply and quite negatively affected by the reality. However, there is little popular or academic discussion of the issue, even in Africa. Not only in the United States, but also throughout the world, people seem to be only dimly aware of the problem of the absent father.

Fatherhood and the Academy

The fatherhood problem is not widely studied, discussed, or understood in either the secular or religious academy, the milieu where I have spent most of my professional life. There are exceptions to this generalization. One outstanding discussion of the problem is a book by David Popenoe published in 1996 entitled *Life without Father*. Before Popenoe's work, there was a neglected tradition that includes Bronislaw Malinowski's *The Father in Primitive Psychology* (1927), David Bakan's *They Took Themselves Wives* (1979), and Samuel Osherson's *Finding Our Fathers* (1986). These books examined the conditions under which males joined the mother-infant dyad and the fragility of this bond, especially in modern societies. Of course, the discipline of evolutionary psychology also has studied the conditions in human prehistory that led human males, in contrast to most other mammalian males, to join the mother-infant family and help his consort care for their infant.

But not until Popenoe's book (and David Blankenhorn's *Fatherless America* in 1995 from outside the academic institutions) were the consequences of fatherlessness for children and society studied in our colleges and universities with a sense of urgency. In spite of the important work of the National Fatherhood Initiative in bringing this issue before the general public, colleges and universities have been slow to respond. Furthermore, Popenoe's work has been accused of exaggerating the problem.

The more usual academic response to fatherlessness is what I call the "cut your losses" approach. This response is represented by James Levine and Edward Pitt in *New Expectations: Community Strategies for Responsible Fatherhood*, published in 1996 by the Work and Family Institute. Their book explicitly rejects the strategy supported by Popenoe, Blankenhorn, and the Council on Families in America in *Marriage in America: A Report to the Nation*. *Marriage in America* called for a number of political and economic initiatives to decrease fatherlessness, but its central emphasis was on encouraging men to marry, remain married, and learn to care responsibly for their children within the institution of marriage. In this report, marriage is promoted as an essential feature of fathering.

Levine, on the other hand, argues that no one really knows how to enhance and stabilize marriage. He believes that it is better to help fathers not living with their children, whether divorced or never married, to learn how to relate positively to their offspring as nonresidential caretakers. In short, much academic writing aspires to help uninvolved and absent fathers become more involved rather than working to reverse the trend toward father absence in the first place. This tendency can be seen in a book by Sara McLanahan and Gary Sandefur called *Growing Up with a Single Mother*. This book sets forth the most compelling evidence presently available demonstrating the disadvantages to children of not having a biological father in the home. Yet, in the last sections of the book, rather than making suggestions on how to slow the rate of father absence, the book primarily concentrates on how single mothers can mitigate the costs to children of the absent father.

What about the religious academy? The fatherhood issue is almost completely ignored in most mainline Protestant seminaries and university-related divinity schools. I cannot speak for more evangelical or Catholic seminaries. But the neglect by mainline theological schools is a mystery since the topic has gotten attention recently in the media, and the writings of Popenoe, Blankenhorn, the Council on Families in America, and the National Fatherhood Initiative are being noticed by the general population. Some of the 12 books from the Lilly Endowment-sponsored Religion, Culture, and Family Project co-edited by Ian Evison and me do address father absence and may help bring the fatherhood issue to theological schools and the liberal academy.[1]

It is difficult to know just why father absence, the declining well-being of children, and the growing impoverishment of single mothers have not been important topics of consideration in liberal theological education. The answer is probably this: Other important topics, such as women's rights, abortion, homosexuality, and matters pertaining to economic justice, have crowded fatherlessness off the agenda of theological education.

Fatherhood and the Liberal Churches

A similar silence can be found in the mainline churches. I have not heard of any major discussion of the fatherhood issue at the national, state, or congregational levels of mainline Protestant denominations. Declining membership and funds, several decades of neglecting family issues, and an understandable but exhausting preoccupation with debates over homosexuality have pushed out of awareness the emerging American and worldwide trend toward declining male involvement in families.

It is true that liberal denominational programs and initiatives sometimes highlight the plight of poor children as a general social problem. But the message of these programs is often very abstract. An example of this can be found in the Children's Defense Fund's laudable program for churches called The Children's Sabbath. This initiative urges churches to hold services, preach sermons, and host other programs that draw attention to the plight of poor, unhealthy, and starving children. The materials provided by the Fund recommend appropriate ameliorating programs for poor children, generally sponsored by government agencies. The goals of this program are so praiseworthy that I hesitate to call attention to one important missing factor—the general omission of the role played by the current culture of divorce, nonmarriage, and fatherlessness in creating the situation of our poor children today. Since the widespread adoption of the Children's Defense

Fund program is one of the first signs that mainline churches are returning to their customary concern with the effects of family disruption on children, we should both applaud it and call for an even sharper diagnosis of family problems. When this happens, the issue of father absence will come into even greater prominence.

In view of the present widespread neglect of this important topic, we have a long way to go before the leaders of various sectors of our society take this topic as seriously as it deserves. My message, however, in the remaining paragraphs, is mainly addressed to the mainline Protestant denominations. Mainline religious groups need to begin taking father absence with seriousness. They have something unique to offer, and the issue increasingly confronts their own congregations. A fatherless society is not just something "out there"—outside the churches in the poor, unchurched, or secular sectors of our society. Out-of-wedlock births, divorce, the culture of nonmarriage, children living away from their biological parents, and fathers only seldom visiting and supporting their offspring are phenomena moving into the mainstream of the population, into the life of liberal churches, into the religious sectors of our society, and into the quarters of the more highly educated and financially comfortable.[2]

Because the fatherhood issue is significantly a cultural issue—an issue pertaining to the meaning, role, and significance of fathers in families and society—it needs to be addressed by religion. Fathers' declining involvement in families should not be handled solely as a policy or economic issue, as important as these perspectives are. Religion traditionally has been one of the most powerful shapers of cultural values pertaining to what it means to be a woman or man, father or mother. This is still true today, especially in the United States, which is one of the most actively religious countries in the world.

The Connection Between Fatherhood and Western Religions

But fatherhood, religion, and the churches are connected in even deeper ways. The fatherhood problem is not just one social problem among many that churches and synagogues should address. Fatherhood has been a central concern of both Judaism and Christianity. In fact, it is not an exaggeration to say that these religions helped bring about something of a revolution in our understanding of fatherhood.

There always has been, in both the Hebrew and Christian Scriptures, a parallel between the image of God and the tasks and responsibilities of a good earthly father. We should not get bogged down by the question of religious language—the issue of whether God should always be spoken of with male nouns and pronouns—to admit the validity of this general claim. As background to the defense of this point, we should recall Bronislaw Malinowski's argument that there was once a time when human males did not understand the relation between sexual intercourse and procreation.

More recently, David Bakan and John W. Miller have argued that when males finally achieved this insight, they developed a new sense of involvement in the life of their offspring. This led to the creation of patriarchy and the social establishment of the special rights of fatherhood.

Miller, a professor of religion at the University of Waterloo, agrees with some anthropologists and evolutionary psychologists that males in general have far more tenuous and ambiguous relations with their offspring than do mothers who carry, give birth, and generally feed their infants. Fatherhood builds on weaker biological ties than motherhood, hence the widespread ancient practices of father's committing infanticide or sacrificing their children to placate the gods. As Margaret Mead has argued in *Male and Female*, fatherhood as an active involvement in the care of offspring is stabilized only when it becomes a socially, culturally, and religiously reinforced institution.[3]

In his small but carefully crafted book, *Biblical Faith and Fathering: Why We Call God "Father,"* Miller gives us several insights into how Judaism and Christianity helped consolidate the fragile ties fathers have with their children.[4] Judaism did this by depicting Yahweh as not only delivering the Jewish people from captivity in Egypt but as protecting the firstborn sons of their families from the power that destroyed the eldest sons of the Egyptians.

The Exodus legend became a paradigm for father-centered rituals such as the Passover feast, which has been celebrated in Jewish homes for centuries. The father—the ritual agent—led the family in remembering how God had delivered the Jewish people and protected their sons. The practice of circumcision was also modeled on the Exodus event. The removal of a baby boy's foreskin by the father was a symbolic way of differentiating a male infant from the exclusive care of the mother, bringing him into the care and direction of the father, reenacting Yahweh's care for children, and directing the infant boy's sexuality toward responsible procreation, that is, toward "the study of the Torah, to the marriage canopy, and to good deeds."

The analogy between the steadfast, loving, and just Yahweh (who possessed certain mother-like qualities) and the good father also extended to the male's role as husband. The parallel between Hosea's steadfast love for his wayward pregnant wife Gomer and God's relation to Israel has been seen in the tradition as an example of how God reinforces responsible manhood.

Miller argues that the Hebrew image of God as a responsible and involved father was quite different from the representation of male gods such as Apsu in Mesopotamia, Osiris in Egypt, and El in Canaan, all of whom were depicted as both detached from humans and rather ineffectual.

Christianity carried forward the tradition of representing God as a creative and caring father. Jesus refers to God as *Abba* (father), blesses the little children, and protects mothers by rejecting the customary practice of husbands unilaterally divorcing their wives (Matthew 19:3-5) for almost any reason. The story of the prodigal son is the most striking analogy between God and a caring, involved, and forgiving father (Luke 15:11-32). Finally, one would not want to overlook difficult passages such as Ephesians 5:20-33 in which husbands and fathers are told to model themselves after Christ's self-sacrificial love for the church. No Scripture has influenced Western religion, law, and art about the responsibilities of husband and father to wife and children more than this passage. It constituted the backbone of the Roman Catholic sacramental theory of marriage and the Protestant covenantal model. This Scripture is foundational for the contemporary Christian men's movement called Promise Keepers. It is the source of their theory of "male servant"—the idea that responsible husbands and fathers lead their families through serving.

I point to these biblical sources not to preach or evangelize, but to make my central point: Male ambivalence about fatherhood has been balanced and stabilized by the stories and beliefs of the Jewish and Christian traditions. Although the patriarchal symbolism of this tradition has often been misused to exploit and dominate women, at another level it created and reinforced a deep commitment to the roles of father and husband.

Fathers, Husbands, and a Love Ethic of Equal Regard

We are now at a significant point in history. There are new threats to male commitment to fatherhood. There are also new demands, and rightly so, for higher levels of mutuality between husband and wife in marriage. It is time to reinterpret the Jewish and Christian traditions in such a way as to continue their strong support of fatherhood while at the same rejecting their lingering patriarchy. This is possible, without doing violence to these traditions, by introducing a love ethic of equal regard.

The effort to renew fatherhood will be most successful if it is not perceived as a pretext for a subtle return of patriarchy—either hard patriarchy or what feminist critics often call "soft patriarchy." Hard patriarchy is the institutionalization of unilateral and arbitrary male prerogatives in family and public affairs. I see no evidence of hard patriarchy in any of the major men's movements in the United States.

Soft patriarchy, on the other hand, is found in men's movements teaching that fathers and husbands should be fair and just but also retain in their own hands the power and authority to make family decisions. As many critiques have pointed out, this is a "monological" rather than a "dialogical" understanding of fairness and justice. Fairness is precisely a kind of relation that requires marital partners to be in *dialogue about what constitutes fairness.* Responsible fatherhood must go hand-in-hand with an understanding of justice that is achieved dialogically between husband and wife.

I see no evidence of any form of patriarchy in the literature and the rhetoric of the National Fatherhood Initiative. Nonetheless, there are great suspicions in our society, especially in liberal academic and ecclesiastical circles, that the fatherhood discussion is a subtle way to reintroduce patriarchy. Some people cannot understand the possibility of promoting responsible fatherhood without implying an arbitrary power on the part of males over their wives and children. From my standpoint, it is supremely simple to disconnect, even on religious and theological grounds, responsible fatherhood from patriarchy in either its hard or soft forms. But we have not discovered the appropriate language to bring together the ideals of responsible fatherhood with a dialogical understanding of love and justice between husband and wife. Yet we must continue to refine our language in that direction if we are to commend the fatherhood movement to society as a whole and especially to the liberal cultural groups who shape higher education and the liberal expressions of American religion, whether Protestant, Catholic, or Jewish.

Recently I have co-authored a book with Bonnie Miller McLemore, Pam Couture, Bernie Lyon, and Robert Franklin entitled *From Culture Wars to Common Ground: Religion and the American Family Debate.*[5] In this book we develop the ideas of a "critical familism" and a "critical marriage culture." We agree with the point developed in *Marriage in America* that society should replace the emerging "culture of divorce" and "culture of nonmarriage" with a new familism and a new marriage culture. Responsible fatherhood should be at the center of this new culture of marriage and familism. But we go a step further. We introduce the idea of a "critical" familism and marriage culture to emphasize the importance of what we call the "equal-regard marriage."

Equal regard is a particular way of speaking about the nature of marital love. It is marital love modeled after the second part of the Great Commandment, "You shall love your neighbor as yourself" (Matthew 19:19) or the neglected model of mutual married love in Ephesians 5:21, "Be subject to one another out of reverence for Christ." This is the kind of marital love in which responsible fatherhood should take place. In the equal-regard marriage, husband and wife treat each other as persons (as human ends and never as means to other ends), work for the good of the other, allow each other in principle to have full access to the privileges and responsibilities of both public and private life (both political-economic and domestic activity), take equal responsibility for parenting, and work out their respective divisions of labor in mutual dialogue.

In the equal-regard marriage, husband and wife exercise family authority with each other and with their children out of a context of dialogue. Ideally, this dialogue would function to interpret and reinterpret the meaning of some authoritative tradition such as a major and tested religious faith. A love ethic of equal regard, however, encourages couples to arrange their respective duties and privileges with a sense of flexibility, giving due attention to individual gifts, inclinations, and the contingencies of life.

A critical marriage culture pays attention to the "blocks" and "power plays" that either husband or wife may sometimes use to retain special privileges for themselves. Self-sacrificial giving is an important part of the equal-regard marriage, but not so much as an end in itself but as the extra effort needed to restore a relation of mutuality and equal regard. In such a marriage, the responsibility of fathers is taken as seriously as the responsibility of mothers. The contemporary fatherhood movements are perceptive in understanding that male relations with children are more tentative, less natural or automatic, and more of a cultural and institutional achievement. As a cultural and institutional achievement, fatherhood requires strong reinforcement by cultural and religious symbols for its creation, maintenance, and renewal.

I am delighted to see the theme of marriage running throughout the literature of the National Fatherhood Initiative. It is impossible to promote the rehabilitation of fatherhood unless one also addresses the entire field of marriage. Marriage as a concept is in crisis in our society. Responsible fatherhood cannot be fully actualized in isolation from the institution of marriage. Although we must learn to talk more and more about the interrelationship of fatherhood and marriage, we also must understand that, for various reasons, some fathers will not be married and that they too have responsibilities that should be honored.

The fatherhood movement needs to be concrete. It must have not only commanding ideas but also practical programs. Furthermore, the fatherhood movement must discover, articulate, and disseminate the good ideas and programs that already exist—something that the National Fatherhood Initiative is already doing. We need to search out the grassroots organizations, experiments, and programs that are successfully working with fathers. Local organizations, churches, and synagogues are often the leaders in discovering the programs that really work.

One gold mine for insightful initiatives with men and fathers is the African American churches of our land. They have been struggling for decades with the effects of discrimination and economic stress on men, fathers, and male youth. Many of these churches have been dealing for a long time with issues that are now beginning to preoccupy the rest of society—how to resist the forces of modern life that pull men away from families and how to make use of our religious and cultural sources to revive and reconstitute responsible fatherhood in both our country and the world.

But there is even more to do. Much can be done early in life to prepare for responsible fatherhood, both in the family and in schools. The family seems a natural place to begin, but what about the schools? Is there anything schools can do to prepare for fatherhood? I believe that there is. If we can address sex education in our schools and universities, we certainly should be able to explore what it means to be a father—and a mother—in the context of a marital relation.

It is possible that we will soon see a renewal of both public and private efforts to educate youth for parenthood, marriage, and family. The new psycho-education movements applied to marriage and parenting—and presently being energetically promoted by the newly created Coalition of Marriage, Family and Couples Education—are influencing schools, divorce courts, and legislatures to educate couples about the essentials of interpersonal communications. Such initiatives are needed for the future. But programs will only work if powerful religious and cultural traditions are mobilized to ground and reinforce fatherhood. Judaism and Christianity both provide rich foundations for fatherhood through their parallels between God's image and an earthly father's tasks, and liberal religious bodies need to be reminded of the biblical concept of equal-regard marriages.

Notes

1. The books of the Family, Culture, and Religion Series are published by Westminster John Knox Press. The ones in print to date are Phyllis Airhart and Margaret Bendroth, *Faith Traditions and the Family*, 1996; Anne Carr and Mary Stewart van Leeuwen, *Religion, Feminism, and the Family*, 1996; Ted Peters, *For the Love of Children*, 1996; Max Stackhouse, *Covenant and Commitments*, 1997; Leo Perdue et al., *Families in Ancient Israel*, 1997; Carolyn Osiek and David

Balch, *Families in the New Testament World*, 1997; John Witte Jr., *From Sacrament to Contract: Marriage, Religion, and Law in the Western Tradition*, 1997; Don Browning et al., *From Culture Wars to Common Ground: Religion and the American Family Debate*, 1997. A book sponsored by the project but published independently of the series is Lisa Cahill, *Sex, Gender, and Christian Ethics* (Cambridge: Cambridge University Press, 1996).

2. Browning et al., *Culture Wars*, 52.

3. Margaret Mead, *Male and Female* (New York: William Morrow, 1949).

4. John Miller, *Biblical Faith and Fathering* (New York: Paulist Press, 1989).

5. Browning et al, *Culture Wars*, 2.

Chapter 12

The Idea of God as Father

John W. Miller

In his seminal work, *Beyond Good and Evil*, the philosopher Nietzsche asked the question "Why Atheism Today?" to which he answered that "the 'father' in God has been thoroughly refuted." Based upon numerous conversations with his peers, Nietzsche concluded that God "does not hear—and if he heard he still would not know how to help. Worst of all: he seems incapable of clear communication."[1] Nietzsche foresaw what the consequences would be—not the *end* of religion but the emergence of new religions. "The religious instinct is indeed in process of growing powerfully," he wrote, "but the theistic satisfaction it refuses with deep suspicion."[2] To fill the void, Nietzsche put forward his own passionately conceived "Philosophy of the Future," at the center of which stood his famous *Übermensch* (superman), the very antithesis of the helpless father: A powerful, self-willed figure, disdainful of pity, ready and willing to enslave others for the sake of an aristocracy "that will grow, spread, seize, become predominant—not from any morality or immorality but because it is *living* and because life simply *is* will to power."[3] In a defining moment of the second millennium, in the middle of the twentieth century, the world experienced what can happen when the "father" in God is refuted in this manner and ideals of this kind are embraced by men of this type.[4] Now analogous developments are recurring as the twentieth century draws to a close.

Arguments Against God as Father

The "father" in God is again being "thoroughly refuted." This time, however, not because he is too weak and does not hear, but in a floodtide of feminist theologies asserting that he is too powerful and that, as such, he privileges men and demeans women and legitimates the sexism that permeates Western culture. Only as the "bellowing" monotheistic father deity who has presided over our androcentric culture for the past several millennia is dethroned, it is being said, will women realize their full humanity and equality with men and the world become what it is meant to be.[5] In this instance, however, refuting the "father" has proven easier than filling the void left by his absence.[6] "We are about to learn," states Naomi Goldenberg, "what happens when father-gods die for an entire culture."[7] But what she observes as now transpiring is a "turn toward inwardness" from which a multiplicity of variously gendered (or genderless) gods or god images (or metaphors) are emerging, not all conducive, she admits, to the "freedom of thought" she herself idealizes.[8] "Image-making itself," she concludes, may be the only common ground achievable among the devotees of these varied religious experiences.[9]

Only slightly less inchoate are the alternative social visions being espoused in these theologies. In them fathers are described as *males* who are part of a system of "legal, social, economic, and political relations that validate and enforce the sovereignty of male heads of families over dependent persons in the household."[10] Therefore, to realize their humanity and equality with men, what women now want to do, writes theologian Rosemary Ruether, is "tear down the walls that separate the self and society into 'male' and 'female' spheres."[11] To do this "demands not just a new integrated self but a new integrated social order" in which males and females will play virtually interchangeable roles, and "maleness and femaleness" will be no more than "reproductive role specialization" with "no necessary . . . psychological or social role differentiation. . . ."[12] Similar ideals are expressed by gender philosopher Sandra Lipsitz Bem, who envisions a "gender neutral" society in which the distinctions between male and female are so "completely dismantled that—except in narrowly biological contexts like reproduction—the distinction between male and female no longer organizes either the culture or the psyche."[13] She acknowledges, however, that "biological contexts like reproduction" do pose problems: "Only women can experience pregnancy, and its impact on a woman's physical condition is such that if not taken into account institutionally, it automatically advantages men as a group and disadvantages women as a group."[14] The care of infants and children poses similar "institutional" problems, she writes.

The solution advocated is professional child care paid at a much higher rate than is now typically the case, along with compensatory advantages for the women needing to sacrifice themselves in this manner.[15] In this emergent social vision, family strength is not judged "by its traditional form (whether there are two parents)," writes Janet Giele, director of the Family and Children's Policy Center at Brandeis University, "but by its functioning (whether it promotes human satisfaction and development) and whether both women and men are able to be family caregivers as well as productive workers."[16]

One is reminded of Plato's thoughts on this subject some 25 centuries ago in *The Republic*.[17] For him, too, the social ideal (at least, for the elite guardians of his society) was full equality of women with men in all spheres of human culture (education, athletics, commerce, politics, war).[18] And he, too, realized that for this to happen new ways would have to be found for mitigating the incapacities resulting from women's ineradicable role in pregnancy, childbirth, and care of young children. He, too, was of the opinion that the two-parent, father-involved family was expendable in this regard and other equally acceptable ways of having and caring for children could be (and would have to be) devised that would allow women to be less tied to the domestic role of mother. His proposal was that the state should assign and supervise certain days of sacred assembly when those duly certified for reproduction would gather for this purpose. The women impregnated by these matings would place their children in state-run nurseries run by professionals. Plato was very confident that such a society would be a happy one in which women would be free now for full participation with men in the tasks and enjoyments of the larger society.

Fault Lines in Feminist Theologies

That Plato could imagine that gender equality might be achieved in this manner says a great deal about his insensitivities to aspects of the human social and emotional condition: the bonds between husbands and wives, the affection parents have for their children, the ways in which children benefit from this affection and suffer without it. There are reasons why his egalitarian vision was never implemented. In our time, too, the feminist crusade against the "father" is bound to abate or be modified as the fatherhood crisis deepens and it becomes ever more apparent how indispensable fathers are for the psychological and social well-being of their children. In the meantime, however, the crusade will continue, and its attacks will inevitably center (as they have) on the literature that still "marks the line of most aggressive resistance to feminist goals," namely, the Bible.[19]

Feminist theologies may be divided into two groups. The first openly reject the biblically based religious traditions of the West, believing that the full liberation of women will require an entirely new religious gestalt, such as worship of the goddess or a bi-gender or genderless divine symbol system. Theologies of the second group, while holding similar views, affirm the basic tenets of biblical faith, but "in doing so seek to keep, but weaken the divine father symbolization."[20] It is this latter, more insidious refutation that must be examined.[21] Three fault lines in feminist theologies appear at this point: (1) misconstruals of what fathers actually are and signify; (2) neglect of developmental issues and needs in the lives of children; and (3) flawed analysis of patriarchy.

Misconstrual of What Fathers Actually Are and Signify

Theologian Ted Peters notes two steps in the strategy of those who "seek to keep, but weaken the divine father symbolization" in the Scriptures and liturgies of Western (biblical) religion, "both taken at the level of critical consciousness."[22] Step number one is "to put distance between the symbol and its referent, between language about God and the being of God. . . ." What is stressed is that God's own being is "ineffable, infinite, indefinable, mysterious, not subject to univocal statements." It follows that God "is not literally 'our Father.' The term *Father* is just a metaphor or symbol." The second step follows closely. It involves the manipulation and interchanging of symbols and metaphors for God. In the process the Father image is demoted, and nonpatriarchal images are advanced. "It is, in short," Peters summarizes, "a divide-and-conquer method."[23]

The ineffability of God is not to be questioned. All language for God (all language, in fact) is analogical, drawn from human experience and no more than an approximation of the reality to which it points.[24] But this does not mean that all God-language, all metaphors, all analogical approximations are equally true. *Some are more appropriate, more adequate, more conducive to evoking or "naming" what God is than others.* And whether consciously or not, we do make judgments in this regard, both as individuals and collectively, so that over time specific ways of naming and talking about God inevitably take hold and become distinguishing features of given cultures or civilizations. The Bible is a case in point. Its pages reflect a culture in which distinctive ways of invoking, addressing, and thinking about God were embraced and then advocated after a prolonged struggle with alternatives of precisely the kind being advanced today.[25] The God central to these Scriptures is *named*. Yahweh (the name), used some six thousand times in the Hebrew Scriptures, is not Baal (son), not Ashteroth (mother), not Anath (daughter). Yahweh is el (father). The identification of Yahweh with El, the god of the fathers (Exodus 3:15) and the father of the gods (Genesis 33:20; Joshua 22:22), is very explicit in the biblical narratives. The assumption that the ascription of fatherhood to God is infrequent in the Hebrew Scriptures is the result of an oversight in this regard. *The name Yahweh itself connotes "father."* When asking, "Have we not all one Father, has not one God created us?" the prophet Malachi was simply stating the obvious (2:10).[26] Jesus taught his disciples to pray, saying, "Our Father, hallowed be thy name" (Matthew 6:9). "Grace to you and peace from God our Father" is the way Paul regularly greeted his Gentile converts in his letters (Romans 1:7; 1 Corinthians 1:3; 2 Corinthians 1:2; Ephesians 1:2; Philippians 1:2; Colossians 1:2). The centrality of this name throughout the corpus of biblical literature is the reason why pronominal references to God are *always* masculine—not because God is male, but because God is father (Yahweh).[27] It is "he" (the father) who is rock-like, warrior-like, husband-like, mother-like. It is "he" (the father) who revealed himself in and through Jesus Christ as a friend of sinners. Father is his name. It is simultaneously a function. God *is* father and acts *like* a father.[28]

The centrality of this name accords with the "intuition" (revelation) that invoking *this* God bearing this name (and not some other), and following in *his* ways, is life-promoting for individuals and cultures. The biblical strictures against worshiping "other gods" is not simply that they are alien, but that they are inadequate, deviant, potentially destructive (Deuteronomy 30:15-20), "empty cisterns that hold no water" (Jeremiah 2:13). Adhering to Yahweh alone will bring "blessings" instead of "curses" (Deuteronomy 28). "Look, today I am offering you life and prosperity, death and disaster" (Deuteronomy 30:15). *The assumptions underlying this biblical naming of God are thus just the opposite of those calling for the refutation of the father in God.* The late twentieth century characterization of this "name" as symbolic of male power demeaning for women and destructive of their well-being is one that is in direct conflict with the biblical assumption that this way of naming and thinking about God is life-enhancing—and not just for men, but for a whole society.

Whose assumptions are correct? These can be empirically tested by looking at communities in which each of these assumptions is operative. Destroy the "father" in God and in culture and see what happens. See what happens in societies where God is honored as gracious effective father and where human fatherhood is vital and strong.[29] The assumptions can also be tested by careful analysis. We can think through what fatherhood is and represents. This ought to be the focus of an intense inquiry, but feminist literature to date is notable for its neglect of this issue. The term "father" itself is avoided. Instead we read of *male* heads of families whose dominance must be curtailed.[30] The man who becomes a father *is* a male, but a male of a certain age and stage. It is thus already a distortion and manipulation of the symbol father to define it solely as male. A father is a male who is such not just by virtue of his maleness nor even by virtue of his insemination of a female or the creation of a child. A father is such by virtue of the recognition accorded him as father by a woman and her children. For this to happen, *knowledge* of the male role in insemination is required. The very concept "father" (in the sense of a male knowing and being father to his own children) does not even exist without this knowledge. But even then, fatherhood can occur only when a specific woman admits a specific man into the reproductive process as the recognized father of *her* children. Fatherhood is thus not even possible apart from the willing collaboration of a woman and her children.

Fatherhood occurs at the conjunction of two relationships, writes anthropologist Peter Wilson—that of the primary bond between a woman and her child and the sexual bond between a man and woman.[31] It is the overlap of these two relationships that produces the *possibility* of a third relationship—that between father and child. "This third relationship differs from the other two in that it is mediate, the product of the conjunction of the other two, which are immediately generated by the biological conditions of reproduction, nurture and attraction." Primary bonds (between mothers and children) and pair bonds (between adult males and females) are rooted in nature, whereas the bond between a father and *his own child* is a sociocultural event arising solely from a male's pair bond with the child's mother. Wilson's remarkable conclusion is that the identity and relation of father and child is thus the primitive or elementary *social* relationship, constructed by transforming natural circumstances and "materials" through thoughts and promises. It is this socializing capacity, he argues, which distinguishes human culture from primate societies.[32] *Fatherhood arises as a potent new mode of social relating (a male's recognition and care for his own progeny) from promises made between specific males and specific females with respect to their children.*

A father is thus a male intelligent enough, socialized enough, mature enough, free enough, decisive enough, healthy enough, with enough foresight, intentionality, and regard for life that he will not allow himself to produce new lives on earth without fidelity and love for the mother of his children and personal involvement in taking care of them. Used of God, the term "father" evokes an analogous sense of God's care and love for all he created. God is father-like in his authoring of human existence, in his commitment and faithfulness to the well-being of the human family. "As tenderly as a father treats his children, so Yahweh treats those who fear him" (Psalm 103:13). His spirit is at work in all who aspire to the creation of the father-involved family. He is the "father of whom every fatherhood in heaven and on earth is named" (Ephesians 3:14f.).

Neglect of Children's Developmental Issues and Needs

A recently published dictionary of feminist theologies, with articles on virtually every facet of feminist thought, has not a single article on children or the developmental needs of children. Nor is there an essay on "father" (or the father's role in the care and maturation of children) to complement its essays on "mothers/motherhood," "mothers at home," "mothers in the work place." It is assumed that women are the preeminent parent and can function well in that role with or without the fathers of their children by their side. "Furthermore," the dictionary states,

> because God calls each woman to tasks that fit her gifts, there are a variety of ways to fulfil one's vocation as mother: adoption provides an equally valid way to become a mother to giving birth; lesbians are as capable of becoming good mothers as heterosexuals; single mothers can provide a loving home as well as married mothers. . . .[33]

The essays on mothering are preoccupied with issues related to women's freedom to be or not be mothers. Their focus is *adult* women achieving personal fulfillment through autonomous egalitarian relationships. "Feminism celebrates woman's ability to conceive, bear, and nurture children without making it a requirement for achieving true 'womanhood.'"[34]

But what then of the *children* whose birth is so celebrated? What about *their* needs? While sensitive to the egalitarian rights of women, feminist theologies are strangely oblivious to the imbalance of power between women *as mothers* and their children, or the bearing this has on adult male-female relations. During pregnancy, birth, and infancy, children are utterly dependent on their mothers. At this stage power imbalances between males and females are enormous. No relationship on earth is more symbiotically powerful than that binding children and mothers. In this light, how *do* children (male children especially) become autonomous human beings with appropriate gender identities and strength to live fulfilled, happy lives on their own, as adults? Failure to attend to this issue has been and still is a puzzling feature not just of feminist theologies but of American culture generally.[35] While children obviously need mothers for acquiring not just life but that bedrock of security and trust that is foundational for everything,[36] they also obviously need fathers for acquiring strong inner identities and a sense of autonomy.

Fathers facilitate this in many ways, among them: (1) by simply being there, right from the start as a "significant other";[37] (2) by their limit-setting (in ways mothers cannot while remaining unconditional caretaker) during the "terrible twos" when ego-controls are fragile and not yet internalized;[38] (3) through fostering secure body-congruent gender-identities in that critical eighteenth to twenty-fourth month of children's lives when this must happen if it is to happen at all;[39] (4) by fostering through their bonds with their wives (and in close harmony with their wives) those relationships with their children (during the crucial oedipal years from three to six) that will enable them to begin to let go of their transitional romantic attachments to the parent of the opposite sex and be reconciled with the parent of the same sex, so that they are then free to move on into a future in which *their* potential for a procreative and parental identity of their own can be realized.[40] It is difficult enough for these transformations to occur in children's lives in homes with caring fathers present—the difficulties are greatly intensified by their absence.[41]

Flawed Analysis of Patriarchy

Feminist scholars are locked in an unfinished debate over the origins of the patriarchy they decry. Recognizing as they do (and must) that all known civilizations are characterized by the presence of families headed by males and believing as they do that this has led to gender inequalities that must be rectified, they wonder how it happened that men became so dominant over women in the first place and what society was like prior to this happening. They imagine this to be a time of greater equality than now when patriarchal monotheism had not yet arisen and the gods were many and of both sexes. Various reasons are given for the changes that occurred, predominant among them, "the change from food gathering and gardening to plow agriculture, private landholding, urbanization, and class stratification."[42] In other words, patriarchy arose on the wings of changed "*material conditions* . . . [which] promoted male dominance for the first time."[43] It is "the product of changing cultural and historical circumstances, rather than a timeless human condition. . . ."[44] Through feminist thought and praxis, it is believed, egalitarian ways once widespread are being recovered.

Missing from this analysis is any attention at all to the marginality of males to the human reproductive process.[45] The reasons for this are puzzling, but I attribute it partly to awareness that its entry would subvert the prevailing patriarchal assumptions. In any case, when tracing the origins of patriarchy, feminist historians typically do not go back far enough, to the point in "human evolutionary ecology" when males were completely absent from the family unit of mothers and children and had no knowledge of, or concern about, their own children. This alone provides a proper framework for grasping what Don Browning has termed the "male problematic."[46]

Throughout the lower orders of life on earth, males have no stake whatsoever in the care of their own offspring. This too is what we find among the higher primates, and even among the chimpanzees (our closest living primate relatives) where males roam in groups and mate randomly. A new kind of sexuality was needed before fatherhood could arise; one in which pair bonds would exist and sexual relating would be more than a momentary impersonal act during specified times of female estrus.[47] Even with this, it seems, fatherhood did not emerge as a cultural norm for many centuries. According to Marija Bimbutas, women were still at the core of community organization and child care ten thousand years ago in Old Europe. Archaeological evidence indicates that males still mated randomly and did not know or care for their own children. The social structure was matrilineal "with succession to leadership and inheritance within the female line."[48] The preeminent religious and cultural symbol was that of a fecund mother with large breasts. "The Goddess of the Paleolithic and Neolithic is parthenogenetic, creating life out of herself. She is the primeval self-fertilizing 'Virgin Goddess'. . . ."[49] The reason likely was that in these cultures males still did not know or understand the role of semen in the procreation of children. Malinowsky found human tribes living in isolation in the Trobriand Islands in which these conditions were still the prevailing ones.[50] Men lived pair-bonded with women, but were not thought of as the fathers of their children since it was not yet understood that women do not bear children of themselves. In fact the word "father" did not even exist, Malinowsky reports. Children regarded the male living with their mother as her "friend"—their lineage was through their mother's family only.

Our oldest evidence of a decisive break and transition from matrilineal forms of human society to that characterized by a family in which males join females in a covenanted relationship oriented toward the care of children they know to be theirs is in those regions where the biological link between male insemination and the origins of a fetus were clearly understood and culturally appropriated by the larger society in ways that supported and favored fatherhood.[51] Evidence of what this entailed is apparent in the literature of the peoples who settled the Egyptian and Mesopotamia river valleys some five thousand years ago.[52] Law codes and instructional texts from these regions dating to the third and second millennia B.C.E. bear witness to the growing importance of the institutionalization of the father-involved family in the emergence of these first great civilizations.[53] The father-involved families of the Bible (ancestors of Israel) were heirs to these cultural innovations. Through Israel's encounter with "mother" cultures of Canaan, Israel's own ideals in this regard were shaken, then solidified and channeled to future generations through the Bible's call for marital fidelity and parental responsibility within a two-parent father-involved family structure. Especially with the advent and expansion of Christianity, these ideals were disseminated to Europe and America and then increasingly worldwide.[54] It is this five thousand year history of the two-parent father-involved family that is now being questioned.

The Father in God Is Key

At the beginning of a recent book of meditations, *Crossing the Threshold of Hope*, Pope John Paul II appeals to his readers not to be afraid to call upon God as father. Near his book's end, he writes about "original sin," which he characterizes as a most disruptive force in the life of humanity, because, he states, it wants to diminish or eradicate the "rays of fatherhood" that shine forth from God into the life of the world. Then (in italics), he adds, *"This is truly the key for interpreting reality,"* for "original sin is not only the violation of a positive command . . ., but [it also] . . . *attempts . . . to abolish fatherhood*, destroying its rays which permeate the created world, placing in doubt the truth about God who is Love and leaving man only with a sense of the master-slave relationship."[55] The thrust of this chapter may be viewed as an exposition of the truth of these insights. Like the state that protects us from anarchy, the father-involved family is a predominantly *cultural* (or spiritual) institution that protects us from dehumanization. Just as there are no more meaningful indices of a healthy culture than one in which fathers are present with mothers in the care of their own children and the two-parent father-involved family is firmly established and strong, so there is no more meaningful name by which to invoke the God who lovingly leads us into our human future than as "father": "Our Father, who art in heaven . . ."

Notes

This chapter is excerpted from John W. Miller, *Calling God "Father"* (Paulist Press, 1999).

1. Frederich Neitzsche, *Beyond Good and Evil: Prelude to a Philosophy of the Future*, trans. with commentary by Walter Kaufmann (New York: Vintage Books, 1966), 66.

2. Neitzsche, *Beyond Good and Evil*.

3. Nietzsche, *Beyond Good and Evil*, 203. Nietzsche wrote: "The essential characteristic of a good and healthy aristocracy is that experiences itself *not* as a function (whether of the monarchy or the commonwealth) but as their *meaning* and highest justification—that it therefore accepts with a good conscience the sacrifice of untold human beings who, *for its sake*, must be reduced and lowered to incomplete human beings, to slaves, to instruments. Their fundamental faith simply has to be that society must *not* exist for society's sake but only as the foundation and scaffolding on which a choice type of being is able to raise itself to its higher task and to a higher state of *being* . . ."(p. 202).

4. For a sobering analysis of the way Hitler and his associates exploited the emotional vacuum resulting from the father absence caused by World War I (through a mesmerizing use of their perverted, "pitiless" pseudo-paternal power), see Peter Loewenberg,"The Psychohistorical Origins of the Nazi Youth Cohort" *Decoding the Past: The Psychohistorical Approach*, (New York: Alfred Knopf, 1983), 240-283.

5. Rosemary Radford Ruether pictures God the Father as seated on his throne and bellowing: "I am the Lord thy God, Thou shalt have no other gods before Me" (*Sexism and God-talk: Toward a Feminist Theology* [Boston: Beacon Press, 1983], 1). For an overview of the literature in which these or similar ideas are now being articulated and of the complex developments that have contributed to their advent and power in our culture, see Francis Martin, *The Feminist Question: Feminist Theology in the Light of Christian Tradition* (Grand Rapids, Mich.: Eerdmans, 1994), especially chapter 5, "An Historical Overview of Feminism and Feminist Theology," 145-167.

6. The complexities and uncertainties involved in this search for alternatives are evident in the work of Naomi R. Goldenberg, *Changing of the Gods: Feminism and the End of Traditional Religions* (Boston: Beacon Press, 1979); *The End of God: Important Directions for a Feminist Critique of Religion in the Works of Sigmund Freud and Carl Jung* (Ottawa: University of Ottawa Press, 1981); and in the work of Carol Ochs, *Behind the Sex of God: Toward a New Consciousness—Transcending Matriarchy and Patriarchy* (Boston: Beacon Press, 1977). Ochs is persuaded that "matriarchy and patriarchy are two fundamental and opposing ways of life in this world and of understanding reality" (p. 110), neither of which is viable. Her alternative is a form of degendered pantheism. The alternative Goldenberg leans toward is the imaginal products of women reflected on in a manner that might be called religious.

7. Goldenberg, *Changing of the Gods*, 37.

8. Goldenberg, *Changing of the Gods*, 72. "When a symbol as pervasive as that of the father-god begins to die," she writes, "tremendous anxiety is generated. Other images arise to take its place almost immediately. Candidates for different god images are already being nominated either to replace the father-god or to

provide him with a female retinue. A survey of these new images shows that some are more conducive to freedom of thought than others."

9. Goldenberg, *Changing of the Gods*, 140. Elsewhere she states: "It seems highly likely that the West is on the brink of developing a new mysticism—post-Christian, post-Judaic. It will most probably be a type of mysticism which emphasizes the *continual observation of psychic imagery*" (p. 120). In this new pantheon of Gods, she states, the father-god will be among them, but no longer will "Christ and Yahweh . . . behave as egotistical, spoiled children in our psyches—they will no longer keep us from giving our attention to other members of our psychic families." (p. 83).

10. Rosemary Radford Ruether, "Patriarchy," in *Dictionary of Feminist Theologies*, ed. Letty M. Russel and J. Shannon Clarkson (Louisville, Ky.: Westminster John Knox Press, 1996), 205.

11. Ruether, *Sexism and God-talk*, 113.

12. Ruether, *Sexism and God-talk*, 111.

13. Sandra Lipsitz Bem, *The Lenses of Gender: Transforming the Debate on Sexual Inequality* (New Haven and London: Yale University Press, 1993), 192. These views are also more or less endorsed by Deborah L. Rhode, *Speaking of Sex: The Denial of Gender Inequality* (Cambridge, Mass.: Harvard University Press, 1997). "Most individuals," she writes, "want neither to relinquish all sense of sexual identity nor to restrict each sex to stereotypical patterns. Yet it is by no means clear that we can have it both ways. Most of what we know about personality development suggests that as long as sex-linked traits remain, the pressures for conformity will limit individual choice" (p. 239).

14. Bem, *Lenses of Gender*, 186f.

15. Bem says, "Full-time parenting when children are young should be regarded as much the same kind of personal career sacrifice for the good of the society as serving in the armed forces—in which case the women who do so should be paid for their effort and should also be helped in their transition into the 'civilian' economy with some kind of analogue to the GI bill" (p. 187).

16. Janet Z. Giele, "Decline of the Family: Conservative, Liberal, and Feminist Views," in *Promises to Keep: Decline and Renewal of Marriage in America*, ed. David Popenoe, Jean Bethke Elshtain, and David Blankenhorn (Lanham, Md.: Rowman and Littlefield, 1996), 101. For similar points of view, see the articles on "Family" and "Mother/Motherhood," by Lee McGee and Nancy J. Duff, in *Dictionary of Feminist Theologies*, 98, 187.

17. Plato, *The Republic*, trans. with an introduction by Desmond Lee, second ed. rev. (London: Penguin Books, 1988), Part VI: Women and the Family (449-470).

18. For a discussion of Plato's feminism, see Nickolos Pappas, *Routledge Philosophy Guidebook to Plato and the Republic* (London and New York: Routledge, 1995), 104-110.

19. Phyllis A. Bird, *Feminism and the Bible: A Critical and Constructive Encounter* (Winnipeg: Canadian Mennonite Bible College, 1994), 40. For many feminists, Bird believes, the Bible is irrelevant, but still engages them as "a sign of

patriarchal bondage to which . . . they cannot and will not return."

20. For this formulation of the issues, I am indebted to Ted Peters, *God—the World's Future: Systematic Theology for a Postmodern Era* (Minneapolis, Minn.: Fortress Press, 1992), 114.

21. On this aspect of the critique, see especially Elizabeth Achtemeir, "Exchanging God for 'No Gods': A Discussion of Female Language for God," in *Speaking the Christian God, The Holy Trinity and the Challenge of Feminism*, ed. Alvin F. Kimel Jr. (Grand Rapids, Mich.: Eerdmans, 1992), 1-16. She writes that "no aspect of the feminist movement has affected the church's life more basically than has that movement's attempts to change the language used in speaking to or about God." (p. 1).

22. Achtemeir, "Exchanging God," 114.

23. Achtemeir, "Exchanging God," 114.

24. This point is acknowledged by virtually everyone who writes on this subject, whatever their perspective. See, for example, the essay by Thomas F. Torrance, "The Christian Apprehension of God the Father," in *Speaking the Christian God*, 120-143.

25. Israel's cultural wars in this regard are either unknown or ignored in feminist writings, or viewed as narrow-minded and tragic in their outcome. Erhard S. Gerstenberger, *Yahweh, the Patriarch: Ancient Images of God and Feminist Theology* (Minneapolis, Minn.: Fortress Press, 1996), is an example of the latter point of view. Rita M. Gross, *Feminism & Religion: An Introduction* (Boston: Beacon Press, 1996), states: "The Bible itself conveys the impression that the acceptance of male monotheism was smooth and clear in ancient Israel; only deviant people are shown objecting to this religious ideal or being attracted by 'foreign' religions" (p. 173). Actually, the Bible gives a detailed account of a prolonged struggle involving major efforts at reform, with only the last of these being successful (those of Ezra and Nehemiah). Regarding this struggle and its bearing on the formation of the Bible, see John W. Miller, *The Origins of the Bible: Rethinking Canon History* (New York: Paulist Press, 1994).

26. For more on this identification of God as father in biblical tradition, see Frank Moore Cross, *Canaanite Myth and Hebrew Epic: Essays in the History of the Religion of Israel* (Cambridge, Mass.: Harvard University Press, 1973), 42-47; John W. Miller, "God as Father in the Bible and the Father Image in Several Contemporary Ancient Near East Myths: A Comparison," *Studies in Religion* 14, no. 3 (1985): 347-354.

27. The father language for God in both testaments has been reviewed many times, recently again in Francis Martin, *The Feminist Question*, 265-292.

28. Yahweh is pictured occasionally as acting with a tenderness and care that is mother-like (Isaiah 42:14; 45:10; 49:15; 66:13), but nowhere in either Testament is he ever *addressed* as mother or said to be mother. On these linguistic distinctions (between simile and metaphor) and their importance, see Roland M. Frye, "Language for God and Feminist Language: Problems and Principles," in *Speaking the Christian God*, 17-43. Frye characterizes the symbol "father" for God as a "structural metaphor" underlying "the entire organism of belief . . . to which

different parts of the living body of faith connect and through which they function" (p. 42). On these issues, see also John W. Miller, "Depatriarchalizing God in Biblical Interpretation: A Critique," *Catholic Biblical Quarterly* 48 (1986): 609-616.

29. The United States of America is today a vast laboratory for discovering what happens when fatherlessness becomes epidemic. For the statistics, see Wade F. Horn, *Father Facts*, second edition.(National Fatherhood Initiative, One Bank Street, Suite 160, Gaithersburg, MD 20878). For a sobering account of the consequences, see David Blankenhorn, *Fatherless America*, especially chapter 2, "Fatherless Society," 25-48.

30. See *Dictionary of Feminist Theologies*, where articles on "father" are missing and "patriarchy" is defined as "male heads of families over dependent persons in the household" (p. 205).

31. Peter J. Wilson, *Man, The Promising Primate: The Conditions of Human Evolution*, second edition. (New Haven and London: Yale University Press, 1983), 59.

32. Wilson explains it this way:

The human situation or the cultural situation is not the metarelation of primary and pair bond; these are the conditions of its possibility. The transformation into kinship marks the point at which the human emerges, as the emphasis shifts from the primary and pair bonds to the kinship bond of father/child. At this point the child replaces the female as the new joint for kinship relations. A series of transformations occurs: the male becomes "father" (a different order of connection from any existing before); and the female now bears to the offspring the kinship relationship of mother" (Wilson, 95).

33. Nancy J. Duff, "Mothers/Motherhood," *Dictionary of Feminist Theologies*, 187.

34. Duff, "Mothers/Motherhood."

35. Regarding this frequently raised, but still poorly understood, issue in the culture generally, see Hans Sebold, *Momism: The Silent Disease of America* (Chicago: Nelson Hall, 1976).

36. For the research on this see Rudolf Schaffer, *Mothering* (Cambridge, Mass.: Harvard University Press, 1977).

37. On the father's critically important role, even during this first year of a child's life, see Fichard Atkings, "Discovering Daddy: The Mother's Role," in *Father and Child: Developmental and Clinical Perspectives*, ed. Stanley Cath et al. (Boston: Little, Brown, 1982), 139-149; Stanley Greenspan, "'The Second Other': The Role of the Father in Early Personality Formation and the Dyadic-Phallic Phase of Development," in *Father and Child*, 123-138.

38. So urgent is a child's own felt need for a father during the second year of his life that one researcher, James M. Herzog, has termed it "father hunger" (see "On Father Hunger: The Father's Role in the Modulation of Aggressive Drive and Fantasy," *Father and Child*, 163-174), and another likens the father in his role at this time of his children's lives to that of a lifeguard rescuing a child desperately trying to reach shore while being pursued by a dragon (Stanley Greenspan, "'The Second Other,'"*Father and Child*, 123-138).

39. Gender itself, of course, is a biological given, but gender-identities are formed in response to subtle distinctions in parenting (many of them father-initiated) right when children are learning to talk. The research leading to this breakthrough discovery is reviewed by Ethel Person and Lionel Oversey, "Psychoanalytic Theories of Gender Identity," *Journal of the American Academy of Psychoanalysis*, 11 (1983): 203-225.

40. For a wealth of studies confirming the reality and importance of these momentous transformations in which the core features of conscience are born (no adultery, no violence), see Seymour Fischer and Roger Greenberg, *The Scientific Credibility of Freud's Theories and Therapy* (New York: Basic Books, 1977), 396-399.

41. For a fuller discussion of these issues, viewed from the perspective of developmental psychoanalysis, see John W. Miller, "The Contemporary Fathering Crisis: The Bible and Research Psychology," *The Conrad Grebel Review*, (fall 1983): 21-37; "In Defense of Monotheistic Father Religion," *Journal of Religion and Health* 21, no. 1 (1982): 62-67.

42. Ruether, "Patriarchy," *Feminist Theologies*, 205.

43. Gross, *Feminism and Religion*, 163.

44. Gross, *Feminism and Religion*, 164.

45. One of the few feminist treatises on this subject that is an exception is Gerda Lerner's *The Origins of Patriarchy* (New York: Oxford University Press, 1986). In it Lerner confesses her surprise at discovering that patriarchal origins did not lie (as she had thought) in slavery or some other violent act on men's part, but in the subordination of women to men sexually in marriage. For this reason she is more cautious than most in predicting what lies ahead. "What will come after, what kind of structure will be the foundation for alternate forms of social organization we cannot yet know," she writes. "We are in the process of becoming" (p. 229).

46. On the importance of the consideration of "evolutionary ecology" for a consideration of the "asymmetrical reproductive strategies of males and females" and a proper understanding of what he calls "the male problematic," see Don Browning, "Biology, Ethics, and Narrative in Christian Family Theory," in *Promises to Keep: Decline and Renewal of Marriage in America*, 121-123.

47. For details and a bibliography, see my essay on "Origins of the Father-involved Family," in *Biblical Faith and Fathering: Why We Call God 'Father'* (New York: Paulist Press, 1989), 13-23; also, Peter Wilson, *Man the Promising Primate*, especially chapter 1, "The Primitive Primate, What Conditions Make Human Evolution Possible?" 11-44.

48. Marija Gimbutas, *The Civilization of the Goddess*, ed. Joan Marler (Harper San Francisco, 1991), 349. The period surveyed is "Old European society" from about 5500 to 3500 B.C.E.

49. Gimbutas, *Civilization of the Goddess*, 223.

50. Bronislaw Malinowski, *The Father in Primitive Psychology* (New York: W. W. Norton, 1927).

51. On this point, see Don Browning, "Biology, Ethics, and Narrative," 123. "According to evolutionary ecologists, paternal certainty is a necessary, but not

sufficient, condition for the development of paternal investment," he states.

52. On this development see my essay entitled, "Male-centered Reproductive Biology and the Dynamics of Biblical Patriarchy," in *Biblical Faith and Fathering*, 24-39.

53. For Egyptian tradition in this regard, see "The Instruction of the Vzier Ptah-hotep," an instructional text from the third millennium (2450 B.C.E), in *Ancient Near Eastern Texts*, ed. James B. Pritchard (Princeton: Princeton University Press, 1950), 413 (lines 200-209 and 330-339); the most extensive collection of Mesopotamian tradition in this regard are the 67 family laws (case laws 128-195) at the heart of "The Code of Hammurabi," dating from the first half of the second millennium, (Pritchard, 171-175). This remarkable collection begins with the decree: "If a seignior acquired a wife, but did not draw up the contracts for her, that woman is no wife."

54. This is the subject of my essays in *Biblical Faith and Fathering*.

55. John Paul II, *Crossing the Threshold of Hope* (Toronto: Alfred Knopf, 1994), 228.

Chapter 13

Emerging Attitudes About Gender Roles and Fatherhood

W. Bradford Wilcox

Since World War II, the dominant cultural story of fatherhood in the United States has changed dramatically. In the 1950s, the father was supposed to be a "good provider," known more for his financial contribution to the family than for his active involvement in parenting or expressive way with the family. The "new father" ideal, which emerged gradually after the cultural transformations of the late 1960s and now occupies the public imagination, suggests that the father share the breadwinner role with his wife. More important, this new father is supposed to be deeply involved with the lives of his children and emotionally open and expressive with his wife and children.[1]

This cultural shift in the story of fatherhood has been accompanied by a marked liberalization in the gender role attitudes of American men. Men are much more likely to profess support for consensual authority in marriage, as well as for egalitarian patterns of spousal employment and parental involvement, than they were 30 years ago.[2] While this liberalization in gender role attitudes has garnered support from most sectors of American life, some religious organizations—especially ones led by conservative evangelicals—have been in the forefront of resistance to some or all of these changes.[3]

Given the fact that many men have embraced more progressive gender role attitudes *and* that religious men—particularly evangelicals—are less likely to hold these values, one might predict (1) that men with progressive gender role attitudes are more involved and emotionally expressive with their children and (2) that religious men, particularly evangelicals, are less involved and expressive with their children. However, this study reveals that religious affiliation, gender role attitudes, and fatherhood are related in ways that largely disconfirm these predictions. Moreover, it appears that religious affiliation is a more powerful predictor of paternal practices and attitudes than are gender role attitudes. But before I explore the relationships between religious affiliation, gender role attitudes, and fatherhood, I will offer a brief history of family and religious life in the United States to provide context for my findings.

Family and Fatherhood Since the 1950s

The 1950s were an exceptional time for the American family[4]; among other things, the marriage rate peaked, the birthrate soared, and the divorce rate (temporarily) stopped its century-long climb. In the midst of postwar affluence and surging suburbanization characteristic of this decade, a familial culture emerged that valued domesticity, motherhood, and child-centeredness. As noted above, fatherhood was tightly connected to breadwinning in this period and only loosely tied to active and expressive involvement in the family; to a lesser extent, fathers were also exhorted to act as role models of sobriety and hard work to their children.[5]

An important dimension of this familialism was religious practice. Although many people, especially members of the mainline churches, had only the vaguest understanding of Christian doctrine, Americans in the 1950s valued basic norms of piety—from grace before meals to church-going—in part because these religious practices served as vehicles of family unity and markers of middle class respectability.[6] Undoubtedly, many parents also attended church so that their children would be taught moral precepts, such as the golden rule, long associated with religious life in this country.

Evangelical and mainline Protestant churches responded to this familialism by developing religious curriculums centered around family life. In the Catholic context, lay movements like the Cana Conference and the Christian Family Movement emerged, stressing family spirituality and Catholic social action. In this period, churches across the theological spectrum lent their moral voice to the familial culture of the era, affirming traditional gender roles, domesticity (particularly for women), and lifelong marriage. The people in the pews reciprocated with increased levels of family piety—unusually high rates of families attending church together, reading the Bible at home, and saying grace before dinner occurred during the 1950s.[7]

For a range of economic and cultural reasons (well beyond the scope of this chapter), the structure and culture of the American family changed dramatically in the next two decades. The birthrate and marriage rate declined as people postponed or avoided children and marriage. The divorce rate doubled, and cohabitation emerged as a viable precursor to marriage. Increasing numbers of women left full-time mothering as women's labor force participation rose from 43 percent in 1960 to 64 percent in 1980.[8] This period also witnessed a cultural shift as 1950s familialism was eclipsed by a "new morality." This new morality was characterized by a turn to expressive individualism that valued self-fulfillment, self-knowledge, liberation from traditional gender roles, and a greater openness to nonmarital sexuality.[9] Amidst these shifts in family life, men adopted disparate strategies: some left marriages or remained bachelors to experience the newfound pleasures of the single life; others continued to pursue a more traditional breadwinning role; and still others—the so-called new fathers—devoted more time to childrearing and active emotional involvement in their families.[10]

Despite the diversity of male practice, the dominant cultural ideal of fatherhood in the contemporary period, as indicated above, has been new fatherhood. This ideal has gained support in the public culture—especially in the media, helping professions, and educational establishments—for two reasons. First, feminists, academics, and parenting experts have portrayed involved and expressive fatherhood as an important dimension of justice in the family, especially since more and more women are sharing the breadwinning burden. Second, parenting experts and men's organizations have argued that this style of fathering is psychologically rewarding for fathers and children alike.[11]

Resistance and Incorporation by Evangelicalism

Religious institutions have responded quite differently to the transformation of family life in the last three decades. Of the three largest religious traditions in America (mainline and evangelical Protestantism, as well as Roman Catholicism),[12] evangelical Protestantism has responded most sharply to these changes, pursuing a public strategy that has been largely resistant to changes in family structure and culture. Evangelical leaders like James Dobson, Beverly LaHaye, and Charles Swindoll argue that the cultural shifts of the 1960s and 1970s placed the "traditional family" under tremendous strain. Accordingly, these leaders press the theme—in books, videos, sermons, and such ministries as Focus on the Family—that the traditional family must be supported at all costs. Partly as a consequence of this defensive posture, evangelical churches and ministries have invested the family with tremendous symbolic importance in this subculture.

Distinct echoes of 1950s familialism can be found in the evangelical understanding of the traditional family. In particular, most evangelical churches promote traditional gender roles and an ideology of intensive mothering. However, this 1950s-style familialism is wedded to an explicit Christian faith that is supposed to transform the dynamics of everyday living. The family is viewed as an embodiment of the love God has for his people. It is also seen as an institution that has been ordained by God for the cultivation of marital love, the transmission of faith from one generation to the next, and for the care and socialization of children.[13]

When it comes to the role of fathers in the traditional family, however, evangelicalism has adopted a strategy that combines equal measures of resistance to and incorporation of the public culture of new fatherhood. Although evangelical groups generally stress men's traditional role as the primary breadwinner and head of household, men are also encouraged to avoid the emotional and practical distance from family life traditionally ascribed to the breadwinner role. In fact, since the 1970s, the evangelical world has incorporated a therapeutic focus on feelings, relationships, and self-esteem into its Christian ethos. This recent development is one of the reasons that evangelical men are being encouraged to adopt many of the behaviors and attitudes associated with new fatherhood. Evangelical concern about the deterioration of family life also seems to be a reason for the evangelical emphasis on active and involved fatherhood. This emphasis is apparent, among other places, in evangelical family advice books. For instance, an evangelical specialist had this to say about the father: "Is Dad necessary? You bet he is! He is part of a God-designed team and his teamwork is essential to the personal growth of his children."[14]

Specifically, fathers are supposed to model the love that God has for humankind to their wives and children. On the one hand, this means taking an active and expressive role in family life. Fathers are encouraged to be involved in the lives of their children and to praise them. But, on the other hand, since God's love also includes the just correction of sin, fathers are supposed to be strong disciplinarians. A spirit of self-control and obedience among children, this script suggests, depends upon fathers' willingness to identify clear rules and back them up with a spanking if necessary. In sum, then, evangelicalism is associated with a fatherhood culture stressing active involvement, expressiveness, and a strict disciplinary orientation.

Accommodation Among Mainline Protestants and Catholics

With some exceptions,[15] a common orientation to the family has emerged among mainline Protestant and Catholic churches. This orientation might be described as one of accommodation. Motivated by values like tolerance and freedom of conscience, these two denominations—especially mainline churches—have largely accommodated themselves to the shifts in family structure and culture of the last three decades.[16] At the same time, active members of these denominations are involved with their children in ways that suggest their religious communities continue to exert influences on them that distinguish their parenting styles from their secular peers.

Compared to evangelical churches, mainline Protestant churches have been unable to articulate a vision of the family or to cultivate vital family ministries.[17] The reasons for this phenomenon are complex but two processes account for mainline Protestantism's inability to offer its members a distinctive message regarding family life. First, operating in light of a religious ethic of prophetic justice, mainline Protestant churches have largely focused their energies on social justice in the last three decades.[18] Accordingly, issues of a more personal nature—such as the believer's responsibilities to his or her family—have received little attention.

Second, mainline Protestant churches have been at the forefront of recent cultural changes, in large part because their clergy and members are drawn disproportionately from the middle and upper ranks of the American class structure.[19] Thus, they have generally adopted a "tolerant" stance to changes in American family life, a stance that often divides their congregations and leaves these churches unable to muster much in the way of a programmatic message or ministry to families. As Don Browning observes, "[Mainline churches] are perceived to be more conflicted, less decisive, and more embarrassed by their family ministries than they once were and than are the more conservative manifestations of the church."[20] It would seem, then, that fathers in this subculture receive little direction specifically aimed at cultivating a distinctively Protestant ethic of fatherhood.

American Catholics were once known for their high regard for authority, tradition, and the family—including the extended family. Although it is hard to know how much of this orientation was caused by religious factors and how much of it was caused by ethnic factors, Catholics had a distinctive familial orientation that included an expectation of obedience from children, the use of corporal punishment, high interaction with members of the extended family, and high fertility.[21]

But in the last three decades, the distinctive Catholic family orientation has largely eroded.[22] Although forces outside of the church have contributed to the erosion of this ethic (such as the socioeconomic mobility of Catholic laity since the 1950s),[23] two processes in the church have also contributed to this transformation. First, in response to post-Vatican II changes in the church and recent cultural shifts outside the church, many lay and clerical Catholic leaders have embraced a more independent attitude toward authority in general and church teaching in particular—especially over matters of sexuality and marriage.[24] Like their mainline counterparts, these progressive leaders have embraced a message of toleration that leaves them unable to offer much in the way of affirmative family advice to the Catholic faithful.

Second, the crisis of authority in the church (especially the controversy surrounding *Humanae Vitae*)[25] has left large numbers of the American Catholic clergy unwilling or unable to address family issues from the pulpit. Clergy seem afraid of offending the sensibilities of their parishioners. Thus, many Catholics don't hear much about family life in their local parishes, even though Pope John Paul II and other members of the hierarchy continue to promote a distinctive Catholic family orientation. For these reasons, Catholic men are almost as unlikely as mainline Protestant men to encounter homilies or ministries dedicated to a consideration of their family roles.[26]

Religious Affiliation and Gender Role Attitudes

Measurements of religious affiliation and attendance are often cause for serious debate in the sociology of religion. Nevertheless, I offer my own estimation of the religious affiliation of American fathers using the National Survey of Families and Households (NSFH), which sampled 13,017 adult respondents in 1987 or 1988, of whom 3,343 were fathers of children ages 18 and under.[27] Operating under the assumption that religious affiliation is meaningful if the respondent has a minimum level of church attendance, I only included men in a religious category if they attended church at least once a year. Men who indicated no religious affiliation or who attended church less than once a year were placed in the unaffiliated category.

By my measure the largest subgroup of fathers were the unaffiliated fathers, who made up 37 percent of this population. Given America's reputation as a religious nation, the large numbers of unaffiliated fathers may be surprising to some. It's important to note, however, that men are less likely than women to be actively affiliated with a church.

Unaffiliated fathers were followed by the three largest religious traditions in America: mainline Protestants (23 percent), Catholics (19 percent), and evangelical Protestants (14 percent). Jewish fathers made up two percent of the fatherhood population, while fathers from other religious traditions (principally Mormonism) made up five percent of the fatherhood population. Because the NSFH did not have sufficient numbers of fathers from Jewish and other traditions to make accurate statistical claims, I do not include fathers from these religious traditions in the rest of this analysis.

Religious affiliation has been associated in recent years with traditional gender role attitudes. This relationship was confirmed in my analysis of paternal attitudes to the gendered division of family responsibilities and to working mothers of preschool children. Evangelical fathers were most likely to agree (56 percent) with the statement "It is much better for everyone if the man earns the main living and the woman takes care of the home and family." Catholics were also significantly more likely to agree with this statement (46 percent). However, mainline fathers were not, in a statistical sense, any different from their unaffiliated peers when it came to attitudes about male breadwinning and female homemaking. Forty-two percent of mainline fathers had a traditional view of male and female responsibilities in the family, as did 41 percent of unaffiliated fathers.

I also analyzed the relationship between religious affiliation and attitudes toward working mothers. Fifty-one percent of evangelical fathers disapproved of "mothers who work full-time when their youngest child is under age 5." Almost equally high numbers of Catholic and mainline fathers disapproved—50 and 49 percent, respectively. Only 43 percent of unaffiliated fathers disapproved of working mothers with young children.

I also determined which fathers were conservative both with respect to their attitudes to male and female responsibilities and in their attitudes to working mothers. I found that evangelical fathers were the most conservative (38 percent), followed by Catholics (31 percent), mainline Protestants (28 percent), and unaffiliated fathers (25 percent). These figures also indicate, however, that many of these fathers were not conservative across both domains, given the discrepancies between support for both items and support for individual items. In other words, some men (principally Catholics and mainline Protestants) did not approve of working mothers but did not agree that men should be the breadwinners and women the homemakers. Another contingent (principally evangelicals) believed precisely the opposite. Thus, gender role attitudes among fathers vary not just by religion but also according to the tasks and scope of activities on which these attitudes bear.

It is also important to note that, on average, more than half of these fathers did not agree or were ambivalent with regard to at least one of these two statements. This suggests that progressive gender role attitudes have become increasingly influential in the United States, even among men.

Moreover, a large number of evangelical fathers, about 40 percent, did not agree with at least one of these statements. This finding confirms other studies that indicate American evangelicalism has also been affected by the fundamental cultural shifts in gender role attitudes that have transformed American life since the 1960s.[28]

Involved Fathering

I examined paternal involvement in four areas: one-on-one activities, youth activities, attendance at meals, and child-care tasks. Although I found no statistically significant differences[29] between religiously affiliated and unaffiliated fathers of preschool children, there were marked differences between affiliated and unaffiliated fathers of school-age children. As Table 13.1 indicates, religious fathers were significantly more involved with their children in one-on-one activities than were unaffiliated fathers. (Please note: whenever I use the word "significant" I am referring to differences that persist even after controlling for factors like income, education, and race.)

Table 13.1
Paternal Involvement with School-Age Children (homework help, private talks, playing, outings)

	Evangelical	Mainline	Catholic	No Affiliation
Infrequent	52%	54%	54%	61%
Frequent	48%	46%	46%	39%

Specifically, Table 13.1 measures the average frequency (from one "never" to six "almost everyday") with which fathers interact with their children in four activities: homework help, private talks, playing (that is, throwing a baseball), and outings (that is, a visit to the park). Fathers who had an average score of four ("about once a week") or higher across the four activities were scored as fathers with "frequent" one-on-one interaction with their children. This means that fathers with a "frequent" score, on average, did all four activities with their children at least once a week. Thus, 48 percent of evangelical fathers had frequent one-on-one interaction with their children, while 46 percent of mainline and Catholic fathers had frequent one-on-one interaction. Only 39 percent of unaffiliated fathers had this level of interaction with their children.

Table 13.2
Paternal Involvement with Youth Activities (Coaching, PTA, Church Group, Scouts)

	Evangelical	Mainline	Catholic	No Affiliation
None	44%	48%	50%	65%
1+ hours	56%	52%	50%	35%

Similar differences are apparent in paternal involvement in youth activities (coaching, Parent Teacher Association, church group, Boy Scouts). As Table 13.2 indicates, 56 percent of evangelicals spent one hour a week or more leading some kind of youth activity. Although only 52 percent of mainline fathers fell into this category, it is important to note that mainline Protestants volunteered more time, on average, than did evangelical fathers. Fifty percent of Catholic fathers spent one hour a week or more leading youth activities, while only 35 percent of unaffiliated fathers did so. When it comes to youth activities, religious affiliation was powerfully linked to paternal involvement.

Table 13.3
Paternal Attendance at Family Dinner

	Evangelical	Mainline	Catholic	No Affiliation
Less than 7	51%	58%	44%	52%
Every night	49%	42%	56%	48%

Although Protestant fathers were more active in one-on-one and youth activities, Catholic fathers were more likely than other fathers to eat meals with their children, as demonstrated by Tables 13.3 and 13.4. Fifty-six percent of Catholic fathers had dinner with their children every night, and 22 percent of them had breakfast with their children every morning. Evangelical fathers were slightly more likely than unaffiliated fathers to have meals with their children, with 49 percent attending dinner daily and 19 percent attending breakfast daily. Mainline fathers, however, were less likely to eat with their children than were unaffiliated fathers (although this difference is not statistically significant). Forty-two percent of mainline fathers attended dinner daily compared to 48 percent of unaffiliated fathers; 16 percent of mainline fathers had breakfast daily with their children compared to 17 percent of unaffiliated fathers.

Table 13.4
Paternal Attendance at Family Breakfast

	Evangelical	Mainline	Catholic	No Affiliation
Less than 7	81%	84%	78%	83%
Each morning	19%	16%	22%	17%

My analysis of paternal involvement in child-care tasks (feeding, bathing, and dressing) associated with preschool children turned up no statistically significant differences between religious and unaffiliated fathers. This finding, when combined with the earlier finding that there were no religiously based differences in one-on-one interaction of preschool fathers, suggests that religious affiliation was more influential for fathers of school-age children than for fathers of preschool children.[30]

Paternal Style

I examined three aspects of fathers' style of interaction: expressions of affirmation (hugging and praising), disciplinary style (yelling and corporal punishment), and expectations of obedience. Once again, religious affiliation was related to distinctive conduct (and attitudes) among fathers. However, I also found stronger differences between religious traditions in this dimension of fatherhood. In particular, evangelical fathers were more likely to embrace an unusual style of parenting that combined acts of affirmation with a strict disciplinary orientation. Mainline and Catholic fathers, by contrast, were more likely to resemble their unaffiliated peers except that Catholics placed a high value on obedience and mainline Protestants were more affirming of their children.

Table 13.5
Paternal Expressions of Affirmation for School-Age Children
(hugging, praising)

	Evangelical	Mainline	Catholic	No Affiliation
Infrequent	8%	10%	13%	17%
Frequent	92%	90%	87%	83%

Although I discovered no religiously based differences in the level of affirmation demonstrated by fathers of preschoolers (who had almost uniformly high scores), my statistical tests indicated that evangelical and mainline Protestant fathers were significantly more likely to affirm their children than were Catholic and unaffiliated fathers (see Table 13.5). Here, "frequent" is defined as a score of three ("sometimes") or more on an affirmation scale (from one "never" to four "very often") that averages reports of praising and hugging. Ninety-two percent of evangelical fathers of school-age children and 90 percent of mainline fathers of school-age children had a frequent score, while Catholic and unaffiliated fathers were significantly less likely to affirm their school-age children, with, respectively, 87 and 83 percent of these fathers receiving a frequent score.

Table 13.6
Paternal Use of Corporal Punishment for School-Age Children
(spanking, slapping)

	Evangelical	Mainline	Catholic	No Affiliation
Infrequent	73%	84%	86%	85%
Frequent	27%	16%	14%	15%

I have found no significant differences between religiously affiliated fathers and unaffiliated fathers of preschool children regarding corporal punishment. However, evangelical fathers of school-age children were much more likely to spank or slap their children than other parents (see Table 13.6). Once again, "frequent" is defined as a score of three ("sometimes") or more on a scale from one ("never") to four ("very often"). Twenty-seven percent of evangelical fathers fell into this category while only about 15 percent of other religious groups and unaffiliated fathers used corporal punishment on a frequent basis.

Table 13.7
Paternal Use of Yelling for Preschool Children

	Evangelical	Mainline	Catholic	No Affiliation
Infrequent	65%	61%	53%	47%
Frequent	35%	39%	47%	53%

Although evangelical fathers were more likely to use corporal punishment than their peers were, they were less likely to yell at their children (see Tables 13.7 and 13.8). Relying once again on a score of three ("sometimes") or higher to denote "frequent" yelling, I found that evangelical and mainline Protestant fathers of preschool children were significantly less likely to yell at their children than Catholic and unaffiliated fathers. Here, 35 and 39 percent, respectively, of evangelical and mainline fathers yelled frequently at their preschool children compared to 47 and 53 percent, respectively, of Catholic and unaffiliated fathers.

Table 13.8
Paternal Use of Yelling for School-Age Children

	Evangelical	Mainline	Catholic	No Affiliation
Infrequent	53%	41%	47%	39%
Frequent	47%	59%	53%	61%

Evangelical and Catholic fathers of school-age children were significantly less likely to yell at their children than mainline and unaffiliated fathers. For this subsample, only 47 and 53 percent, respectively, of evangelical and Catholic fathers yelled at their children compared to 59 percent of mainline fathers and 61 percent of unaffiliated fathers.

To determine paternal valuations of obedience, I created a scale by combining attitudes to the following questions: "How important is it to you that your children always follow family rules?" and "How important is it to you that your children always do what you ask?" Respondents indicated their attitudes to these two questions by placing themselves on a scale of one ("not at all important") to seven ("extremely important"). I determined that fathers who averaged a score of six ("important") or higher across these two measures were fathers who considered obedience "important."

Table 13.9
Paternal Valuation of Obedience from Preschool Children

	Evangelical	Mainline	Catholic	No Affiliation
Less Important	25%	50%	42%	52%
Important	75%	50%	58%	48%

As Tables 13.9 and 13.10 indicate, evangelical and Catholic fathers were significantly more likely to value obedience from their children than mainline and unaffiliated fathers. For fathers of preschool children, 75 and 58 percent, respectively, of evangelical and Catholic fathers considered obedience important compared to 50 percent of mainline and 48 percent of unaffiliated fathers. More than 60 percent of evangelical and Catholic fathers of school-age children considered obedience important compared to 55 percent of unaffiliated fathers and 47 percent of mainline parents.

Table 13.10
Paternal Valuation of Obedience from School-Age Children

	Evangelical	Mainline	Catholic	No Affiliation
Less Important	36%	53%	37%	45%
Important	64%	47%	63%	55%

Religion and Fatherhood

The larger portrait of religion and fatherhood that emerges from this data analysis is as follows. Evangelical fathers, particularly those who have school-age children, were largely living up to the standards of the public story of fatherhood offered by evangelical churches, ministries, and leaders. They were consistently more likely than unaffiliated fathers (the largest subgroup of American fathers) to be involved in one-on-one activities, youth activities, and meals. They were also more likely to be affirming or expressive with their school-age children than Catholic and unaffiliated fathers were. In my view, these patterns suggest that the therapeutic turn evangelicalism took in the 1970s, combined with this subculture's vigorous advocacy of family life, has had a marked influence on evangelical fathering. In this respect, ironically enough, the subculture most known for its gender role traditionalism has produced men who seem to be strong candidates for new fatherhood.

But evangelical fathers also continued to be influenced by their Puritan heritage. They were much more likely than were other fathers to value obedience from their children and apply corporal punishment when they don't get that obedience. At the same time, in keeping with classically Protestant norms of restraint, evangelical fathers were significantly less likely to yell at their children than other fathers. In fact, their disciplinary style seems indebted to the advice of evangelical authors like James Dobson, who extolled the virtues of obedience and corporal punishment even as he counseled against yelling in his best-selling book *Dare to Discipline*, published in 1970.

Despite the paucity of explicit guidance on family life from their churches, mainline Protestant fathers were more involved and expressive than were unaffiliated fathers. Specifically, they were significantly more likely to be involved in one-on-one activities and youth activities than unaffiliated fathers. They were also significantly more likely to hug or praise their children than were unaffiliated fathers.

Since very little scholarship has been done on the role of religion in mainline families, I will hazard three explanations for these patterns of mainline fathering. First, because large numbers of mainline Protestants report that they attend church to experience a sense of community or to provide their children with a moral code to live by,[31] it may be that the type of fathers who attend mainline churches are, compared to unaffiliated fathers, simply more engaged parents and citizens. In other words, one of the factors driving the higher involvement of mainline fathers may be an underlying commitment to family and community among these men that propels them to be active both in their children's lives and their local churches.

Second, many mainline fathers hail from the middle and upper classes, which tend to take their cues from progressive parenting experts like Benjamin Spock who occupy a prominent position in the secular book market and popular media (*Dr. Spock's Baby and Child Care* [1985] has sold 40 million copies thus far).[32] If mainline fathers are indeed more engaged than unaffiliated fathers, they may be more likely to follow the advice found in these books, and the culture more generally, exhorting fathers to be active and expressive with their children. The influence of progressive parenting experts may also account for the fact that mainline fathers don't value obedience as much as evangelicals and Catholics.

Of course, it probably is the case that mainline churches do exert some kind of independent influence on the fathers who attend their services. The religious messages conveyed by sermons and the ethos of care and concern found in many mainline churches may implicitly promote an ethic of involved and expressive parenting even though an explicit familial message is lacking. In fact, churchgoing may lend additional strength to the ethic of familial and communal engagement that propelled these men into the pews in the first place.[33] All three of these factors, in all likelihood, account for the fact that mainline Protestant fathers were more active and expressive than were their unaffiliated peers.

Catholic fathers were more involved than unaffiliated fathers were, especially when it came to attendance at meals; they were also significantly more likely to value obedience from their children than were unaffiliated and mainline fathers. What accounts for these distinctive patterns given the fact that Catholics, like mainline Protestants, haven't experienced strong direction in family matters, at least at the parish level, in recent years? I suspect that one of the reasons that Catholic fathers are more involved with their children is that many of them share the underlying commitment to family and community that drives their mainline brethren. Thus, when compared to fathers who were raised Catholic but no longer attend church, these men may be more involved in civic, religious, *and* familial activities.

However, it is also important to note that the nature of Catholic involvement differs in some ways from Protestant fathering. While Catholic fathers are slightly less involved in one-on-one activities and youth activities, they are more likely to share daily meals with their children. The Catholic paternal presence at meals may be an outgrowth of the sacramental ethos, and the eucharistic focus of Catholic worship in particular, which has been and continues to be so integral to the Catholic tradition. It is also possible that the recent influx of Latin American, Central American, and Asian immigrants into Catholic churches is replenishing aspects of "ethnic Catholicism," including emphasis on family meals.[34]

The Catholic paternal emphasis on obedience is, in all likelihood, related to these two factors. Despite recent declines in hierarchical obedience in the American Catholic Church, the Church's traditional emphasis on obedience in the church and family may still have a hold on the imagination and the habits of the lay faithful—in this case, Catholic fathers. Here again, the influence of Hispanic and Asian cultures, which tend to stress the importance of obedience,[35] may also be contributing to the Catholic paternal valuation of obedience.

Gender Role Attitudes and Fatherhood

Although gender role attitudes did not influence as many aspects of fatherhood as did religious affiliation, they did have a discernible impact on a number of paternal practices and attitudes. In particular, gender role attitudes had contradictory effects on paternal involvement but consistent effects on the disciplinary practices and attitudes of fathers.

My research indicates gender role traditionalism was associated with lower paternal involvement in one-on-one activities. However, I also found that religious fathers were more involved with their kids even after controlling for the effects of gender role attitudes. Thus, even though religious fathers, especially evangelical ones, were more conservative than unaffiliated fathers, they were still more involved.

Although gender role attitudes were also related to paternal involvement in youth activities, this relationship is markedly different from the previous one. In this case, gender role traditionalism had a significant positive effect on paternal involvement. Once again, religious affiliation was positively related to paternal involvement, regardless of whether or not the effects of gender role attitudes were controlled for.

Surprisingly, gender role attitudes were not related to paternal involvement in child-care tasks associated with preschool children (feeding, bathing, and dressing). They were also unrelated to meal attendance and to involvement in one-on-one activities for fathers of preschool children. Thus, gender role attitudes exercised less influence on paternal involvement than did religious affiliation.

However, gender role traditionalism was strongly associated with higher rates of corporal punishment. For fathers of preschoolers, conservative gender role attitudes had a significant positive effect on the use of corporal punishment even though religious affiliation did not. For fathers of school-age children, conservative gender role attitudes also had a positive effect. Nevertheless, evangelical or mainline affiliation was positively associated with corporal punishment of school-age children regardless of whether or not the effects of gender role attitudes were controlled.

Gender role traditionalism was also related to higher paternal valuation of obedience. Conservative fathers of preschool children were much more likely to value obedience than liberal fathers. In this case, when the effects of gender role attitudes were controlled, the distinctive mainline valuation of obedience disappears (though evangelical and Catholic fathers maintained their distinctive status). This means that mainline fathers' higher valuation of obedience, compared to unaffiliated fathers, was largely a product of the fact that mainline fathers held slightly more conservative gender role attitudes than unaffiliated fathers.

Conservative fathers of school-age children were more likely to value obedience from their children than were liberal fathers. The positive effects of evangelical and Catholic affiliation remained even when the effects of gender role attitudes were controlled. With regard to paternal style, traditional gender role attitudes were related to a strong disciplinary orientation, such as a greater willingness to use corporal punishment and an expectation of obedience. However, gender role attitudes were not related to paternal rates of yelling or affirmation. Again the influence exercised by gender role attitudes was smaller than that of religious affiliation.

The *Real* New Fathers Are Religious

One of the ironies found in the literature on fatherhood is that the ideal of new fatherhood has, in many ways, not yet been borne out by marked changes in paternal practice. Although fathers who marry and stay married (a declining percentage of all fathers) have made some changes around the home, women still perform the lion's share of child care, housework, and emotional work associated with family life.[36] As Ralph LaRossa observes, "Yes, fatherhood has changed if one looks at the culture of fatherhood—the ideologies surrounding men's parenting. No, fatherhood has not changed (at least significantly), if one looks at the conduct of fatherhood—how fathers behave vis-a-vis their children."[37]

How can we account for this gap between the culture and conduct of fatherhood? This study implicitly suggests that one of the reasons the conduct of fatherhood has not substantially changed in the last three decades is that the culture of new fatherhood, for the most part, is not associated with institutions that have power over the conduct of family life. This conclusion is suggested by the first finding of this study: namely, that *religious affiliation, particularly an evangelical Protestant affiliation, was a much stronger predictor of fatherhood conduct than were gender role attitudes.*

When it comes to fathering, communities of faith appear to have a more dynamic impact on the domestic "habits of the heart," to borrow Tocqueville's phrase, than do gender role attitudes. Religious affiliation was positively related to three areas of paternal involvement—one-on-one activities, youth activities, and meal attendance. Gender role attitudes were only related to two areas (and their influence was contradictory). Looking beyond involvement, religious affiliation—particularly an evangelical affiliation—was associated with four aspects of father-child interaction (hugging and praising, yelling, corporal punishment, valuation of obedience), while gender role attitudes were only related to the latter two. The relationship between evangelical affiliation and fatherhood conduct was particularly striking since evangelical patterns of fatherhood—high levels of involvement, affirmation, and expectations of obedience combined with low levels of yelling—tracked so closely with the cultural cues offered by churches and leaders.

The powerful influence of religious affiliation can be attributed to the institutional power—moral authority, informal communal supports and sanctions, and ethos—churches can bring to bear on family life. By contrast, gender role attitudes—and the culture of new fatherhood more generally—are not connected to institutions that wield similar power over family life conduct. Thus, their influence on paternal conduct is constricted.

I turn now to the predictions that I posed at the beginning of this chapter: namely, (1) that men with progressive gender role attitudes are more involved and emotionally expressive with their children and (2) that religious men, particularly evangelicals, are less involved and expressive with their children. Both predictions proved false. With regard to my first prediction, progressive gender role attitudes were not consistently related to paternal involvement or an expressive style with children. In fact, my findings reinforce existing scholarship about the minimal influence of gender role attitudes on male involvement in family life. Scholars have found no consistent evidence that gender role attitudes are related to more involved or expressive fathering[38]; in the arena of household chores, the evidence is conflicted—some scholars have found evidence of a positive effect but others have not.[39] Ironically, then, fathers with progressive gender role attitudes are—for the most part—no more likely to conform to the ideal of new fatherhood than are other fathers. (However, this study indicates that gender role attitudes were related in conventional ways to paternal styles of discipline and authority in that conservative fathers were more likely to use corporal punishment on their children and to value obedience from them.)

What about my second prediction? As this chapter makes clear, religious fathers—especially evangelical ones—have more traditional gender role attitudes. But this religious traditionalism was not associated with consistent differences in involvement or expressive fathering. In fact, evangelical fathers, despite the fact that they were also more traditional, were as involved as other religious fathers were and more expressive than most fathers. (However, the gender role traditionalism of evangelicals and, to a lesser extent, Catholics was associated with higher rates of corporal punishment and expectations of obedience from children).

In sum, the second major finding offered by this study is that the *real* new fathers, to the extent that fathers are in fact moving in this direction, *are religious fathers, even ones—like evangelicals—who hold traditional gender role attitudes.* Given the strong relationship between religion and fatherhood, it will be interesting to see if movements like the Promise Keepers further solidify the relationship between religion and active and expressive fathering.

Notes

Portions of this chapter were adapted from W. Bradford Wilcox, "Religion and Fatherhood: Exploring the Links Between Religious Affiliation, Gender Role Attitudes, and Paternal Practices," working paper 13, Sociology Department of Princeton University, Princeton, N.J., 1997.

1. See Robert L. Griswold, *Fatherhood in America* (New York: Basic Books, 1993), 1-9, 185-210.

2. Arland Thornton, "Changing Attitudes Toward Family Issues in the United States," *Journal of Marriage and the Family* 51 (1989): 845-871.

3. I am thinking of groups like Focus on the Family, Promise Keepers, and Concerned Women for America.

4. I am referring here to the white, middle-class family that dominated the imagination and practice of most postwar Americans.

5. See Griswold, *Fatherhood in America*, 185-210; David Popenoe, *Life Without Father: Compelling New Evidence That Fatherhood and Marriage Are Indispensable for the Good of Children and Society* (New York: Free Press, 1996), 38-39, 126-134.

6. Thomas C. Reeves, *The Empty Church: The Suicide of Liberal Christianity* (New York: Free Press, 1996), 124.

7. For a discussion of Protestant churches and the family in the 1950s, see Penny Long Marler, "Lost in the Fifties: The Changing Family and the Nostalgic Church" in *Work, Family, and Religion in Contemporary Society*, ed. Nancy Tatom Ammerman and Wade Clark Roof (New York: Routledge, 1993), 33. For a similar overview of the Catholic Church in this period, see Christine Firer Hinze, "Catholic: Family Unity and Diversity within the Body of Christ," in *Faith Traditions and the Family*, ed. Phyllis D. Airhart and Margaret Lamberts Bendroth (Louisville, Ky.: Westminster John Knox Press, 1996), 59.

8. For overviews of changes in the American family since World War II, see Andrew J. Cherlin, *Marriage, Divorce, Remarriage*, rev. ed.; and Daphne Spain and Suzanne M. Bianchi, *Balancing Act: Motherhood, Marriage, and Employment Among American Women* (New York: Russell Sage Foundation, 1996).

9. See Daniel Yankelovich, *The New Morality* (New York: McGraw-Hill, 1974).

10. See Katherine Gerson, *No Man's Land: Men's Changing Commitments to Family and Work* (New York: Basic Books, 1993); and Barbara Ehrenreich, *The Hearts of Men: American Dreams and the Flight from Commitment* (New York: Anchor Books, 1983), 117-143.

11. See Griswold, *Fatherhood in America*, 245-252; and Steven Brint, *In an Age of Experts: The Changing Role of Professionals in Politics and Public Life* (Princeton: Princeton University Press, 1994), 81-103.

12. Because my sample size was not large enough, I did not perform independent analyses on black Protestants, Jews, and members of other religious traditions. Thus, African Americans who did not identify with mainline Protestant or Catholic churches were subsumed under the evangelical category because black Protestant churches generally have theological beliefs and cultural values that parallel those

found in evangelical churches. Fathers from the other dominant religious traditions in America—primarily Mormonism and Judaism—were dropped from my analyses because they could not be easily associated with the three largest religious traditions.

13. See James Davison Hunter, *Evangelicalism: The Coming Generation* (Chicago: University of Chicago Press, 1987), 76-83.

14. Dan Benson cited in Hunter, *Evangelicalism*, 79.

15. There are resurgent conservative movements among mainline Protestants and Catholics that stress support for the "traditional family." This conservatism is particularly strong among some Catholics, who have been inspired by Pope John Paul II's commitment to the traditional family. Nevertheless, religious conservatives currently constitute a minority in both communities.

16. See Phyllis D. Airhart and Margaret Lamberts Bendroth, "Introduction: Churches and Families in North American Society," in *Faith Traditions and the Family*, 3.

17. See Don S. Browning, "Religion and Family Ethics: A New Strategy for the Church," in *Work, Family, and Religion in Contemporary Society*, 158.

18. Browning, "Religion and Family Ethics," 159.

19. Wade Clark Roof and William McKinley, *American Mainline Religion* (New Brunswick, N.J.: American Mainline Religion, 1987), 106-117, 227.

20. Browning, "Religion and Family Ethics," 158.

21. Gierhard Lenski, *The Religious Factor* (New York: Doubleday, 1963).

22. Duane Alwin, "Religion and Parental Child-Rearing Orientations: Evidence of a Catholic-Protestant Convergence," *American Journal of Sociology* 92 (1986): 412-440.

23. Richard D. Alba, "The Twilight of Ethnicity among American Catholics of European Origin," *Annals of the American Academy of Political and Social Science* 454 (1981): 86-97.

24. William V. D'Antonio and Mark J. Cavanaugh, "Roman Catholicism and the Family," in *Families and Religions: Conflict and Change in Modern Societies*, ed. William V. D'Antonio and Joan Aldous (Beverly Hills, Calif.: Sage Publications, 1983), 141-162; and Andrew W. Greeley, *The American Catholic* (New York: Basic Books, 1977).

25. Andrew W. Greeley, *The Catholic Myth: The Behavior and Beliefs of American Catholics* (New York: Scribner, 1990).

26. The principal exception to this claim is Marriage Encounter, a ministry dedicated to marital enrichment.

27. All tables and analyses reported in this chapter are based on statistical analyses conducted on the National Survey of Families and Households.

28. See Hunter, *Evangelicalism*, 93-106.

29. Only statistically significant results are reported in this chapter.

30. An alternative explanation is that I did not detect the religious effect among fathers of preschool children because the sample size for this group was substantially smaller (419 fathers) than the sample size for fathers of school-age children (2,924 fathers).

31. Dean R. Hoge, Benton Johnson, and Donald A. Luidens, *Vanishing Boundaries: The Religion of Mainline Protestant Baby Boomers* (Louisville, Ky.: Westminster John Knox Press), 109.

32. Sharon Hays, *The Cultural Contradictions of Motherhood* (New Haven: Yale University Press, 1996), 51.

33. For evidence that churchgoing is related to volunteerism, see John Wilson and Marc Musick, "Who Cares: Toward an Integrated Theory of Volunteer Work," *American Sociological Review* 62 (1997): 694-713.

34. For a discussion of the familial norms and values associated with Latino and Asian American families, see Bryan Strong and Christine De Vault, *The Marriage and Family Experience*, 6th ed. (St. Paul, Minn.: West Publishing Company, 1995), 620-621.

35. Strong and De Vault, *The Marriage and Family Experience*.

36. See Arlie Hochschild and Anne Machung, *The Second Shift* (New York: Avon Books, 1989); and Michael E. Lamb, Joseph H. Pleck, and James A. Levine, "Effects of Increased Paternal Involvement on Fathers and Mothers," in *Reassessing Fatherhood: New Observations on Fathers and the Modern Family*, ed. Charlie L. Lewis and Margaret O'Brien (London: Sage Publications, 1987), 109-125.

37. Ralph LaRossa, "Fatherhood and Social Change," *Family Relations* 37 (October 1988): 451.

38. William Marsiglio, "Paternal Engagement Activities with Minor Children," *Journal of Marriage and the Family* 53 (1991): 973-986.

39. See, for instance, Rosalind C. Barnett and Grace K. Baruch, "Determinants of Fathers' Participation in Family Work," *Journal of Marriage and the Family* 49 (1987): 29-40; and Theodore Greenstein, "Husbands' Participation in Domestic Labor: Interactive Effects of Wives' and Husbands' Gender Ideologies," *Journal of Marriage and the Family* 58 (1996): 585-595.

Chapter 14

Men as Promise Makers and Keepers

Bill McCartney

America is suffering from a severe shortage of integrity, and men are behind some of its worst manifestations. Men are more likely than women to break their marriage vows through adultery, violence, or abandonment. Men are impregnating young women in record numbers and leaving them to deal with the consequences—a stint on welfare, an education cut short, or a trip to an abortion clinic. Men are also more likely to abuse drugs and alcohol and then engage in a wide range of criminal behavior. Indeed, it is men, overwhelmingly, who commit most of the nation's violent crimes and dominate its prison system: At least 94 percent of all inmates are male.

Social problems are moral problems, which ultimately have a spiritual cause. For those of us involved in Christian outreach programs, the connection is inescapable: The failure of large numbers of men to live up to their family and social obligations represents a failure of faith.

More to the point, the growing irresponsibility of men points, in large part, to a failure in our Christian churches. Men are much less likely than women to set foot in a church, less likely to say they are absolutely committed to Jesus Christ, less likely to read the Bible during the week or strongly affirm the role of religious faith in their lives. Many—perhaps most—men see church mainly as a place for women and children. A similar separation of men from religious life is found in non-Christian communities as well. Uninspired by any religious vision for their lives, more and more men are becoming disconnected from any moral vision.

All of this is taking a tremendous toll on our culture. The absence of responsible men from the home is now widely regarded as the most important cause of America's social decline. If America is truly in the throes of cultural breakdown, then the shallow faith of so many men, and the kind of behavior that follows from it, has contributed to this breakdown.

The Need of the Hour

But here is where many feminists and others who scorn traditional virtue have it wrong: If men are a principal cause of family meltdown, crime, and racial strife, then men also are central to the solutions to those problems. What America desperately needs today is men who take responsibility for their actions, who are faithful to their families, and who keep their word, even when it's difficult or costly.

America is crying out for a generation of "promise keepers." Five years ago, when I was still the head football coach at the University of Colorado, I realized that too many men were getting their priorities out of alignment. I'd seen too many men who called themselves Christians and attended church, but had little idea what it meant to live out a Christian ethic, either on the playing field or in their homes. To be honest, I watched my own family suffer as I poured myself into my career. I rationalized my workaholism, of course, but in reality I was abandoning my most basic responsibilities. Family members and friends finally helped me to see that, in essence, I had been directing my own life without reference to God. Because I failed so miserably, I've been able to see that many men today are doing exactly the same thing I did.

I resigned my coaching position in order to help bring together men who were interested in succeeding in the most important areas of their lives: their personal relationships with Almighty God, their wives, and their children. Just over 4,000 men met in 1991 at the Coors Event Center in Boulder, Colorado, for the first conference of our new organization, Promise Keepers. It was not a gathering of angry white males or an exercise in chest-beating or in lifting male self-esteem. This was about men taking stock of their moral and spiritual inventory. We asked men to publicly proclaim their love and allegiance to Jesus Christ and their commitment to their families. Since then, more than two million men have attended conferences in which they are challenged to make, and keep, a series of promises to honor God, to remain faithful to their spouses, and to support their churches.

Now we have taken Promise Keepers a step further. We called on men to come to Washington, D.C., for a day of heartfelt confession and prayer. Men from all over the country gathered not for any political cause, but for the purpose of being honest with each other and, most important, with God himself, about our shortcomings. We saw God spark personal renewal in the lives of tens of thousands of men, the kind of spiritual commitment that radically changes attitudes and everyday decisions.

Why Washington, D.C., and why now?

The nation's capital has historically served as the geographical soul of America, the place where national tragedies are mourned, where victories are celebrated, where protests are most keenly felt, and where the nation's attention turns in times of crisis. Many believe we are in such a crisis. Many Christian leaders correctly see the crisis not only *out there* in the larger culture, but *right here*, inside the church. That's why, despite what our critics claim, we aren't interested in political agendas; politics simply can't touch issues of the heart.

Prayer can reach the heart, for it involves communicating with our Creator. It means bowing down before Almighty God. For Christians, humble prayer unlocks the door to a personal, life-transforming relationship with Christ. It is perhaps the most important tool for moral and spiritual rebirth. And so, what better place to spark such renewal, to help address our national ills, than in the symbolic heart of the nation?

Signs of the Times

In the game of football, if your team is getting trounced, you'd better have a serious talk with the men at halftime and identify the problems. There is plenty of blame to go around to explain the ills afflicting America, but the decline in responsible manhood is surely one of the worst culprits.

Could it have anything to do with the fact that fathers are less and less likely to live with their sons? In one generation, the proportion of children entering a broken family has more than quadrupled. Patrick Fagan of the Heritage Foundation, using data from the National Center for Health Statistics, calculates that in 1950 about 12 out of 100 kids entered a family torn by divorce or illegitimacy; last year the number was 58 out of 100. More children are growing up without fathers than at any time in our nation's history. And though many women are courageously raising children on their own, kids—especially young boys—need the firm guidance of a loving father.

Why have crimes against American women—assault, rape, spousal abuse—hit new highs among the industrialized West? Is it a coincidence that America leads the world as a peddler of pornography? According to *U.S. News & World Report*, the number of hard-core pornographic video rentals rose from 75 million in 1985 to 665 million in 1996. Last year, the money that Americans (mostly men) spent viewing hard-core videos, peep shows, live sex acts, adult cable programming, computer porn, sex magazines, and the like exceeded all of Hollywood's domestic box-office receipts. Any clearheaded man can tell you: The more that men are exposed to images of women as objects created only to satisfy their needs, the more likely they are to treat women in exactly that way.

In a breathtaking range of categories, America ranks as a leader in vice. "If God withholds judgment from America," Billy Graham said, "he will owe Sodom and Gomorrah an apology." Graham echoes the warning of founding father Thomas Jefferson: "Indeed, I tremble for my country when I reflect that God is just, and that his justice cannot sleep forever."

A Weakened Church

One of the most important reasons for America's declining morals is the lack of powerful restraints on people's worst impulses. In my view, every society needs the restraint of the people of God, who act as bulwarks against their own and others' ill-informed and destructive choices, like offensive linemen protecting the quarterback. People attuned to God are the ones most likely to discourage evil, to argue for moral reform, and to perform heroic acts of kindness. Russell Kirk put it this way: "Without Christian culture and Christian hope, the modern world would come to resemble a half-derelict fun fair, gone nasty and poverty-racked—one enormous Atlantic City."

Yet today the church in America is grievously compromised. In a 1991 poll conducted by George Barna, 25 percent of regular church attendees admitted that their Christian beliefs made no significant difference in their lives. The problem is especially acute among men: Barna found that men are half as likely as women are to attend a church during any given week. Men are also 33 percent less likely to say they are religious and to claim they are absolutely committed to their faith.

Pollster George Gallup reports that, while almost half of Americans attend church services, only 6 to 10 percent are what he terms "highly spiritually committed." Gallup's research has compared behavior of churched and unchurched people in a variety of categories: people who call in sick when they are not, pad their resumes, cheat on tax deductions, and so on. His research has found little difference in the ethical views and behavior of the churched and the unchurched.

How can this be? Despite evidence of interest in religion at the popular level (books about angels, the growth of "psychic hotlines"), people seem to be looking for support, not salvation; help, rather than holiness; a circle of spiritual equals, rather than an authoritative church or guide. Too many churches are pandering to this trend.

One of the major functions of the local church should be to help Christians continuously deepen their devotion to God, to become more like Christ. That means facing up to personal failures, shedding selfish attitudes, and exchanging destructive habits for healthy ones. In countless practical ways, Christian faith ought to affect how men resolve conflicts, control their tempers, juggle work and family responsibilities, and discipline their children. Without such devotion, there is little reason to expect most men to make good choices most of the time.

How can we recover a healthy fear of God in our lives, our churches, and our communities? How can people of faith reemerge as a powerful, nearly irresistible force for good in our society? It will not happen without prayer: prayer for repentance, reconciliation, and renewal.

The failure of men to live out their responsibilities as husbands and fathers reflects a profound failure in the American church. The church must teach and practice biblical repentance, reconciliation, and renewal.

Biblical repentance means taking personal responsibility for our actions, admitting to God where we've gone out of bounds, and asking for his forgiveness and for the strength to change course. Reconciliation means taking whatever steps necessary to repair relationships that we've helped to damage. Renewal involves pledging our best efforts to honor God and meet our God-given responsibilities in our families and communities.

This is what our sacred assembly in Washington aimed to bring about. We spent most of the day in prayer, worship, and confession. Pastors and other Christian leaders spoke about these subjects. Men were challenged to admit their failings and sins not only to God but also to one another. The adage "confession is good for the soul" is much more than a religious platitude. It is an affirmation that there is a spiritual dimension to life and that when we neglect our spiritual lives, we damage our own souls.

A New Game Plan

We realize that conferences might produce a lot of heat, but not much light. As a former coach, I know it's not enough simply to get men worked up in the locker room about winning a ball game. They need a game plan.

That's why Promise Keepers, since its founding, has worked closely with local churches, which are still the key to revitalizing men's commitment to spiritual growth. Promise Keepers has three roles, all of which we believe will strengthen local congregations: First, we use stadium conferences to challenge men to rededicate their lives to Christ, through biblical teaching, worship, and the Seven Promises of a Promise Keeper (see chapter's end). Thousands of men have made decisions to follow Christ that have profoundly and positively changed the way they regard their family responsibilities.

Second, we offer pastors the tools to challenge men to grow in their faith and in their ability to live out the promises they make to their wives, children, and churches. When it comes to influencing men through our congregations, the role of spiritual leaders is absolutely crucial; yet while men are catching the vision at the conferences, few churches have established men's ministries that are prepared to help them live out that vision. We distribute study materials aimed at men that can be used both in the pulpit and in group discussions.

Finally, we want to see men become significantly involved in serving people in their congregations and in their local communities. From a biblical standpoint, serving others must involve real sacrifice: At a recent conference in Washington, D.C., for example, we mobilized 1,500 men to help clean and repair 47 dilapidated school buildings. On October 3, 1997 approximately 5,000 men went to 90 D.C. schools and did the same thing, all as unpaid volunteers.

Behind our goals is an assumption that one of the ways to help people make real life changes is through relationships. This is why churches are so important: They offer numerous opportunities for men to build friendships with other men, especially in the context of small groups. Whether task-oriented (fixing a church member's car or mowing the lawn for a single mom) or study-oriented (poring over a passage of Scripture), small groups allow men to get involved in each other's lives.

How does that make a difference? Only in the context of meaningful friendships can men hold one another accountable for their behavior, seek advice about their marriages or careers, and be candid about the struggles they're facing. The authors of the Bible understood this when they wrote that "plans fail for lack of counsel, but with many advisors they succeed" and that "as iron sharpens iron, so one man sharpens another" (Proverbs 15:22; 27:17).

In our best moments, we want to do the right thing, but often we don't. If men are regularly getting together as friends, with a common Christian commitment, then they'll be asking each other some tough questions about their behavior: Who was that woman you were having dinner with the other night? How are you handling the temptation to pad your expense account at work? The men could lie, of course. But the better a man knows his friend, the easier it is to sense when he's fudging the truth.

Men and Manhood

Many have asked us, why only men? Won't another men's-only club just worsen the relationship between the sexes?

There's no doubt that when men are simply left to themselves, whether roving in gangs or gathering in locker rooms, they often are trouble waiting to happen. That's exactly what our conferences are not about.

Men can meet and work together for positive purposes, whether it's fixing up schools or coaching Little League baseball. And when they do so to establish or deepen their relationship to Christ, something extraordinary happens. It's a dynamic that is hard to describe, but our events seem to reach a level of lasting honesty, vulnerability, and commitment. Our conferences and the friendships that grow out of them help to create a healthy pressure among men to do the right thing. It's a sense that we're in this thing—this journey of faith and commitment to God and our families—together. When I talk to men about the impact of the conferences on their lives, this is one of the first things they tell me.

I've worked closely with hundreds of men over the years, and at least one common denominator stands out: Men are eager to make and keep promises; they want to be challenged to "be all they can be"—that is, to adopt a thoroughly Christian vision for their lives. Promise Keepers is about helping men see a picture, giving them concrete goals and helping them move toward those goals, whether that's spending more time with their children, honoring their word to their wives, or owning up to failure on the job. It is about becoming men of integrity, because integrity is impossible without keeping promises.

There's another reason to bring men together for training and encouragement. We live in a society that is, almost daily it seems, redefining manhood. That men are carrying more responsibility in childrearing is a great step; it is one of the most important ways that men can demonstrate their love for their families. But it's not the whole story of what it means to be a husband and father.

From a Christian perspective, men have a unique, God-given responsibility for the spiritual health of their families. Some suspect that in emphasizing this leadership role for men, we seek to put women down or turn back the clock on women's recent gains. On the contrary, by challenging men to take their faith seriously, we think they will work harder at nurturing their wives and children and helping them fulfill their own God-given potential.

Whenever the Bible discusses the issue of male leadership, for example, it is always for the purpose of serving and sacrificing for others—for the family, the church, and the world. To read the teachings of Christ and the apostles in any other way is to distort the Scriptures. Period. Ironically, it is men's masculine qualities, their willingness to provide for and protect their families, for example, or their ability to draw strong boundaries for their children, that seem to be in greatest demand by women today. And so one of the specific promises of a Promise Keeper is to support his family through love, protection, and biblical values.

We realize that many people, even those sympathetic with our goals, remain suspicious about Promise Keepers' challenge to men. Let me suggest that much of this skepticism is a result of some lousy examples of men, even supposedly religious men, who manipulate and exploit the women around them. No woman wants—nor should want—to love and support a husband who acts like a predator or a tyrant. Those who remain skeptical ought to ask the wives and children of men who attend our conferences if they resent or are troubled by their husbands' determination to follow Christ. He is, after all, our supreme model for manhood.

On October 4, 1997, men from around the nation and from other countries assembled on the Mall in Washington, D.C., in a national sacred assembly. There are great precedents for such a gathering. Spiritual assemblies such as these played an important role in some of America's greatest spiritual awakenings—which always led both to transformed lives and to significant moral reform.

During the early nineteenth century, for example, tens of thousands of men and women converted to Christianity in revival campaigns that became known as the Second Great Awakening. The movement began in England and had its roots in a Call to Prayer issued by pastors in Northamptonshire in 1784. The flame of revival eventually spread to America, where it shaped the course of the great national debate on abolition. Large numbers of new converts, determined to follow Christ wholeheartedly, freed their slaves. Many began to preach publicly against slavery. Others helped with the Underground Railroad, which shuttled slaves to freedom in the North.

We sense that America faces a cultural crisis as potentially destructive as that facing the nation in the era of slavery. That's why we called the October 4 event "Stand in the Gap: A Sacred Assembly of Men." The name is taken from the prophet Ezekiel's plaintive cry for his own people to return to God. In Ezekiel's day, the people of Israel had wandered far from God, their first love. The result for Israel was national disaster: military defeat from without, moral rot from within. Ezekiel despairs that no one is willing to come forward to climb the literal breach in Jerusalem's walls and act as a human rampart against the evils of his day. In Ezekiel 22:30, God tells the nation: "I looked for a man among them who would build up the wall and stand before me in the gap on behalf of the land so I would not have to destroy it, but I found none."

We believe that God is again looking for a few good men who desire to honor him in every area of their lives. In so doing, such men will refuse to abandon their wives during the tough times; they will balance their obligations at work with those at home; they'll gladly lose sleep to calm a child who hears ghosts under the bed. Today, more than ever, America needs men like these, men who will "stand in the gap" and stand against a culture that mocks commitment, sacrifice, and virtue. A multitude of such men gathered in our capital. We pray that God will use them to stand in the gap for our nation.

Seven Promises of a Promise Keeper

A Promise Keeper is committed to:

- Honor Jesus Christ through worship, prayer, and obedience to God's Word through the power of the Holy Spirit.
- Pursue vital relationships with a few other men, understanding that he needs brothers to help him keep his promises.
- Practice spiritual, moral, ethical, and sexual purity.
- Build strong marriages and families through love, protection, and biblical values.
- Support the mission of his church by honoring and praying for his pastor and by actively giving his time and resources.
- Reach beyond any racial and denominational barriers to demonstrate the power of biblical unity.
- Influence his world, being obedient to the Great Commandment (Mark 12:30-31) and the Great Commission (Matthew 28:19-20).

Chapter 15

Restoring Civil Society Through Fatherhood

Don E. Eberly

The emerging movement to renew fatherhood in America takes place against the backdrop of a society caught in an anxious mood over the general well-being of its basic cultural and political institutions. To an astonishing degree, American citizens and their leaders, across the political spectrum, have arrived at a consensus that the weakening of American society is indeed serious and portends a potentially devastating erosion of social cohesion and democratic health. Much of the anxiety in this country has to do with the condition of the culture; there is a generalized sense that the fabric of our communities is weakening and that our institutions, public and private, are burdened with seemingly intractable problems and pressures. In a few short years, public attention has shifted markedly from economic recession to social regression. Social regression reflects a real decline in the health of our social institutions, especially the family, a weakening of citizenship, and an erosion of the psychological and spiritual strength that citizens must possess in order to sustain a free society.

Americans Want a Healthier Society

Public opinion polls reveal a sense of loss, and even anger, over what has happened to our families, communities, and spiritual values. Americans today are deeply concerned about the need to recover a healthier, lovelier society. In important ways, America's social debate has itself begun to reflect the seriousness of our condition. For example, faced with convincing evidence of societal disorder, many now recognize the need to curb the hyper-individualism that has come to dominate our culture.

The ideology of autonomy cripples our capacity to renew society, reducing every decision to a matter of private, personal choice. In its shadow, communities possess almost no claim on the individual and hence have virtually no voice. Vying to replace this excessive individualism is a new ethos emphasizing what was once called the common good, which entails curbing the impulse toward self-interest and seeking the welfare of others, especially the welfare of children. This shift portends improved prospects for renewing community, for increasing social cooperation, and for coalescing around a common moral and civic vision.

The public debate over fatherhood also appears to have matured well beyond infancy. For many years, the fatherlessness debate was regarded by many as more polarizing than constructive. Some observers worried that fathers were being used as a handy ideological club to score points in a broader cultural debate, however sincere father advocates might actually have been. Though still occasionally rancorous, the question of fatherhood's preeminence in society, and the inescapable importance of fathers, seems to be settled within mainstream debate. As evidenced by both party conventions in 1996, whatever else the notion of family presently means for the political left or right, its irreducible components now include parents, preferably both, committed passionately to the care and nurturance of their children. Surely, conflicting visions of fatherhood and the family will continue to generate important debate, especially over public policies, but one now senses we are debating means, not ends.

The proposition that attracts almost no opposition from policy or social science experts is that family fragmentation and fatherlessness are the chief contributors to many forms of maladjustment among children. The scale and consequences of father absence are now routinely cited by scholars and commentators as a prime explanation for numerous negative outcomes among children. The maturation of this debate has enabled us to pinpoint and to acknowledge the relationship of father absence to specific pathologies in society, such as crime, drugs and teen pregnancy. What we have not captured, however, is the contribution fathers make in nurturing children. Social well-being as measured by such things as trust, cooperation, and social generosity among citizens are conditions commonly discussed in connection with civil society. What relevance does fatherhood have to these equally important, though less quantifiable social conditions?

Fatherhood Is Essential to Society

To what extent, in other words, is the restoration of committed fatherhood integral to the renewal of American civil society? The restoration of fatherhood is essential—in the context of declining civil society. It is central, and it is causal. Assumptions regarding cause and effect will differ, of course. One must accept that social outcomes have multiple explanations, especially in a society as complex as ours.

These differences should be acknowledged and respected. Still, acknowledging differences of assumption need not prevent us from drawing certain elementary conclusions. The basic proposition set forth in this chapter is as follows: The decline in fathering, whether through the growing prevalence of physical absence or merely emotional disengagement by fathers, contributes to socially underdeveloped citizens who often lack the necessary disposition for healthy participation in society. Fathers can be powerfully positive in making better citizens. In short, there can be no healthy democracy without dads.

Whatever role the reform of policy and economic structures may have in restoring fatherhood, these reforms are unlikely, by themselves, to produce more than modest change at the margins of the problem. The work of renewing fatherhood offers a role for everyone, policy makers included, but the primary responsibility will very likely fall to precisely the kind of sociocultural movement that is the subject of this volume.

Social Capital Creates Democratic Habits

Democracy, we are frequently reminded, is an "experiment." The continued use of the term experiment after over two centuries of practical success implies persistent doubts over democracy's basic durability. Those who supplied the philosophical foundations of American democracy assumed that our basic republican system was fragile because mankind is morally frail, and that it was thus, as Madison put it, "chimerical" to assume it would endure without a rich supply of virtue. Public well-being flowed from the private wellspring of virtue. In our system of government, whether one prefers a lot more or a lot less of it, much responsibility is left to individual citizens to maintain communities that are safe, civil, and humane. Liberal democracy cannot survive without a large endowment of human capital and individual competence. From the beginning, the framers of the American democratic experiment presupposed the existence of individuals possessing democratic habits and dispositions.

Much of the analysis of democratic disorder in America centers on process flaws, not on our failure as a society to maintain positive democratic habits. In our public conversation, we frequently speak the language of the technical and procedural aspects of public life: the language of lawmaking, elections, appropriations, and fiscal projections. There is such a thing as democratic character, and it flows not from formal constitutions and congressional acts, but from vital, character-shaping institutions in society. According to Mary Ann Glendon, professor at Harvard, "Governments must have an adequate supply of citizens who are skilled in the arts of self-government." According to Glendon, these arts consist of "deliberation, compromise, consensus-building, civility [and] reason-giving."[1]

Free people need written constitutions and representative institutions, of course, but they also need unwritten social bonds that make the work of deliberation and compromise in democracy possible. Countries that are moving successfully toward democracy, such as the recently liberated nations of Eastern Europe, are also recognizing the need to rebuild the social institutions that supply democratic habits and skills. Because many of these fledgling democracies have badly weakened institutions of civil society, they are being crippled by a range of social diseases, from pervasive public corruption and crime to private greed and distrust among citizens.

The most insightful observer of American democracy, Alexis de Tocqueville, was careful to draw this important connection between societal health and democratic functioning. Strong civic institutions, he said, were essential to democracy: "[F]eelings and opinions are recruited, the heart is enlarged, and the human mind is developed only by the reciprocal influence of men upon one another" through voluntary associations.[2]

Recent research by Robert Putnam of Harvard University and Francis Fukuyama of the Rand Corporation points to the unbreakable link that exists between strong social institutions and the healthy functioning of both democratic government and the market economy. Putnam, whose research focused on the relationship of regional governments in Italy to robust civic life, found that democratic government was far more effective when surrounded by strong civic communities.

Citizens in civic community, Putnam said, "are helpful, respectful and trustful toward one another." In effect, they take upon themselves much of the work of democratic deliberation and consensus-building. Individuals in civic community are bound together, not by rigidly enforced rules or "vertical relations of authority and dependency," says Putnam, but by "horizontal relations of reciprocity and cooperation."[3]

Francis Fukuyama has looked at the role that trust and collaboration now play in empowering individuals to compete in a rapidly changing, interconnected global marketplace. Economic life, he says, is maintained on "moral bonds of social trust," which he describes as an "unspoken, unwritten bond between fellow citizens that facilitates transactions, empowers individual creativity, and justifies collective action."[4] Fukuyama concludes that societies with strong bonds of social trust and collaboration will increasingly gain important advantages over those characterized by individual isolation and social fragmentation.

The success of capitalism, as we are beginning to discover, depends on a rich supply of social capital, consisting of knowledge, aptitude, skills, and positive habits. This is even more true in a post-industrial age where softer forms of human capital become dramatically more important than hard capital assets such as factories, tools, and machines. Tragically, at the very time when individuals need plentiful social capital in order to compete in an unregulated, rapidly changing, global information society, that capital has been severely depleted.

A nation's reserves of social capital, like its stock of more tangible and measurable economic capital, can be drawn down. The common phrase "living on borrowed capital" speaks to the failure of one generation to renew and pass on the social endowments it inherited. The result is a decline in what Fukuyama calls "spontaneous sociability," rooted in the loss of social trust, all of which portends worrisome consequences for a democratic society.

At a time of social disintegration, greater care must be given to understanding how human development takes place and what is required for individuals to flourish and function in society. The good society requires good institutions, starting with good fathers, pursuing good ends. James Coleman, who popularized the term "social capital," utilized the phrase to describe a range of personal strengths that are cultivated in the family, especially the ability to form ties of cooperation and to work toward common purposes.[5]

The capacity to collaborate in trustful and helpful ways with one's associates is clearly affected by patterns of trust and interdependency learned in families. It is fathers who cultivate a spirit of reasonableness and compromise, a capacity to trust and be trustworthy, a willingness to be helpful and empathetic, and a capacity to act with self-restraint and respect toward others. Responsible fathers, engaged first of all with their families, provide a model of the virtues necessary for good citizenship.

In sum, liberal democratic values flower when rooted in the subsoil of virtuous and vibrant institutions. Functioning families and communities are able to subordinate individual interests to the concerns and needs of the larger group.

Fathers Foster Trust in Society

The central task of a democracy, in view of the above, is for older generations to devote themselves to socializing infants into adults, a process which transforms self-interested private individuals into public-spirited citizens. Democracy is heavily dependent for its success upon those institutions that socialize infants into adult citizens. What concerns us, then, is the unique socializing role fathers have been assigned in the social order. Is it possible that the maintenance of our democratic regime falls largely to families, and perhaps in some unique way to fathers? Tocqueville thought so. He observed that the basic democratic prerequisites—the "habits of the heart," as he put it—would be nourished and transmitted from generation to generation through the family. The private voluntary associations, so strongly favored by Tocqueville, played a critical but secondary role in his analysis to the more central role of the family.

For years we have seen that large majorities are distrustful of their public institutions. Now we have discovered the unsurprising fact that American citizens are more and more distrustful and suspicious of each other. Contrary to convenient myth, our discontents are not confined to governmental malfeasance and feckless politicians. A more likely source of our cynicism is the rupture of our primary relationships within the family, of our marriages, and our fellowship with our fathers. Disillusionment with our primary relationships leads to distrust of kin and community.

As inherently social and meaning-seeking creatures, human beings possess a need for membership in human community, for connection, and for coherence. When these needs are not met, society atrophies and individuals experience painful isolation. Tocqueville captured this when he said: "Without ideas in common, there is no common action. There may still exist human beings, but not a social entity. In order for society to exist and, even more, to prosper, it is necessary that the spirits of all citizens be assembled and held together by certain leading ideas."[6]

When the social norms that bind people together weaken, people feel an acute sense of unease—what Emile Durkheim called "anomie." While there are other causes of America's anomie, namely, the fast pace of life and the danger of being assaulted in public places, the principal culprit in the erosion of trust is the declining reliability of a growing number of parents to preserve the bonds of trust with their own children. Since most absent parents are men, we are referring primarily to fathers.

Trust is nurtured in the family. In bonding to the child, the parent puts in place the rudiments of trust: a process which, according to Urie Bronfenbrenner, conveys "a strong, mutual, irrational, emotional attachment" offered through a person who is "committed to the child's well-being and development, preferably for life."[7] Who can doubt that a child will be less trusting and cooperative as an adult if he has experienced a painful loss of trust in the person in whom he thought he could surely place his trust, his own father. Sadly, for many children this betrayal occurs not once, but several times during childhood.

By the time an adolescent develops impressions of the institutions beyond the home, he or she has already developed attitudes based upon relationships that exist in the home. If the child's experience of adults and the exercise of authority in the home was positive, attitudes about authority in the broader society are likely to be positive. If adults in the home were caring, fair, and faithful under all circumstances, then that is what the child will likely expect beyond the home.

Conversely, if the experience the child had of home was one of abuse, neglect, or betrayal, the projection of attitudes of cynicism and distrust toward the broader society is not surprising. It is hard to imagine attitudes of general trust taking shape toward more remote political and social institutions when a child is abandoned or betrayed by a mother or father.

Fathers Are the Bearers of Outside Norms

Fathers are the first encounter kids have with male authority, and perhaps authority generally. How interaction with that intimate form of authority takes shape will likely determine the child's success at navigating his or her way through the more challenging territory of authority and conflict in the school, on the playground, or at the mall. In many ways, healthy fathers serve as a bridge between the more protected life of the home and the more demanding environment of the world beyond. Fathers raise their children mostly with an eye toward their inevitable encounter with the rules and norms of the world beyond the nest. Good fathers tutor their children toward developing positive habits of self-control and respect toward others.

Committed fathers perform other important functions in the socialization of children. Wade Horn, president of the National Fatherhood Initiative and child psychologist, points out that proper socialization requires the development of the ability to delay or inhibit impulse gratification. According to Horn, "Well-socialized children have learned not to strike out at others to get what they want; undersocialized children have not. Well socialized children have learned to listen to and obey the directions of legitimate authority figures, such as parents and teachers; undersocialized children have not."[8] He notes that studies which demonstrate the differences between the way fathers and mothers parent indicate that fathers are essential in helping the young develop impulse control.

Fathers give to society children who are capable of self-restraint and cooperation with others, precisely the personal qualities that polls indicate people desire to see increase. America's current public debate has filled the air with expectations of a more humane and socially cooperative society. With these expectations raised, we must consider the steps needed to meet these expectations. We must acknowledge the source of trust and the methods necessary to renew it.

The unfolding debate over civil society raises many important topics for discussion, including the need for a new public philosophy elevating the common good over private self-interest, renewing social values, and encouraging wider civic participation. But none of these, as important as they are, will produce a civil and humane society by themselves. Only involved fathers, undergirded by family-friendly communities, will accomplish this goal.

Fathers Model Involved Citizenship

Civil society refers, in one meaning of the term, to a society that is civil. But it also denotes a distinct social realm, an "intermediate sector" consisting of our families, churches and synagogues, charities, civic networks, and voluntary neighborhood associations. This realm mediates between the individual on the one hand, and the state and market on the other, tempering the negative social tendencies associated with each.

Fathers make an important contribution to creating citizens and community members, but it also works the other way: These community-based institutions create important roles for the father, and recognize and reward his work.

Attitudes about the importance of fathers are imbedded in communities: in a community's civic associations and social give and take. These attitudes quickly surface in local schools when a school board is asked to decide whether it should advocate childbearing exclusively among married fathers and mothers or whether it is acceptable to offer programming to teen mothers while completely withholding judgment on father-absent households. Attitudes about the importance of men as fathers quickly surface when the Boy Scouts and Boy's and Girl's Clubs are asked to address young people as generic future parents, not as future fathers and mothers bearing unique responsibilities.

Until recently in the vast majority of communities, there were no attempts made by any major civic, educational, philanthropic, or religious body to explicitly reach out to fathers or, for that matter, to send a strong signal to men, women, and children alike that fathers matter, that every child deserves a father, and that communities need fathers in order to remain strong and healthy. Fortunately, that is changing somewhat, although most communities have a long way to go.

The National Fatherhood Initiative recommends ten steps to make a community father-friendly, including such basic ideas as organizing fatherhood forums, distributing information on the contribution fathers make to civic and media outlets, encouraging employment practices that are supportive of fathers, developing special community events for Father's Day, and putting fathering as a topic on the local civic and service club agenda.

Renewing Fatherhood as a Social Norm

If the renewal of fatherhood is central to the restoration of civil society, we cannot afford to be agnostic on several related questions that concern not just whether fathering takes place, but how and under what circumstances it is likely to be carried out.

It is nearly impossible to discuss the renewal of fatherhood in isolation from other social and cultural realities that are now common in America. For example, the vagueness of our recent discussion of family reflects our need to accommodate a steep rise in separated, divorced, blended, and never-formed families headed predominantly by young single mothers. To some, family now means little more than a collection of adults bound together by temporary needs and agreements. This relativization of the family also fits comfortably with the broadly felt desire among adults to embrace the dramatic expansion of private lifestyle choices.

Because all circumstances do not lend themselves equally to engaged fathering, this dilution of the meaning of family is not inconsequential. While our collective consciousness has been raised regarding the importance of family, the broader, fuzzier definition of family that has gained acceptance will likely make married, full-time fatherhood harder to attain.

It is important that a discussion of fatherhood be addressed to all fathers. Even though many fathers are removed from the households in which their children are being raised, we must acknowledge their desire to care for their offspring and the importance of such care, even under circumstances that are extremely difficult. This is important, especially in urban America where nonmarital births are the large majority and where fathers, if they are engaged at all, are involved through noncustodial arrangements with the mother(s) of their children. Thus any legitimate discussion of restoring fatherhood will need to include noncustodial fathers.

Having said this, however, it is necessary to point out that embracing an elastic notion of family out of a legitimate desire to improve today's fathering may have the unintended consequence of making the job harder to accomplish in the future, raising the likelihood that more children will be raised without fathers. To put the problem plainly, the immediate consequence of this relativization of the definition of family is that fathers are the first to be written out of the family script. When the cutting and pasting begins on the ever-changing family portrait, it is the father who is typically thrown away. In the vast majority of cases, children from fragmented families live apart from their biological father and, in many cases, see him infrequently.

Much of this has been made possible by society's acceptance of the myth that fathers are optional and that while children may prefer having fathers around, they'll get by without them or with only occasional contact. In other words, fathers are dispensable because they are assumed to play no unique, gender-specific role in raising children. With this assumption, it is easy for fathers to be relegated to the sidelines of childrearing in society. Even the most motivated father is likely to find these impediments daunting.

Little in the modern cultural script favors the father, and thus, not surprisingly, little in the law favors the father either. Frequently, dad is presented in popular culture as an extra set of hands, a deputy mom, a provider of child support payments, possibly "the nearby guy,"[9] more akin to a relative than a devoted, nurturing father.

Not infrequently, popular entertainment portrays the father as a dunce. Still worse, literature from the women's movement often raises the ugliest specter of all: Dad is a danger. Domestic abuse is nothing to be trifled with—it is a criminal offense and should be treated accordingly—but factual distortions should not be permitted to become yet another wedge between fathers, mothers, and children.

Reasserting a basic family norm of two parents, preferably the biological parents, preferably parenting cooperatively in the context of marriage, depends largely on the validity of the claim that fathers are essential in the contribution they make. This in turn means recognizing that fathers differ significantly from mothers and need stronger reinforcement in their parental roll. Historically, societies have not really had to worry that mothers might fall short of fulfilling their biologically determined role; voluntary mother-absence has not occurred broadly across time and human societies. This is obviously not true with fathers.

The case for family restoration, and improved child welfare, rests almost entirely on whether, in fact, fathers are unique and irreplaceable and should thus be expected by society to carry out a role less biologically determined but nevertheless vital to children. If fathers are disposable, then the current expanded definition of family is justified—we might even want to expand it further.

Instead of getting caught up in debate over secondary issues, however, let us instead attack the problem of father absence in a different way: Let us acknowledge that the current scale of absence by fathers from their children is unprecedented, that it is tragic for children, that it must be reversed in future generations, and finally, that in order to reverse father absence we must reduce the incidence of both family nonformation and divorce for the coming generations. In short, we can do better, and for the sake of our children—who have far more settled opinions on this matter—we must.

If we cannot yet accept a universal imperative, perhaps we can lend support to a desirable norm. We can acknowledge that whereas father absence was once the exception to the rule it is rapidly becoming the rule, and this is not good for children. Societies, including our own, have always had a certain percentage of father absence in various forms: Fathers have always left the home for work or war, sometimes for long periods of time, frequently never returning. Moreover, we have always had a certain amount of divorce and a certain amount of nonmarital births. And in all too many cases, dating back to the beginning of recorded human history, there have been fathers who have been largely dysfunctional—perhaps physically present, but in all other respects disengaged. The family revisionists are correct in at least the limited sense that the family has always been under some stress. The revisionists are wrong, however, in refusing to acknowledge that what American society is having to cope with today is radically different, both in its scale and its nature.

Cultural Foundations of Fatherhood

Fatherhood has very real social and cultural components. Fatherhood must be understood, in part at least, as a cultural institution. Fathering, says John Miller, family sociologist, is "a cultural acquisition to an extent that mothering is not." Since there are few biologically compelling reasons for the male to care for his offspring, "a set of overlapping largely cultural developments" are required. When a culture "ceases to support a father's involvement with his own children (through its laws, mores, symbols, models, rituals) powerful natural forces take over in favor of the mother only family."[10]

Of course, increased economic opportunity is essential, and policy reforms recognizing fathers through a range of social programs will help. But the restoration of fathers to their children will happen when an all-fronts mobilization takes place within society to reinforce adult male responsibility for children. Durable social structures, including stable families, cannot be legislated into existence. They derive their strength from a people's habits, customs, and social ethics, which are drawn partly from social norms, partly from religious and moral beliefs.

Periodically in American history, citizens have reacted to the general disregard of social standards and obligations and, with the help of society-wide social reform movements, moved individuals toward restraint and social obligation. In the nineteenth century, for example, society witnessed an explosion of voluntary associations and organizations aimed at social reform and moral uplift. Spiritual awakenings, temperance movements, and many private and public efforts were made to strengthen character and responsibility. These were dynamic movements, which transcended politics and partisanship.

James Q. Wilson, who has tracked social reforms, says that "throughout history, the institutions that have produced effective male socialization have been private, not public." If this is true, he says, "then our policy ought to identify, evaluate and encourage those local, private efforts that seem to do the best job at reducing drug abuse, inducing people to marry, persuading parents, especially fathers, to take responsibility for their children, and exercising informal social controls over neighborhood streets."[11]

The renewal of fatherhood and the renewal of civil society go hand in hand. Fathers have much to offer in strengthening communities, and community-based institutions can be mobilized to strengthen fathers—to reinforce their importance, to offer training and assistance, and to help them pass on to their own children a strong fathering heritage.

Notes

1. Mary Ann Glendon, "Forgotten Questions," introduction in *Seedbeds of Virtue*, ed. Mary Ann Glendon and David Blankenhorn (Lanham, Md.: Madison Books, 1995), 4.

2. Alexis de Tocqueville, *Democracy in America*, vol. 2, ed. and trans. Henry Reeve (New York: n.p., 1954), 114.

3. Robert B. Putnam, *Making Democracy Work: Civic Traditions in Modern Italy* (Princeton: Princeton University Press, 1993), 88.

4. Francis Fukuyama, *Trust* (New York: Free Press, 1995), dust jacket; see also p. 10.

5. James S. Coleman, "Social Capital in the Creation of Human Capital," *American Journal of Sociology* 94(1988): 95-120.

6. Alexis de Tocqueville, *Democracy in America*, vol. 2 (New York: Vintage

Books, 1945), 1-2.

7. Urie Bronfenbrenner, "Discovering What Families Do," in *Rebuilding the Nest: A New Commitment to the American Family*, ed. David Blankenhorn, Steven Bayne, and Jean Bethke Elshtain (Milwaukee: Family Service America, 1990), 29-32.

8. Wade Horn, "Character and Family," in *The Content of America's Character: Restoring Civic Virtue*, ed. Don Eberly (Lanham, Md.: Madison Books, 1995), 80.

9. For further analysis of the cultural scripting of fatherhood, see David Blankenhorn, *Fatherless America: Confronting Our Most Urgent Social Problem* (New York: Basic Books, 1995), 65-185.

10. John Miller, *Biblical Faith and Fathering: Why We Call God Father* (New York: Paulist Press, 1989), 2.

11. James Q. Wilson, "Culture, Incentives, and the Underclass," in *Values and Public Policy*, ed. Henry Aaron, Thomas Mann, and Timothy Taylor (Washington, D.C.: Brookings Institution, 1994), 74.

Part Four

Faithful Fathers:
The Journey Back

Chapter 16

One Denomination's Initiative

Larry Malone

The United Methodist Church established a new agency in 1996 at a time when downsizing and streamlining was the trend. The decision reflected an urgency to reach men in important new ways and to address issues that affect them. The new agency, the General Commission on United Methodist Men, has as its number one priority the spiritual development of men. Men are called on a journey to become servant leaders together. The journey helps men to become more like Christ and to do the hard work in committed partnership with other men. On a spiritual journey together, men move forward in expeditionary teams on treks to the next checkpoint, taking on the challenges together.

The world of the servant leader is upside down. Men learn to lead as they humble themselves, put others first, and serve others sacrificially as Jesus did. As men learn to practice God's brand of leadership, everyone is blessed, the church is strengthened, and God is honored.

Many men who attend church do not have a faith that gives them joy and overflows into blessings for others. Often burdened, these men have not developed spiritually. The revival of the church requires the renewal and spiritual growth of these men. Their hearts must be reached *before* their minds and hands are useful for God. So the first priority must aim at the hearts of men; programs and projects follow.

Heart work is done at weekend gatherings across the nation where men are being revived and equipped for their personal spiritual journeys. Since establishing United Methodist Men, events previously held as men's retreats are transformed into expeditions to rarely traveled places inside each man's heart and mind. These expeditions have been held in each of the 60 conferences of the United Methodist Church. We continue to refine and learn from each event as we seek to standardize the retreat sequence that we now refer to as a Heartland Expedition.

Fathers and Faith

How do the issues of fatherhood, servant leaders, and men's expeditions connect? Simply this: Fatherhood is the most highly leveraged role that men will ever hold on the planet. Period!

Fatherhood as defined here is not limited to biological bloodlines or even marital status. Every man was designed to function in a father role during his lifetime. Think about this: What can you do *well* or *poorly* today that will *last 100 years* or more? Answer: Something that *profoundly influences a young life*, for better or worse.

Leaders, if you want to make an investment that lasts an eternity in your own life and many others, teach your men to be the best men they can be. Invest in the arena of fatherhood, and you will reap the return on that investment in your own life and in the lives of generations to come.

Reconnect Men

The hearts of many men are broken, and the pain runs deep. Behind men's "game faces," private tragedies go unexpressed and repressed. We men have been taught that real men fly solo. It is too easy for Christian men to take an "I'm okay, you're not" attitude. The truth is, many of us are hurting.

Friendship has always been a frontline remedy for life's troubles, but American men have almost no friends. Men need a catalyst to bring friendship into their lives, since the world we live in tends to preclude deep friendships. For men in the United Methodist Church, such a catalyst is provided at weekend men's expeditions.

These events are intended to bring personal healing, support, friendship, and revival to men. Friendship is not the goal; it is a means to healing and personal renewal. Heart work is needed before head work. Healing must precede programs, projects, and works for men who are hurting and broken. When Christian brothers tend to the dying and wounded among themselves first, they build and strengthen men who will become servant leaders and impact the lives of many.

A Heartland Expedition

At a high mountain camp in New Mexico, a lake retreat in Texas, a wooded hideaway in South Carolina, and across the nation, United Methodist Men can experience a new kind of men's retreat. It is not a place to learn prepared lessons from others; it is a place to journey inside one's heart.

The journey is navigated best in teams. Each man goes to places where the support of other men is needed and appreciated. When a few men who share core values are committed to one another, they develop mutual respect, deep trust, and fierce brotherly love. Men are assigned to teams of three to five with as much range in age, race, and backgrounds as possible. Teams maintain integrity throughout the weekend, forming bonds that can and do continue after the expedition has ended.

Participation demands the best individual and team effort the men can give, plus a liberal covering of God's protection, guidance, grace, and mercy. Leaders for the expedition are required to get out in front, cover some new paths, and serve men as Journey Guides.

Finding Fathers

The first session, called "Finding Fathers," lets men experience the impact of fatherhood, rather than learning information about it.

As men gather, the Journey Guide, or leader, offers brief instructions: "Gather in your teams and sit in a circle." Instructions are then given for the exercise described below.

- Round One: You each have 60 seconds to *say something about yourself.* Stop immediately when directed. In 60-second intervals, the Journey Guide calls out, "Man #1 - go," "Man #2 - go," and so forth.
- Round Two: Same rules as above, but this round *say something about your father.*
- Round Three: Same rules as above, but *describe the significance that you felt in your father's eyes.*

The Journey Guide notes that only a short time has been spent on this little trek. Yet *remarkable things happen in this brief male encounter.* Round One is a cakewalk, and men are wondering, "What's the point?" During Round Two, some men begin to struggle at the mere thought or mention of their fathers. In Round Three, the easy stuff is *over*, and the agony and ecstasy begins. Daddy's view of his son is a blessing or a curse. Waves of emotion penetrate the men as they hear of fathers who loved and cared and other fathers who deeply scarred their boys—now grown men who are fathers and grandpas.

- Round Four: Men are asked to say a prayer for one another, praising God for the blessing of a loving father or asking God to begin healing the wounds that run so deep, and hurt so much.

In less than 30 minutes, the short journey has ended. Men are asked to reflect upon the following questions:

- When, if ever, did you last say these words? To whom?
- How many men that you spend time with, or consider friends, have no knowledge of how it was [or is] with your dad?
- Did it surprise you that men could go that far, that deep, that fast?
- How do you think the pain of this issue affects you and/or other men?

Fact is, daddy stuff is crucially important throughout a person's life. For better or worse, the lives of all men and women carry the mark of their fathers and mothers. The church can and should be a place for healing wounds.

Broken Brothers

The Journey Guide now asks the men to "imagine 100 American men of any and every description standing before you." The Journey Guide tells men that we will ask three questions of each man in the group. Their first "yes" response is to *step forward*; their second "yes" response is to *fall to their knees*; and the third "yes" response is to *fall on their faces* to the floor. Keep in mind, the participating men are not asked to do this; we are asking them to imagine the response of 100 men. The three questions are these:

- How many of the 100 are headed for or have experienced divorce—last year, next month, next year, ten years, and so forth? Men are asked, "How many?" Their answer is usually, "50 or more!"
- How many are in employment chaos? Meaning they are out

of work, expect to be soon, cannot earn enough to meet current obligations, or are required to learn new skills and start brand new careers. Answer: "One-third to one-half of them!"

• How many have a relationship or health-related issue causing great pain in their lives now? A wayward child, family conflict, terminal/grave illness, and so forth. Answer: "most of them!"

Men are asked to imagine the 100 men again: "How many are unaffected, standing forward, on their knees, and on their faces?" The mental image is now one of collective grief, pain, and brokenness. The Journey Guide makes a final comment to the group: "Men, we are them!"

The Acid Test

Next, the Journey Guide asks each man to consider his friendships with other men, applying the "acid test of true friendship." Men are asked to make an inventory of the men in their lives today who really *know* them. True friends are defined as those who actually know the places where you struggle, fall, and suffer. These friends also know where perseverance and commitment have resulted in personal victories and joy. The friend named should also be known by the man naming him in the same deep way.

An uncomfortable silence pervades the room as men think about their friendships. The Journey Guide knows that pain has been exposed in this short trek. Each man is left on his own to reflect upon his friendships.

In less than one hour, the expedition has taken men into well-guarded places intentionally left untouched: fathers, brokenness, and friendlessness. Such fun this is! These are major issues for American men, and they are linked together in important ways.

Past Times, Other Places

At the start of this session, the Journey Guide challenges men to think about the past and to compare it to today by using the sample narrative below:

"Imagine a different world for a moment. This world, however, is real for most men today, and all men of the past centuries. In your mind, you need change only one thing—the date is the same, 100 years ago.

"Life was simple and hard. Families were the nuclear center of life. You lived with or very near your grandparents and relatives. All of your local community knew you and your name, and took some ownership in your development. No one you knew was divorced. Early death or work in far away places was usually the cause of homes without fathers. Work and life skills were passed to you directly by your parents and community. Fathers put a claim on a boy as an apprentice as soon as he was physically able to carry his own weight. The days and years of young life were made up of countless hours of time spent with loved ones and friends, uninterrupted by twentieth century media, frenzy, and technology. Life was simple and hard. Relationships were the center of it.

"Now, think about the lives of men in most Western cultures today. What we have experienced is distinctly different from the past. We may not know our father or our bloodlines. We may move every three to five years to places where we do not know anyone. We change jobs and careers frequently. Often far away from kin and community, many men have no significant connection with other men.

"Across the world, through the centuries, men have gathered in small groups to be with men. They chat and cajole, laugh and lie, meet and eat, compete and confront, play and console. Even across rural America, we still find men in coffee shops and barber chairs, on benches and in pool halls. Men are hard-wired for friendship with a few men, forged and built on adversity, and tested over time.

"Today men compete with other men in the workplace, and often view them as adversaries. In 'less advanced' cultures, relationships between men are very different. Without supermarkets, men provide food by growing, gathering, or killing it. Without contractors, men build their homes and communities. Without police protection and the armed forces, men band together to protect and defend each other's families. Without schools, men teach work and life skills to their children and spend time with them. Men perform these roles by working together, side by side, not in competition with them.

"Trust and respect are essential elements of deep relationships among men. These qualities are forged over time and through trials by doing things together for a right purpose. Relationships among men that exist purely in a conversational realm lack ingredients essential to the development of mutual trust and respect. In essence, these relationships are hollow; they lack a seal of authenticity because words have not been tested or backed up with actions. The anemic bonding of contemporary man is rooted in the violation of this principle."

The Generation Gap

Men today are separated and disconnected. Even among men of faith, we are often isolated racially, socially, and across other barriers. One crucial way men in our culture are divided is generational isolation; we spend time with men only of our similar age.

To illustrate this situation, the Journey Guide asks men to imagine themselves divided into age groups:

- Sages - men 70 years and older
- Eagles - men in mid-50s and 60s
- Bulls - men from mid-30s to mid-50s
- Bucks - men in 20s and early 30s
- Spikes - young men in teens

Men are asked to identify strengths and liabilities of each age group. Invariably, testosterone enters the discussion, and the group mentally plots a graph of male sex drive along a life span axis. Now the Journey Guide poses some questions:

- What was an Eagle, in his previous life stage? What does an Eagle know about, that a Bull might need?
- A Sage and a Spike have an entire day together. What does it look like? What happens? Who benefits the most?
- How many men have important, active relationships within one age group? Two? Three? And so forth.
- What is the price paid for the absence of generational connection among men? Who pays it?

By the time the above session occurs, men have already discovered first-hand that contact with men from different generations is beneficial. They have spent much of the weekend with the other men of their team. We strive for great diversity when making team assignments. Teens are put with grandfathers and great-grandfathers. By this time men have discovered through experience that they naturally fall into their God-ordained roles. What happens between sons and fathers is very different from what happens between sons and grandfathers. And it should be different. The social order of almost every society follows this pattern, except ours.

Think of society as a mosaic with each generation represented by a different color tile. The beautiful pattern the artist intends will not be complete when one color of tile is missing. Not until every tile is present and integrated with those around it will the mosaic be complete. Men do not need to be forced or orchestrated into their roles, but they do need to be made aware that today's fragmented society is not normal. Each generation has a unique relational role to play. When they are put in contact with one another, men naturally fulfill their roles as God ordained it.

The Elder Blessing

After being challenged to their personal limits for two days, men are asked to make one final trek, finishing the expedition. Men are invited to find some quiet space alone to reflect on what God would have them do differently and to respond by making personal commitments. The Sages (those 70 years and older) are asked to remain in the assembly room and to gather in four elder councils in each corner of the room.

When the younger men return, they are asked to wait quietly to meet with one of the four elder circles. When called by the elders, they are to present themselves by name and present their commitments to the elders. The elders are encouraged to ask them questions about their commitments. Then the men are free to ask questions of the elders about the commitments.

Finally, it is time for the elders to perform a sacred role. Elders stand over seated men and huddle around them closely with their right hands placed on them. Together, the elders *present* the man, and his commitments, *to God.* They ask God to hear his plea and to protect and empower him as he makes the difficult choices and changes. They petition God on behalf of the man and ask that the blessing of God be passed through their old, knurled hands.

As director of men's ministries and a frequent Journey Guide, I have discovered that a reverent, sacred spirit permeates the place. God orchestrates the event, right down to the match of men and elders. The experience of being "presented to God," by godly elders, is indescribable. It is a beautiful thing—both powerful and tender. The elders listen well and give good counsel. But the power of their prayers and the spiritual energy that flows through their right hands is from God. The process itself feels profoundly right, as though it is part of the natural order of things. It is intuitively appropriate.

One expedition was particularly memorable because I brought the personal commitment to renew and rebuild my 30-year marriage despite turbulent waters. As I left the elder circle where I verbalized my commitment, I asked, "Are you men married?"

"Yup," they nodded.

"Same women?"

"Yup."

"How long you been married?"

"Fifty-six years." "Fifty-three years." "Forty-nine years." "Fifty-four years."

"Thanks!"

"Yup."

I wondered who in the world might have been more perfectly suited to hear my commitment. *No one!* It doesn't get any better than this.

On this occasion when all the men had been "presented" by the elders, I asked the group what they thought of the experience. None spoke, because there were no words that fit. The most senior elder (bull sage) was asked to speak for the elders. Halfway through he lost control. His final words were, "I felt so honored . . ."

The Expedition Examined

Sacred space. Sacred ceremonies. Male soul-work. There is something vital and life giving that is missing from the world of most modern men. Whatever it is, men mainline it at our expeditions. Let's call it *JUICE*!

Male life force, or juice, has several levels of authenticity and potency. The most superficial level, and the level that possesses the least power, is macho bully juice. Authentic men of character, men who have a transforming effect for good upon their environs, have a much more potent source of juice. Pure juice, 100 percent undiluted, in concentrated form is *profoundly* spiritual. Men who access and radiate this kind of juice are vessels—the juice is not theirs to claim or to keep—it flows through them. The source of this crystal clear artesian spring is the Almighty One.

Juice is an element that can be strongly sensed by others. Police know that the very first assessment that must be made of a potentially dangerous man is to determine if he is armed. Everything depends on that assessment. They must know, "Is he packing heat?" This is a good question for all men. What kind of heat do you pack? Is it the stuff of a weak, cowardly, honorless world? Is it heat that degrades women, and beats up on men? Or is it the authentic male Juice that flowed abundantly from a humble servant named Jesus?

A behind-the-scenes look at what happens to men on an expedition will help us to understand its impact and to see how Juice flows through the event into men. The expedition contains four stages: grief, grace, growth, and giving.

Grief: The Descent to the Past

Deep within the souls of men there is a well of grief. The well is deep, cold, and full of pain. The well is carefully avoided but at a terrible cost. No one really knows everything in each man's grief well, or exactly how it got there. The important thing is that it is there. Until the well is visited, there is no healing and no wholeness. The well is a spiritual place—the healing is God's work.

Ministry leaders should be aware of a few things that might be in men's wells. Father hunger is a ravenous demon that lives inside many men. It is a cannibal. Generational bondage and baggage passed from ancestors may be in the well—until men disconnect from it. The grief wells of modern man are overflowing, because many have never been shown the way or the reason to go there.

The "Finding Father" trek takes many men to their well. An important purpose of the expedition is to show men where the well is located and to encourage them to pull something up from it. When a man is allowed to share what is pulled up in the bucket from another man's well, he is given a position of great honor and trust. He knows it, and often wants to respond with a bucket from his own well. And so the building of true friendship begins. It really can be that simple, having a few true friends.

Sometimes the well contains things that really hurt a man, or are presently killing him. Good friends sense when a man needs a very competent, highly trained guide to navigate dangerous territory. They point him toward professional help.

Grace: The Event at the Well

What happens at the well really controls a man's emotional or spiritual well-being. Everyone has demons to wrestle with that define and confine one's life. If a man is unwilling or unable to deal with his past, his life becomes defined or determined by those hidden things that act as roadblocks. He becomes emotionally or spiritually limited.

A man can be cleansed at the well because God's grace and mercy is the source of healing. Here are some things that can happen at the well:

- The wound is bared and is grieved.
- Heartfelt confession and genuine repentance occurs.
- God's forgiveness and blessing are received.
- Renewal occurs; forgiveness is given to self and others.

A changed life is begun.

Growth: The Present Work

Jesus Christ says to everyone: "Come to me, all you who are weary and burdened, and I will give you rest. Take my yoke upon you, and learn from me, for I am gentle and humble in heart, and you will find rest for your souls. For my yoke is easy, and my burden is light" (Matthew 11:28-30).

"Even youths grow tired and weary, and young men stumble and fall; but those who hope in the Lord will renew their strength. They will soar on wings like eagles; they will run and not grow weary, they will walk and not be faint" (Isaiah 40:30-31).

At the well, healing, blessing, and a repentant heart produce spiritual growth. Forgiven and forgiving, rejuvenated by God with his pure juice, men find power to change. Here is where broken manhood is given up, and where healthy, vital masculinity is forged. It doesn't occur in a single event; the well has to be visited often. A good life is tough because we would not change unless something forced us to change. Every trip builds muscle and strength to take the next trek. God knows that hauling some of those buckets will require great effort from men and supernatural help from God, including the men he sends to help you pull! God knows exactly what is required for each man to get it done. The choice to *do* it, however, always remains personal.

God provides men everything necessary to grow from their present condition—no matter how bad it is. Men's will and courage to change, however, differ. Here is the fork in the road at which the church stands. A successful expeditionary force is one taken by a team of men who have trained with one another and who share commitment and core values. Churches can instill a desire to go to the well, to change. Most men do not get to the well often enough, or haul muck from the bottom without the help of other men. It is for this reason that our wells are so full.

Giving: The Gift That Keeps on Giving

An overflowing well spills out the same stuff that is in it! Whatever it is we are full of (so to speak), we give to others. If what you give were being offered by another, would you want any?

When men get their wells flowing with the pure *Juice from the Source,* the demand for the stuff is insatiable. Men would order it by the boxcar load if they thought they could get it. One man who is changed will revive others. This is evangelism at its best: men radiating the goodness and love of their

Creator. Giving is God's plan for all of us. We can't out give Him; giving is like a perpetual motion machine because God has unlimited resources.

Giving is the blessing, or curse, at the end of the expedition. It is literally the gift that keeps on giving. The Law of the Farm always applies: Reap what you sow, get what you give.

The Results of Our Efforts

The Heartland Expeditions have resulted in renewed men who are profoundly influencing others for the better. The most important result occurs first and is personal within each man. A man experiences a renewal or revival of his spirit. The event gives men a place to examine priorities and to choose to do some things differently. Men focus on things to let go and things to pick up. Here are several other important results:

- Men experience the blessing of trusting one another and building friendships. They learn that men can trust and work in teams. After the expedition, some teams continue to meet together.
- Men learn the power of generational connection and reach out to form relationships across generations. During the response times at the close of expeditions, younger guys talk about how it feels to interact with older men. "We want a relationship with older men," young men say, "and we want you to come after us." Older men hear this and make a personal commitment to be initiators. Now those older men are initiating—pursuing—relationships with younger men. These older men are leading by serving.
- A shift of focus toward spiritual growth has been initiated among men who have been more oriented toward meetings and projects. Mission work and outreach grow since they are formed on solid spiritual foundation.
- The expedition is a means to reach younger men and many other men of the UMC and the friends they invite.

United Methodist Men also offers a comprehensive training program. At the individual level, men are encouraged to study a 12-lesson series on servant leadership. Each man is given a personal journal with lessons and related Bible studies. Men study together in small teams and build relationships as they learn. The lesson notebook is augmented with video training to be viewed by the men in teams.

Leader training will be conducted nationwide, equipping men to train others in more than 500 districts within the United Methodist Church. Patrick Morley, author of *Man in the Mirror* said, "A man is a hard thing to reach." We want to reach more than three million of them in 35,000 congregations nationwide.

In addition to the servant leader training, United Methodist Men has several major initiatives to meet the needs of men:

- Pastoral Partnership—encouraging men to pray for, support, and serve the male and female clergy.
- Prayer focus—elevating prayer to the very highest priority through our Prayer Advocate Program. Prayer initiatives include support of the Upper Room Prayer Line Ministry, establishment of a prayer room in every congregation, and pastoral prayer support.
- UMMen Missions—inviting men to support missions with their time, money, and talents. A featured national UMMen ministry is the Society of St. Andrews Meals for Millions program, which feeds the hungry in America through crop gleaning and excess food distribution.
- Men in Teams—encouraging, supporting, and equipping men to build vital relationships with one another in small groups by using the model established over 200 years ago by the founder of Methodism, John Wesley.

Our theme at the General Commission on United Methodist Men is building servant leaders. A servant leader is not the typical Type-A driven person. Everything in servant leadership is upside down. Before a man becomes a leader, he must become a servant; he must learn to focus on the needs of others, to do things the way Jesus did them.

If church leaders want to make an investment that lasts for eternity, invest in the lives of men so they become the best men they can be. Build men into servant leaders.

Chapter 17

One Pastor's Personal Struggle

DeForest "Buster" Soaries

I approach Father's Day every year with a sense of haunting ambiguity because the emotions that saturate my psyche are hard to describe. Part of me is challenged by the continued pain and sense of loss that I feel since the death of my father. Many people wish I would stop talking about my father's death that occurred 23 years ago. They assume that after such a long time a seasoned Christian, especially a minister, should have accepted and learned to cope with the death of a loved one. Of course, I consider myself a relatively mature Christian, and I am aware that the Holy Spirit provides healing and power. But frankly, that knowledge has not erased completely the reality of my pain.

Another part of me faces the pastoral challenge on Father's Day to summon fathers to be better fathers. Year after year I ask myself, "Why beat up the good fathers with a message intended to reach the bad fathers?" Most of the men who need to hear that message are not in church pews. Then, of course, there are so many people who did not have or do not have good relationships with their fathers.

Father's Day is always a tough day for me. But there is a story in the Bible that gave this past Father's Day new meaning. This story is about a Jewish leader named Jairus who requested Jesus' help on behalf of his sick daughter.

> When Jesus had crossed again in the boat to the other side, a great crowd gathered around him; and he was by the sea. Then one of the leaders of the

synagogue named Jairus came and, when he saw him, fell at his feet and begged him repeatedly, "My little daughter is at the point of death. Come and lay your hands on her, so that she may be made well, and live." So he went with him . . . (Mark 5:21-24, NRSV).

This fellow Jairus illuminated the meaning of *father* for me in an unprecedented way. As I consider the notion of fatherhood and apply basic principles to myself, the achievements of my own fatherhood pale in comparison to this leader named Jairus. According to Scripture, he was one of the rulers of the synagogue. To be Jewish during Jesus' time was in some ways very similar to being a minority in the present age in the United States of America. The synagogue played a similar role for the Jews that black churches have played for African Americans. For example, consider the office of deacon in black churches. Historically, in the black church, the deacon is highly regarded. Our history attests that when we were denied the opportunity to be recognized as "somebody" in every other arena, we could be recognized as "somebody" in our churches. When we were denied access to responsibility in every other arena, we had responsibility in the church. Likewise, this man Jairus, a Jew in a land dominated by foreign and adversarial political powers, was empowered in the synagogue in ways that are similar to the experience of empowerment for many African Americans in churches.

Scripture portrays Jairus as an important man—a leader in his community and in his "church." Jairus was a hardworking man, settling disputes, distributing resources, going to meetings, selecting rabbis, planning strategy, sitting on boards, and negotiating with the government. Yet, when his 12-year-old daughter became sick, he said, "I'm stopping everything on behalf of my child." This suggests that Jairus knew what and how his child was doing. He was in touch with his daughter and her needs. We can get so busy that we do not even know what and how our children are doing. Unlike the father who sent his wife to see Elisha when their son got sick and died, Jairus took paternal responsibility too seriously to send a surrogate to get medicine for his daughter. Jairus did not send his daughter with his wife to the hospital. Jairus did not restrict himself to the patriarchal gender roles of his day. Jairus said, "I'm this girl's daddy, and I'm going to see Jesus." Then Jairus stayed with Jesus until Jesus said, "Let's go."

The Daddy Personality

Jairus understood the meaning of the word *father*. He had a daddy personality. That is the challenge to all fathers today. In spite of all of his legitimate responsibilities, Jairus clearly had a relationship with his daughter. This meant that Jairus understood fatherhood as a full-time commitment, not something that he did every now and then. For Jairus, being a father meant more than making entries on his calendar to note the intermittent visits with his daughter. Instead, the word father was a part of his *personality*.

We need more fathers whose personality is absorbed by their fatherhood. Our total personality is what Jesus meant when He said, "Love God with all your mind, your body, and your soul" (Matthew 22:37). Too many of us want to be fathers with our money only. Too many of us want to be fathers every other Saturday morning. Too many of us want to be fathers with our birthday cards only. In contrast, being a dad was part of Jairus's personality. It was part of his character. Jairus would not be caught saying that he was "baby-sitting" for his own child. This was his baby. He was not baby-sitting. He was being daddy. One cannot baby-sit one's own child. One gets a teenager to baby-sit. One gets a college student who needs some extra cash to baby-sit, but one cannot baby-sit one's own child. When we care for our children, we are being daddies. It should be a part of our personalities.

The Daddy Priority

Jairus not only had a daddy personality, but Scripture indicates that Jairus understood his daughter to be his *priority*. Bob Bennett, a Washington attorney, was described by his wife of 27 years as having always kept his children as a priority. Mrs. Bennett said regarding her husband, "He's always been a successful lawyer, but he has never *not* had time for our children." I have been married for 13 years, and I have already flunked that course! For most of us it is completely inconceivable that after 27 years, the mothers of our children are able to tell the *New York Times*, "He has never *not* had time." Grammatically, that double negative is incorrect. But as fathers, that would be the most correct we could be! That means that Bob Bennett has always been there!

I have been increasingly impressed as I have come to know the children of Martin Luther King Jr. and the children of Malcolm X. These men were both killed at 39 years of age when their children were very young. But it shocks me to hear their children talk about their daddies. How on earth could the Shabazz children know anything about Malcolm in light of his travels all over the world? How could the King children have any fond memories about Martin, the man whose work changed the social landscape of America? Yet, if you peruse their biographies and look at the pictures, you will discover that, despite their greatness and profundity, somehow these men found time for their children. Being a father must become a priority for this generation, including ministry leaders.

The story of Jairus began impacting me a few weeks before Father's Day. My sons were out of town on a church-sponsored camping trip. While the boys were on that wonderful retreat, I bought them new baseball gloves and a Ken Griffy Jr. baseball bat. My boys like baseball and can hit a baseball so far that you need to send someone out to get the ball. I bought two balls so that when Martin hit the first ball into the bushes, we would have a replacement ball. When the boys came home, I surprised them with the gifts. "Okay," I said. "I have to preach a revival every night this week, but on Tuesday night I will be home at five o'clock to play ball. Between work and revival, we are going to go out and I'll show you how to use your glove, your bat, and your ball."

But my new priority was tested.

I was at the office preparing to leave by 4:30 p.m. when one person said, "Buster, I have to see you for a minute."

Someone else said, "Reverend, I have to see you for a minute." One minute turned into five, five turned into twenty, twenty turned into twenty-five, and when I looked at my watch, it was five minutes past five o'clock.

To sneak out of the building, I used the back door. When I reached my car, a fellow on a bicycle approached me. The man appeared to be poor, helpless, and homeless. He looked like he was in desperate need. "Reverend," he said, stopping my car. "Can I talk to you for just three minutes?"

Then I did something I had never done.

I said, "No. I don't have three minutes. I'm late. I was supposed to be at home five minutes ago to play ball with my boys." Pointing across the way, I continued, "Do you see that big building over there? There are about 39 people who work in that building. They are ministers and psychologists and social workers and secretaries. There may even be some deacons hanging around there. You walk right through that door, and tell them that I sent you. They will do whatever they can to help you. I have to go home and play baseball with my boys."

As I left, I felt so guilty that I actually drove around the block to see if the man had followed my directions. Then I remembered Jairus. The Holy Spirit used his story to say, "You are the only father your boys have. Right now, you are the only baseball coach they have. You are the only man in their lives, and if you do not teach them how to play baseball, the devil is going to teach them how to play something else. If you do not teach them how to swing a bat, the devil is going to teach them how to swing something else."

I rose above my guilt, and I said, "Lord, have mercy. I hope someone helped that fellow, but I have two sons at home waiting for me." I started to feel better. As I started to feel better, I said, "I am going to get used to this! I'm going to do this more often."

People will two-minute me to death, and then talk about me when my boys get into trouble. The same people that keep me running all over town will be the first ones to say, "You see! He was so busy trying to help everybody else, that he could not help his own children."

The real question for church leaders is, If we were to die today, what would our children say about us? If I were to die right now, what would my eight-year-old boys have to say about me? If we were to leave the planet today, what child could say about us the same thing a young man said about a member of our church—that he is his spiritual hero?

We talk a good game, but Jairus made his daughter his priority. Jairus said, "Forget about the synagogue. I'm going to see Jesus." While he was gone, he may have missed a committee or board meeting. He may have missed a choir rehearsal. He may have missed an election. He may have missed a fundraiser. He may have missed a "fish-fry." He may have missed Sunday morning worship, but he said, "I am going to see Jesus because my daughter is dying."

Some of us who minister in the church or community have children who are dying. Some of us have children who are dying intellectually. The teachers think that they cannot pass a test, and the children have begun to believe it themselves. Some of us have children who are dying emotionally. They do not know what to do with their lives, and they are being persuaded to participate in frivolity and reckless living. Some of us have children who are dying politically, detached from all of the social structures that are designed to serve them. Some of us have children who are dying spiritually. They have had no one to teach them to pray.

Some parents, some fathers, may need to spend less time in church and more time with their children. Some of us may need to take a leave of absence from our duties and from our service to others in order to dedicate that time to our children. We need each other's assistance in the raising of our children. But how can I help you with your child, if I cannot raise my own child? How can I mentor neighborhood children if I am not a father to my own children? How can I coach a Little League team if I am not a coach for my own child? Jairus took a leave of absence from the synagogue. He said, "I know I am in charge. Yet, right now, someone else will have to take care of the offering. I am going to take care of my daughter."

The Power Behind Daddy

Although Jairus was politically connected, when he saw the condition of his child, he went to the source of real *power*. As fathers we must be careful not to confuse our children about the source of true power. We have to be careful not to "thing" our children to death, to substitute material possessions for fathering. Some of us are so preoccupied with making sure that our children have it easier than we did that we make it too easy. Our children have become spoiled brats and good for nothing. If making it easier for our children means that they do not know how to pray, then maybe they do not need it to be easier. If making it easier means that our children know more about television than they do about Scripture, then maybe they should not have it easier. If having it easier means that they get a car at an earlier age, but end up driving drunk at 19, then maybe they should not have it easier. Perhaps to make it easy is not the right remedy. Maybe our children need to know what it's like to walk a mile in order to buy a pint of milk. Maybe our children need to know what it's like to sleep two or three nights without food in their stomachs. Maybe our children need to know those things that some of us knew and that served to develop our character. Maybe we are giving our children too many things.

Perhaps it is for this reason that when they get in trouble, they do not know what to do. Don't get me wrong. I love young people. I love their brilliance. I love their vocabulary and their technology skills. I love their capacity to think things through that we did not even know existed when we were growing up. Nevertheless, when I look at this generation and their inability to deal with disappointment, I am scared to death. This generation is unable to deal with obstacles. They are unable to deal with teachers who dislike them, the way some teachers disliked us, our grandmothers, and our great-grandmothers. Since when does one's future depend on whether or not one is liked? We are raising a generation that cannot deal with disappointment because we have "thing"-ed them to death.

A young child spoke in our church one Sunday and said that her father has helped her to learn how to talk to God. We have to teach our children what Jairus knew. We have to teach our children how to access real power.

Jairus was the ruler of the synagogue. Jairus had connections in high places, and still Jairus said, "For my daughter's illness, I need the power of Jesus!" He was not a disciple of Jesus. He did not even believe that Jesus was the Messiah. But he knew that Jesus had the power to heal the sick. He was a ruler in the synagogue. But his child was sick, and he loved his child. Therefore, Jairus was willing to go wherever he had to go to get real help for his daughter. He could not settle for political or economic influence—he needed real power. That is what I loved about my father. He believed in going to the one who had the power to solve problems.

When I was a boy, I loved baseball. I played baseball well. I was thrilled when I made starter for the Little League baseball team. When they sent us the schedule, 90 percent of the games were scheduled during the same time as a church worship service. I went to the coach and I said, "I can't play baseball and go to church at the same time. Unless I am going to live in your house, I have to go to church."

"If you can't make 80 percent of the games," the coach said, "you can't be on the team." It broke my heart. Joe was on the team, and Larry was on the team. Everyone else in town was on the team. I went home and cried.

"What's wrong?" my daddy said.

"The coach said I can't be on the team," I said.

"Why not?"

"Because the majority of the games are during a church worship service."

"Don't worry. I'll deal with it."

"The coach already made up his mind," I said.

"I am not going to see the coach," my dad said. "I am going to see the head of the league."

My father went to the power source. He rang Mr. Blair's doorbell. Mr. Blair was a big shot. He smoked a cigar and wore three-piece suits. Mr. Blair answered the door and said, "Do I know you?"

"You're going to know me in a few minutes," my father said. We sat down in Mr. Blair's house, and my father said, "You are not going to keep my boy off the Little League team because he goes to church. If there is only one game on Wednesday, you are going to let him play on Wednesday night."

Mr. Blair agreed with my dad and gave me permission to stay in the league and on the team. There was only one game scheduled for Wednesday night. But Mr. Blair was going to let me play in that one game if that was the only game I could make. My dad got him to use his power on my behalf.

The man with the power solved my problem just as the man with the power solved Jairus's problem. Jesus returned with Jairus and raised his daughter from the dead. If we want our children to live, we must rely upon the One who has the power to give life.

But then, after Mr. Blair used his power to help me, I was introduced to another level of power. As God would have it, it rained every weekend that summer. The rain dates were on Wednesday nights. I actually played in every game, and I made the all-star team. When it rained on the weekend, I went to church and said, "This is my Father's world!"

The Ultimate Daddy

This is my Father's world! That is what is most profound about fatherhood today. The world is desperately seeking a Daddy. Some may never have a daddy who teaches them to pray or who will make them their priority. Others may never know a father that takes the time to teach them baseball. Despite that, if someone is living without a father, it is really his or her own fault. There is another Father besides our earthly father. This is the Father of whom Jesus was talking when he said, "No man comes to the Father, but by me" (John 14:6). And I like this Father, because this Father has a Father personality. Everywhere I go, my Father is there. Everything I need, my Father has. Paul said that my Father "will supply all of my needs, according to his riches in glory" (Philippians 4:19). Not only does my Father have a fatherly personality, but my Father has made me his priority. Jesus said, "Look at the lilies of the field" (Matthew 6:28) and "consider the little bird, it neither sows, nor reaps" (Matthew 6:26). If God would take care of a little lily, if God would clothe a little sparrow, then God will take care of you and me!

The black church offers these words in a favorite song, "I sing because I'm happy. I sing, because I'm free. Since God's eye is on the sparrow, I know God watches me." A man's earthly father may have been an alcoholic. Yet, if God is his heavenly Father, God is watching over him. One's earthly father may have been delinquent and irresponsible, but there is another Father. We all can have another father, a Father who is rich in houses and land. My Father, God, not only has a father personality. Not only has God made me his priority. God not only sends the power. God not only goes to the power, but God is the Power! God has the power to dry my weeping eyes when I long for my earthly father. God has the power to make my body straight. God has the power to make my enemies leave me alone. Although my earthly father is not present, I have a heavenly Father who always walks with me. I have a heavenly Father who always talks with me.

The world is desperately seeking a father. He may not be found in the home, but He can be found. The mission and responsibility of the church is to show the way to the ultimate Daddy. Individual churches can and should be things to bring the Father to fathers.

At First Baptist Church we approach the issue of fatherhood within the context of our overall ministry to men. This ministry is coordinated through our Men's Fellowship and includes the following activities:

- Quarterly breakfasts that feature guest speakers
- Annual men's retreats

- Outreach activities to neighborhood boys
- A mentoring program
- Recruitment of men to work in all church ministries
- Annual men's conferences
- Various fellowship activities such as golf outings
- Involvement in Promise Keepers
- A men's Bible study
- Involvement in Boy Scouts

The objectives are to provide instruction, accountability, and encouragement to men as they attempt to be disciples of Christ. The idea that God has a plan for men as fathers is integrated into all of our various activities while understanding that there are different categories of men that need to be reached. These categories include married men who are fathers and living with their children, men who are fathers and not living with their children, men who are not married and living with their children, men who are not married and not living with their children, men who are married and would like to be fathers, single men who will become fathers, men that we have recruited to become foster or adoptive parents, men who have had good relationships with their fathers, and men who have not. Rather than completely segregating all these categories and developing different activities for each group, we assume that everyone needs to hear everything to be able to deal with the diversity of issues in the body of believers.

Ultimately, we believe that a man will become a good father if he understands God's purpose for men in general and accepts that purpose as he is. Of course, the only way to accept that purpose is complete surrender to the Lordship of Christ and complete dependence on the Holy Spirit for power.

The ultimate power for good fathering comes from God because this is my Father's world! The Father to whom I refer said, "Let it be," and it was. This Father parted the Red Sea and let the people of Israel walk through without getting their feet wet. He said, "I will never leave you, nor forsake you" (Joshua 1:5).

I do not have to be depressed on Father's Day. My father died in 1975, but my heavenly Father watches over me. He watches over me when I am driving my car. He watches over me when I am sleeping in my bed. He watches over me when I am eating in the restaurant. He watches over me when I am flying in an airplane. He watches over me when my enemies rise up against me. This is my Father's world! I am not going to forget it.

God is a good God. He will be the father I no longer have. He will give me power to be the father he called me to be. He will do the same for you.

Chapter 18

Recovering the Rites of Male Passage

Gordon Dalbey

Jesus' parents were astonished when they saw him, and his mother said to him, "Son, why have you done this to us? Your father and I have been terribly worried trying to find you."

He answered them, "Why did you have to look for me? Didn't you know that I had to be in my Father's house?" (Luke 2:48)

"When Jesus was 12 years old," begins the ancient Bible story, his family makes their annual pilgrimage to Jerusalem to celebrate the Passover. But for a Jewish boy on the threshold of manhood, this year is different from all other years.

When the extended family and friends begin their journey home to Nazareth, Jesus does not go with them. His parents don't realize he's gone until a full day into their journey. In a panic, they rush back to the big city to find him. Likely out of desperation, they go first to the Temple to pray for their son's safety and are shocked to find him there among the men, even as a peer, questioning and commenting with authority.

His mother, predictably, is confused, hurt, and angry. Like every good mother, she has taught her boy not to leave her side without her permission. But now, at 12, the boy's own emerging agenda and identity as a man must take precedence, even over Mom.

It's time for the boy to become a man.

It's time to be with the Father.

For some two thousand years Christians have read this simple but powerful story. Yet strangely, tragically, we have not acknowledged and acted upon its simple truth, which cries out with longing from every masculine soul: *It's the father who calls the boy into manhood.*

At its root, the issue here is neither a cultural custom nor a religious duty. It's a human need—which culture and religion ignore to their peril.

The ancient prophet Malachi both promised and warned: "See, I will send you the prophet Elijah before that great and dreadful day of the Lord comes. He will turn the hearts of the fathers to the children and the hearts of the children to the fathers; or else I will come and strike the land with a curse" (Malachi 4:5-6).

How can we fathers today meet this need in our sons to be called into manhood—and thereby bear a blessing to the land, and not a curse?

Indeed, dare we recognize the need, so long buried, unmet in our own wounded, masculine souls?

Certainly, when a society has lost touch with so basic a need, only input from another society can reawaken it.

How the Ibo People Call Boys to Manhood

Early in the fall of 1964, at the adventurous, indestructible age of 20, I was invited by the U.S. Peace Corps to teach at a boys' high school among the Ibo people in rural Nigeria. Freshly equipped with my bachelor's degree in math and a minor in physics, I set out for the "Dark Continent," as it was then called—asking not what my country could do for me, but how I could share the boons of Western civilization with other, apparently less fortunate, people.

After several months of teaching young African men about congruent triangles, however, I was startled—and appropriately humbled—by a simple question while chatting with a student about family life in America.

"In American villages," he asked, matter-of-factly, "how is it that a boy is called out by the men?"

Puzzled, I hesitated, wondering if maybe my student was misusing his English words. "What do you mean?"

"In your village in America," he replied, "how did the men come for you, when you were reaching the proper age to come out from your mother's house?"

At once, I thought of how in that polygamous society, each of a man's wives had her own separate hut, in which her children were raised. "Oh," I said, smiling graciously at last. "In America, unlike here in your village, the mother and father live in the same house, so that sort of thing really isn't necessary."

How naive I was! Today, some 35 years later, I'm dismayed by the irony at how our changing American society has since become more like that Ibo village. "You Americans scoff at our polygamy," one Ibo friend of mine countered, "but you just have serial monogamy." Indeed, could our rising divorce rate be linked to the fact that we American men are not called out into the fellowship of older men, and therefore lack the mentoring and manly confidence necessary for enduring commitment to a family?

In any case, the statistical norm in our broken American families is that, like my Ibo village, the mother and father do not live in the same house. Most often, in fact, the son lives with the mother and the father lives elsewhere. The major difference is that we Americans don't appreciate the boy's need for his father.

I understand now why my young Ibo student was confused by my response. I recall he moved as if to speak, and then sat quietly, knitting his brow. Unsure what more to say, I changed the subject.

Fortunately—though I couldn't appreciate it at the time—I had occasion later to ask an Ibo teacher on our staff to describe for me his own initiation rite as a boy. Like a seed planted in dry ground, his story remained dormant in my mind and heart for some 20 years, until at last I began to soak in the brotherly longings of my fellow men. Today, I treasure it, sharing it as often as possible.

Once, a man told me, he took my book to work with him to read on break. Halfway into the chapter describing initiation rites, however, he couldn't withhold his tears and had to put the book away. Later that night, alone at home, he let the dam burst and rivers of painful longing flowed. At such times, I wish I could contact that Ibo student who asked me the question that I, in my narrow vision, simply had no way of understanding then.

In the rural village where my teacher friend grew up, a boy lives in his mother's house until he reaches the proper age, usually around 12. The father has been watching his son grow, and when he decides the boy is ready, he goes at once to the village elders to officiate this sacred rite of passage for his son.

Unlike our American compulsion to eliminate men when they become 65, among Ibos the older a man gets, the more authority he gains. Old Ibo men are not paid; they make the currency—which is simply the blessing of manhood.

The men of the village have never read Hebrew Scriptures. But they know the truth which the God of Israel proclaimed thousands of years ago through the prophet Malachi: If they as fathers do not do their sacred job and call their sons into the fellowship of men, a curse will be unleashed on their village. Boys will grow up unable to feel like men, and shrink from the masculine calling to bless, to call forth giftings, to lead, to protect, and to serve.

Males will fear and dishonor manhood because it stirs the shame of their inadequacy.

Men, are you listening?

Dads, are you ready?

When the several elders agree, therefore, one night they and the boy's father gather on the edge of the mother's compound, perhaps 50 feet from her door. They are joined by a drummer, whose beat sets the pace, and by a man wearing a large mask over his head, called the *nmoo*—which in Ibo translates two ways: "mask" and "spirit." When all are together, they wait quietly for the *nmoo* to move.

The father and elders are not allowed to approach the mother or the boy. This is a job for the spirit. Ibo men understand this dynamic and essential truth, largely lost to our Western scientific pride: *It is the spirit who initiates the call to manhood.*

As the spirit/mask then begins to move away from the men into the mother's yard, the drummer picks up a beat—which echoes for some distance through the surrounding palms. The *nmoo* does not make a beeline for the mother's house, but first dances in her yard, essentially to claim the territory between her and the men.

And when the *nmoo* is ready, he turns and faces the mother's door. The drummer switches to a sharp, pounding beat, and the spirit rushes ahead to pound loudly on the door: Bam! Bam! Bam!

The boy inside the house has likely already been awakened by the drumming, and now the loud crashing against his mother's door makes his heart pound with fear. Isn't mother's place supposed to be safe from all things fearful?

Ah, but the call to manhood is an awesome thing. No mother can protect a boy from it.

After several retreats, drum shots, and more pounding, the *nmoo* pauses outside—and finally, the mother goes to the door and opens it.

"Who are you?" she cries out into the darkness, shielding the boy behind her. "What do you want?"

At that, the boy's father bursts forth with a loud cry, with a supporting chorus from the elders: "Come out! Son of our people, *come out!*"

Significantly, the mask/spirit does not enter the mother's hut to seize the boy. Coming out is not his job. It's the boy's job. He has to be willing to step out from behind his mother to face the spirit and the men.

Therein, really, lies the fear. Like vertigo, it's not that someone else will push you, but that you'll jump.

Louder the elders chant, sharper the drum beats, more feverishly the *nmoo* dances, more firmly the mother protests, and more deliberately the father and the elders insist—until finally, the mother steps aside.

It's the moment of truth for every boy in the village.

Standing there before the threshold of his mother's house, as the spirit beckons from the darkness, the boy hesitates. Likely, the comforting scent of his mother's dinner yet fills the room. Beside and behind him holds everything that's tender and reassuring and soft and secure.

While there, before him—*and within him*—cries out everything that is sharp and powerful and clean and true:

"Come out!" the men shout.

Uneasily, wanting but not daring to look at his mother, the boy steps forth from the dark womb of his mother's hut into the night—born again, this time as a "son of the father" (1 Peter 1:23).

At once, the spirit/mask seizes his wrist and rushes him over to the father and elders—in case he might have second thoughts!—where he is joined with other boys for this year's initiation. As he reaches the company of men, a wail of mourning breaks from the mother. At once, a great, masculine chorus of victory shouts bursts forth and overwhelms the mother's cries—suggesting, indeed, the mother's first painful cries at the boy's birth and the father's joy.

The drummer picks up a sharp and decisive beat, which together with the shouts, slowly fades as the men move farther into the forest to the next boy's house.

And the mother's wail fades to sobs. For indeed, her grief is deep. She has lost something tonight, never to be regained.

The mother's little boy has died.

And the man has been born.

There is no other way. Until he has become secured in the fellowship of men, a man cannot keep the commandment to honor his mother, but can only fear his mother's power to reduce him, and so withdraw from her.

Once gathered, therefore, the entire group of boys to be initiated are led out of the village area to a special place in the forest, where they are turned over to several old men who instruct them in manly disciplines for the next few weeks. Skills from thatch roof construction to hunting are taught first.

Then the boy enters a period of fasting for several days, thus turning his focus from physical gratification to spiritual discipline. During this time, the boy is circumcised and, while he is healing, taught clan history.

Circumcision, of course, is a symbolic cutting of the penis, that is, a yielding or sacrificial offering of manhood to the power in whose name the cut is demanded—in this case, the clan gods. The immense physical pain of the operation would seem to connect the boy graphically with the sufferings of the men in his tribal heritage.

Meanwhile, back in the village, the father builds his son a small hut of his own. Upon returning from the wilderness ordeal, the boy is regarded as a young man at last; when he enters the village, his mother is not permitted to greet him. He proceeds directly to his own new house, now separate from his mother's. That evening, he receives from his father a gun for hunting, a piece of farmland, and a hoe—his stake with which to establish his manhood in the clan.

Hearing this story at age 20, as a world traveler romantically "on my own," I scoffed. Today, in middle age, I weep. For I have grown strong enough to face what my fellow twentieth-century Western males and I have lost. The pounding on your mother's door, the cry of the man-affirming spirit to "Come out!," the chorus of older men waiting to receive you, the father's gift of accouterments—all these tap deep, deep longings in me that words cannot express.

Hearing such a story, I'm humbled, emptied—no, revealed as empty.

How America Calls Boys to Manhood

What does my own culture offer as a validation of manhood? The driver's license at 16, freedom at 18 to join the Army, attend pornographic movies, smoke cigarettes, and drink beer. The message is clear: Becoming a man means operating a powerful machine, killing other men, masturbating, destroying your lungs, and getting drunk.

Young men today are literally dying to be included in the company of men. Recently, an article in my local paper reported that a college fraternity was suspended after three pledges were hospitalized for "massive dehydration" following a weekend "boot camp." The article noted that no less than 56 students have died in initiation-related accidents since 1973.[1]

We are lost males, all of us: cast adrift from true community, cut off from our masculine heritage—abandoned to machines, organizations, fantasies, drugs.

Is it any wonder we're often terrified of fatherhood? We haven't even become men yet.

I realize the depth of our predicament when I describe the Ibo male initiation rite to groups, for the most frequent question afterward is, "Does the mother *really* hold the boy behind her when the mask/spirit approaches her hut, and cry when the mask/spirit seizes him? Or isn't she just playacting, going along with the game, so to speak?"

I have come to see such a question as similar to the unspoken attitude of Western Christians before the sacrament of communion: Does anything *really* happen to people who take the bread and the wine? Or isn't the congregation just playacting, going along, as it were, with the game that the church insists on perpetuating?

God help us when we have so forgotten who we are, and so lost our experience of the event that brought us into being, that we wander in such spiritual amnesia.

Gently, I explain that yes, the drama of the initiation rite anticipates a certain response from the mother. But in doing so, the rite does not define that response, but authenticates it. In fact, no mother who has enjoyed the devotion of her son can readily give it up. The release and proper growth of the boy require a community-ordained ritual to which her natural, self-centered impulses must yield.

The ritual, through the spirit who initiates and presides over it, allows the mother both to express her genuine pain and submit at last to the larger authority of the spirit—thus yielding to the boy's new emotional/spiritual "birth" even as years earlier she yielded to the boy's physical birth in labor itself.

Clearly, without such a ritual, the mother is not likely to be confronted with this, her essential role—and her natural, self-centered desires for the boy then prevail over his life, even into adulthood. In a convoluted myopia, the boy in later physical maturity cannot look beyond the woman to find manhood, and therefore seeks it in women, perhaps through sexual "conquests." If his manhood has never been confirmed by identifying with the larger community of men through his father, he constantly seeks it with woman after woman, remaining forever "invalid" in his manhood.

In the face of such realizations, I am overwhelmed. How in the world—indeed, how in *our* world—can we Western men begin to rediscover this basic male need and meet it? If, in fact, the father is the key to a boy's crossing the threshold into manhood, what can those do who had no father, or perhaps, whose father did not appropriately call him out from his mother?

Certainly, the origin of manhood cannot lie in the father alone, but only in some greater masculine Source from which the father himself must draw. The father becomes the sole focus of manhood only in a society such as our own, which lacks communal bonds of male "tribal" fellowship—not in societies such as the Ibo village, where the boy's father appears before the mother's hut as part of a larger group of men, who themselves stand in the background, behind the mask/spirit.

Yet Dad remains the gatekeeper to manhood. On the one hand, a man must beware the temptation to skirt the pain of being cut off from his father;

to do so is to let that pain bind and control him from the deeper unconscious to which he banishes it. He must start where he genuinely is, however painful, if he is to get where he needs to go.

At the same time, he must beware the companion temptation to judge and condemn his father for not giving him what he needed. As one man in his eighties rose unsteadily to proclaim at one of my conference question-and-answer sessions, "Whatever a man does not forgive his father for, he will do to his son."

The man who confesses his pain by bringing it to Jesus at the cross will begin to see the truth that sets him free: Dad was not called out by his own father, so didn't know how to call out his son. Dad is thereby revealed as not the oppressor, but rather, a fellow victim, a brother in mutual need of manly affirmation. When a man allows Jesus to carry his tears for his own loss into tears for his Dad's loss when Dad himself was a boy, he has begun to become a man of God at last.

Weeping for generations of loss, however, cannot by itself make you a man of God. Perhaps more significantly, neither can it save your own son from being so wounded. The communal dimension of manhood, largely discounted by our "modern" society, must be rediscovered and reaffirmed, as must the larger Source of manhood that beckons both fathers and sons.

When enough men have begun to face and cry out their longings for manly affirmation, the time comes to act. The man who would move through and beyond his individual pain into an authentic, viable manhood today must acknowledge and connect with the deeper masculine Source which calls a man out—even from his father—to fulfill his unique, individual calling in life.

How the Church Can Call Boys to Manhood

The Christian man may trust that such a transcendent manhood is rooted in the Father God who created all men and beckons him through Jesus.

And so at last, I wonder: What might an authentic Christian male initiation look like? Surely, it must be called a sacrament, that is, the outward and visible sign of the inward and spiritual grace of godly manhood.

I think of our modern church and shudder at the task. So many, many of our members are women—two-thirds of all church members, according to one survey, and as any pastor knows, an even greater portion of active members. Dare I begin such a portrait?

Dare I not?

For I feel the longing in myself, and in so many men I've prayed with, and know that I must forge ahead.

And so I pray: Help us, Father God. We're tired of slavery, frightened of the desert, yet longing for the Promised Land. Lead us with your vision. Awaken in us the truth; stir the hunger.

I imagine: One evening after dinner, Dad gets up, mentioning casually that he's going out to the store for a few minutes. Outside, he drives to the church, where he's met by the male elders and the other fathers of boys to be initiated. The men gather in the sanctuary to worship and rededicate their own manhood to God, praying that together they might be a fitting channel for God's spirit of manhood to each boy. All lay hands on each father, one at a time, and pray for God's strength and wisdom to fill him for guiding his son. For boys who have no father available, godly men are appointed as surrogates.

All the men then drive to the first boy's house—perhaps in one or two vans—and while a male pastor approaches the door, the men stand on the front lawn singing hymns.

The doorbell rings. The mother opens the door:

Faith of our fathers, living still . . .

Surprised to see the pastor and the men outside singing, she stands there, uncertain.

"We've come for Dan," the pastor says.

In spite of dungeon, fire and sword . . .

"But . . . but what for?" she asks. "I didn't know there was a youth group event tonight?"

O how our hearts beat high with joy
When e'er we hear that glorious word!

"This is not for the youth group," the pastor explains; "this is for the men."

Faith of our fathers, holy faith!
We will be true to thee till death.

"Well, I-I don't know," the mother says, glancing uneasily at the men singing out front. "Actually, Danny's father's not home just now, so you'll have to wait until—"

"What's that singing outside, Mom?" the boy calls from the living room. "What's going on?" He comes to the door, beside his mother.

Rise up, O men of God! Have done with lesser things . . .

Seeing the men out front, the boy draws up, tense.

"We want you to come with us tonight, Dan," the pastor tells him.

Give heart and mind and soul and strength
To serve the King of kings!

"Dan!" his father calls out from the group.

"What's your father doing out there with those men?" the mother exclaims.

"Dad!" the boy calls back—still uneasy, but encouraged to see his father there.

Lift high the cross of Christ
Tread where His feet have trod . . .

"Come on out, Dan!" his father shouts. "Come out with us!"

As brothers of the Son of man, rise up, O men of God!

The boy looks up at the minister, who nods—and waits.

"But it's cold outside," the mother protests. "And Danny hasn't finished his dessert . . ."

Stand up, stand up for Jesus, the trumpet call obey . . .

"I appreciate your concern," the pastor says, then turning to the boy: "You can go and get your coat. Your dad has already put together the clothes you'll be needing."

The boy hesitates, licking a trace of apple pie from his lips.

Forth to the mighty conflict, in this his glorious day . . .

"Come on, Dan!" his father shouts again. "Let's go!"

Ye that are men now serve him against unnumbered foes
Let courage rise with danger, and strength to strength oppose.

A pause . . . then all at once, the boy spins on his heels and dashes to his bedroom, comes running back grasping his coat. As he steps out the front door, the pastor nods graciously to the mother and puts an arm around him. The two head out onto the lawn as a mighty chorus arises:

A mighty fortress is our God! A bulwark never failing;
Our helper He amid the flood of mortal ills prevailing.
For still our ancient foe doth seek to work us woe;
His craft and power are great, and armed with cruel hate,
On earth is not his equal.

Did we in our own strength confide, our striving would be losing,
Were not the right man on our side, the one of God's own choosing;
Dost ask who that may be? Christ Jesus, it is he;
Lord Sabaoth his name, from age to age the same,
And he must win the battle.

When all the boys have been gathered this way, they are driven to a church campground for a period of discipline and instruction. This would include the following:

- An opening worship service in which each boy is taught to

memorize Romans 12:1-2, offering himself to God's service and opening himself to let God transform him inwardly during the initiation period
- Time to remember the men from whom the boy comes: stories of his father and grandfather, stories of American history
- Time to remember the God from whom all men come: Bible stories and biblical standards of behavior
- A period spent learning to pray, both alone and with others
- A time of fasting, during which the boy is taught its biblical basis and purpose
- A span of teaching on the nature of sexuality and how to relate to women with both compassion and strength
- Aptitude testing for professional skills, followed by a general session in which the men sit as a panel and share frankly about their jobs, inviting questions afterward
- Rigorous physical exercise
- Daily individual prayer, Bible reading, and journal-keeping
- Prayer and counseling for each boy to heal inner emotional wounds
- Talks by much older "grandfathers in the faith" about what life was like when they were boys, and what their faith has meant to them
- A closing worship ceremony in which the men call each boy forward, lay hands upon him, and pray for him to receive the Holy Spirit, as in the traditional rite of confirmation.

Clearly, all this requires considerable planning and organization—the sort of gifts that most churches rely upon women to exercise. To make such a commitment, the men of the church must of course be convinced it's necessary. That is, they must have dared to face their own need to be affirmed as men, their own emptiness and longing for that out of their own boyhood.

Only a man can call a boy into manhood.

Since this chapter first appeared in 1988 in my book, *Healing the Masculine Soul*, I have received numerous letters and calls from men asking, essentially, "Can you send me a step-by-step plan for calling out the boys of our church into manhood?"

I have no program, no CD-ROM that makes it happen. Only the Spirit of the Living Father God can do it, through men surrendered to him.

We must build a community of men to call our sons into. And we must start, as always, at the beginning—here manhood itself begins. Get on your knees and surrender to God. Confess you can't do it. Cry out to God to do it in and through you.

Dare to believe that your heavenly Father is calling you out. Get together with other men. Call each other out. Commit yourselves to each other. Get real with each other about your wounds and needs. Pray for each other.

Stand on Jesus' promise that wherever two or three gather in his name he—who is one with the Father—will be there. Cry out to God to send his Spirit to you for healing. Ask God to give you his heart for your sons.

Then step out together in faith and try something with the boys. Trust your Father that he will lead, and redirect where necessary. It's easier to turn the car wheel, after all, when the car is moving.

Above all, trust that God wants *even more than you do* to see your son walk in godly manhood, that as you reach toward God on your son's behalf, He will meet and honor you as "the Father from whom all fatherhood in heaven and on earth receives its true name" (Ephesians 3:14).

Notes

1. "Fraternity Suspended at UCLA," *Santa Barbara News Press*, April 12, 1998, A-13.

Chapter 19

One Son's Rite of Passage

Myron Stoltzfus

The story you are about to read was the culmination of an idea that had been percolating in my mind for several years. The idea was brought into focus through conversations with friends, books I read, and my own thoughts about an event I wanted for my son on his 13th birthday. I was hoping the experience would be a benchmark for him. I made this evening a matter of prayer. I really had no agenda. As I walked out the door, my wife asked if I wanted the video camera. I replied, "No." I did not want anyone or my son to feel pressure, and I did not want our time to be forced or staged. I could not have foreseen that our evening would be touched by the hand of God himself.

My son, Zachary, turned 13 on June 20, 1997. Prior to this date, I thought about creating some type of special event for him to mark the occasion. I had heard of some friends who had rites of passage for their sons at significant times of their lives, and I wanted to do something similar.

I decided to have a ceremony to commemorate Zachary's entrance into his teenage years. I invited our pastor, youth pastor, both of his grandfathers, and his eighth grade teacher, Mr. Rienford.

I planned a cookout beside the Pequea Creek in our Amish neighbor's meadow. Pequea Creek is the site of many memories of my own, including trapping for muskrat and raccoon, camping and picnicking with family, and sometimes walking alone, just to clear the cobwebs that accumulate in my head.

I chose some exquisitely marbled rib-eye steaks and cut them 1 1/4" thick. At a farmer's market, I bought some freshly picked corn on the cob—a real man's meal. The evening weather was created to order: warm and sunny with low humidity.

After throwing all of our supplies in the back of my pickup truck, we jumped in and headed to our spot by the creek. Nestled in a sort of cove, in an area that may have been a small quarry decades ago, is a little haven from which we could watch the sun set over the water. Trees surrounding this spot always keep it a bit cooler and more comfortable in hot weather.

The steaks were delicious; no doubt the best I had ever made. Throughout our meal we regularly had to chase away a small herd of the Amish farmer's heifers that were curious about our activity and didn't seem to appreciate us invading their meadow.

Finally, as the sun dipped low in the western sky, the heifers trotted off in a cloud of dust to look for greener pastures. It was time to move to the ceremonial part of our evening.

I had asked each man to come prepared with a message for Zach. They were allowed to bring symbolic gifts, but were asked not to bring traditional kinds of gifts. Each gathered what they had brought to share with Zach, and then we all sat in a circle.

Pastor Leon was the first to address Zach. He described a "recipe for greatness." He referred to James and John's mother asking Jesus how they could become "great" in his kingdom. Of course, Jesus stunned his listeners by saying the key to greatness was servanthood. Pastor Leon presented Zach with a handmade pottery bowl and towel that represented Christ's servant-spirit when he washed the feet of his disciples. He instructed Zach how to display it with the towel draped over the side. He noted how unnatural it is to be a servant. He pointed to imprints of two nails the potter had placed on the inside. Turning the bowl to examine its outside, Pastor Leon showed Zach some imperfections left there by the potter. He emphasized that we are earthen vessels just like the bowl. And yes, we are imperfect. But with Christ dwelling in us, represented by the nail imprints, we can become perfect. It was a most profound truth that Zachary was able to grasp.

My wife's father, Zach's Grandfather Mervin, spoke next. He presented Zach with several owl figurines. He told Zach that through his teenage years he will ask lots of questions. The owls would be good symbols of this because an owl stands for wisdom. He defined wisdom as the power of discernment—good common sense. He pointed out several Scriptures and gave Zach many more, written on the bottoms of the owls. Grandfather Mervin was careful to point out the difference between God's wisdom and the world's wisdom. He explained that true wisdom comes from above and told when and how one receives wisdom.

Zach's teacher, Neil Reinford, was next. He began by telling Zach that he wasn't sure what to get for him, but that he was at K-Mart recently and purchased a bottle of "Patience lotion." (He had doctored a bottle of suntan lotion with white adhesive tape, inserting appropriate words at specific spots on the bottle.) He said it was #45—the highest strength one could buy and that it was selling fast. The lotion was "anger" resistant, "Satan" proof, and "frustration" free. On the back the directions read: "Apply liberally at all times. In case of an emergency, dial *1-800-GOD-HELP!*"

Todd, our youth pastor, was next. He blessed Zach and said he observed a sensitive and caring heart in him. Out of wood, Todd had scroll-cut an apple and painted it. One side had Galatians 5:22 written on it: "But the Fruit of the Spirit is love, joy, peace, patience, kindness, goodness, faithfulness, gentleness, and self control." The other side said: "Dear Zach, May God develop in you all the Fruit of His Spirit as you continue to grow in Him!" He also presented Zach with another wooden apple that had a bite taken out of it. He invited Zach to partake of this fruit, to make it a part of himself—a part of his being. Fruit is everywhere (God), tastes good (Jesus Christ), gives energy (Holy Spirit), and is healthy (Bible). On the back of the apple with a bite missing, Todd had written an acrostic:

Zealous for God
Always Faithful
Committed to Christ
Honors God

My dad spoke next. He asked Zach to think about what had been said. To chew on it as our animal visitors to our campsite chew on their cud. Dad reminded him of his heritage of faith. He read 1 Timothy 6 to Zach. He then blessed Zach in the mighty name of Jesus.

Now I was the only person yet to speak. I knew that my time with Zach would be full of feelings. Throughout the week as I thought about this night, I was often overcome with emotion. The sun was below the horizon, and the last rays of light were fading fast. Off to the southeast, the full moon appeared brilliantly from the rocky knoll behind us. Shining through a few scraggly trees on the upper edge of the quarry, it provided almost as much light as the waning sun.

I recalled for Zach how pleased I was when God blessed us with his birth. I remembered taking Sally to the hospital around 2:00 a.m. and getting her settled. After I was sure I wouldn't miss the birth, I took time to move our car from emergency parking to the general lot around 4:30 a.m. Robins, stirred by the first hint of morning light, added merriment to my soul by serenading me as I walked back to the hospital. Around 8:15 that morning Zach was born. I felt like bursting into song along with the birds; I was so proud to have a son.

"In a new personal way, I understood the love our Heavenly Father had for his son," I said. "You probably have no idea how much Mom and I love you. I am a father who is well pleased with his son!

"God has a special plan for your life, Zach. I believe that he can and will use you to have a most significant impact on the world." I read to Zach from *Raising a Modern Day Knight* by Robert Lewis and explained all that went with knighthood. In the book, Lewis quotes historian Will Durant's description of a memory-making event, known as "dubbing":

> The candidate began with a bath as a symbol of spiritual, perhaps as a guarantee of physical, purification. . . . He was clothed in white tunic, red robe, and black coat, representing respectively the hoped-for purity of his morals, the blood he might shed for honor of God, and the death he must be prepared to meet unflinchingly.

> For a day he fasted, he passed a night at church in prayer, confessed his sins to a priest, attended Mass, received communion, heard a sermon on the moral, religious, social, and military duties of a knight, and solemnly promised to fulfill them.

> He then advanced to the altar with a sword hanging from his neck; the priest removed the sword, blessed it and replaced it upon his neck. The candidate turned to the seated lord from whom he sought knighthood, and was met with a stern question: "For what purpose do you desire to enter the order? If it be riches, to take your ease, and be held in honor without doing honor to knighthood, you are unworthy of it."

> The candidate was prepared with a reassuring reply. Knights of ladies then clothed him in a knightly array of hauberk, breastplate, armlets, gauntlets (armored gloves), sword, and spurs. The lord, rising, gave the accolade—three blows with the flat of the sword upon the neck or shoulder, and sometimes a slap on the cheek, as symbols of the last affronts that he might accept without redress; and "dubbed" him with the formula, "In the name of God, St. Michael, and St. George I make thee knight."

> The new knight received a lance, a helmet and a horse; he adjusted his helmet, leaped upon his horse, brandished his lance, flourished his sword,

rode out from the church, distributed gifts to his attendants, and gave a feast for his friends.

The book gave me the idea to present Zach with a "coat of arms." Several weeks before our evening by the creek, I had designed one especially for Zach. Sally bought fabric and sewed it together for me. The coat of arms was royal blue with gold bands separating it into quadrants. The bottom was lined with gold tassels. In the upper left quadrant, to signify Zach's heritage of faith, I put a silhouette of an Amish farmer walking behind a one-bottom plow. Zach comes from a people who were honest, trustworthy, and industriously toiled in the field. In the upper right quadrant, I set a collage of spiritual armor. Zach knew each piece of armor and described its spiritual symbolism. In the lower left quadrant, I placed an open Bible with a cross in the background. I explained to Zach that God's Word was the ultimate truth, that Christ reveals himself through his Word, and that his Word always prevails. In the lower right quadrant, I put the Promise Keepers logo. We have been to two Promise Keepers conferences together. This symbol was to remind Zach to be faithful in keeping his promises to both man and God.

I commissioned Zach to be a "spiritual" knight. I told him he will need courage and steadfastness to stand firm in righteousness in the coming years. I pointed out that he has several tools at his disposal. Zach can draw strength from wearing his spiritual armor; remembering his heritage of faith, the commitment of his forefathers; and learning God's Word and its promises. He will be able to remain faithful by being a promise keeper, a man of integrity. Just like knights of centuries past who were faithful and loyal to their king, Zach must be devoted to his King, his God.

For a few seconds there was silence as we all meditated on these thoughts. Then, remembering the setting, an almost unbelievable thing happened.

From the distance, we heard a set of rapidly approaching hoofbeats. Suddenly, as if on cue, a *white horse*, at full gallop, appeared out of the darkness. It raced up over the knoll behind us, right across the full moon. The white horse, its mane and tail streaming behind it, nostrils flaring and snorting, thundered by. It was gone as fast as it came. The sound of its hoofbeats disappeared into the night.

I firmly believe that God sent us that sign to confirm the moment. To give us a glimpse of his glory. How else could it be explained? I couldn't have scripted that to happen in a thousand years!

This day was also my Dad's birthday. For a long time I had wanted to honor my Dad in an appropriate way. The time had come. With my 39th birthday only days away, I decided to verbalize my feelings. I told Dad how much he has meant to me over the years and how much I loved him. I thanked him for standing by me during some recent decisions I needed to make regarding the family business. I don't remember ever telling my dad these things. It had gone long enough. Painful things were left unsaid. I felt so good saying what I had longed to say!

Now it was time to end the evening. Earlier I had felt some apprehension about what to do. I didn't want to force anything or have anything appear hokey to Zach. All of my anxiety faded as I felt led to ask the men to gather around Zach. We all laid our hands on him. I said a prayer for Zach, and each man added a special blessing for him.

It was one of those times that you wish you could freeze and save. A moment to remember forever, especially for Zach. As we piled into my pickup for the short ride home, Zach leaned over and said, "Dad, that was awesome. I'll never forget this evening!"

Neither will I, son, nor will any of the other men! It was a time touched by God. A time that he chose to shine his face upon us, letting *us taste and savor his goodness!*

In the months that have passed since that evening, I have come to appreciate and understand the significance of that evening in a broader sense. Zachary is 13. I have spent the past few months seeing him bloom into adolescence with all the changes that brings as a child begins to try to find his place in life. I know that the timing was right. It was at the threshold of his going from childhood to manhood. A stake was driven, a benchmark made. The details of the evening may fade in the coming years, but its memory will always be there, just a thought away.

Chapter 20

The Power of Male Initiation Ceremonies

Robert Lewis

During my 20-plus years in the ministry, I've preached hundreds of sermons and led more Bible studies, counseled more people, and attended more planning meetings than I care to count. While I have many warm memories from these experiences, they are not as clear in my mind as those special moments that occurred during *ceremonies*.

Ceremonies are those special occasions that weave the fabric of human existence. Weddings. Award banquets. Graduations. The day you became an Eagle Scout or were accepted into a fraternity. *We remember them because of ceremony.* The value of those moments was sealed by a ceremony. Someone took the time to plan the details, prepare the speech, and purchase the awards—so you would feel special. And "special" is what ceremony is all about.

Ceremony should also be one of the crown jewels for helping a boy become a man. In many cultures throughout history, a teenage boy is taken through some type of ritual to mark his official passage into manhood. One of the great tragedies of Western culture today is the absence of this type of ceremony.

I cannot even begin to describe the impact on a son's soul when a key manhood moment in his life is forever enshrined and memorialized by a ceremony with other men. What I will share in the following pages are the powerful experiences two other dads and I have had in using ceremony to shape a boy's life and direction.

For our sons we followed a knighthood motif. We concluded that there are three ideals of modern-day knighthood: a vision for manhood, a code of conduct, and a transcendent cause. These "weapons of the spirit" are transmitted from father to son through *character, instruction,* and finally *ceremony.* A ceremony is like the "spike" in a volleyball game. It drives home the point with unmistakable certainty.

Our medieval counterparts understood this all too well. While a knight's identity was shaped by instruction, his journey to manhood was "spiked" by an elaborate act of ceremony.

Historian Will Durant describes this memory-making event, known as a "dubbing":

> The candidate began with a bath as a symbol of spiritual, perhaps as a guarantee of physical, purification. . . . He was clothed in white tunic, red robe, and black coat, representing respectively the hoped-for purity of his morals, the blood he might shed for honor or god, and the death he must be prepared to meet unflinchingly.
>
> For a day he fasted; he passed a night at church in prayer, confessed his sins to a priest, attended Mass, received communion, heard a sermon on the moral, religious, social and military duties of a knight, and solemnly promised to fulfill them.
>
> He then advanced to the altar with a sword hanging from his neck; the priest removed the sword, blessed it, and replaced it upon his neck. The candidate turned to the seated lord from whom he sought knighthood, and was met with a stern question: "For what purpose do you desire to enter the order? If it be riches, to take your ease, and be held in honor without doing honor to knighthood, you are unworthy of it."
>
> The candidate was prepared with a reassuring reply. Knights or ladies then clothed him in knightly array of hauberk, breastplate, armlets, gauntlets (armored gloves), sword, and spurs. The lord, rising, gave the accolade—three blows with the flat of the sword upon the neck or shoulder, and sometimes a slap on the cheek, as symbols of the last affronts that he might accept without redress; and "dubbed" him with the formula, "In the name of God, St. Michael, and St. George I make thee knight."
>
> The new knight received a lance, a helmet, a horse; he adjusted his helmet, leaped upon his horse, brandished his lance, flourished his sword, rode out from the church, distributed gifts to his attendants, and gave a feast for his friends.[1]

He was now a knight! Do you think this young man would ever wonder if he *really* became a knight? Would you ever find him in the dark corner of some medieval tavern, anxiously wrestling with the question, "Who am I?" I don't think so.

To this powerful picture let me add a quotation by Richard Barber. Read the words slowly: Drink in every syllable. This is precisely what American sons are missing. "From early days of knights who were simple fighting men to the extravaganza of the most elaborate kind of chivalry, the ceremony of knighting was the central moment in a knight's life. Its roots lay in the initiation ritual, by which primitive societies marked the coming of age of adolescents."[2]

We need celebrations like this today to mark the passages from adolescence to manhood. *Boys need manhood ceremonies that will live on in their memory*—elaborate occasions that will "spike" forever the defining moments of their passage to modern-day knighthood.

Ceremonies come in all shapes and sizes. But the truth is, good ceremonies share four common characteristics.

First, *memorable ceremonies are costly*. The more time, thought, planning, effort, and money you give to a celebration, the more memorable it will be.

For example, you can celebrate your wedding anniversary by giving your wife a nice card with your signature. You might get by with such a meager offering—but I doubt it! Or you can include roses with the card. Better still is a card, roses, and dinner at a nice restaurant.

Second, *memorable ceremonies ascribe value*. By setting aside time, making the effort, spending money, and employing meaningful ceremony, we declare the high value of an individual. At the same time, ceremonies ascribe value to the beliefs and morals we hold important. Effective ceremony says, "You are important!" and "This moment is important!" It ascribes dignity with worth.

Third, *memorable ceremonies employ symbols*. Weddings are symbolized by a ring, Christmas by a star, graduation by a diploma. Each of these symbols calls to mind a host of pleasant memories.

Finally, and perhaps most importantly, *memorable ceremonies empower a life with vision*. The wedding ceremony points to a new life together rather than two individual lives; the graduation envisions a new career; the fraternity ceremony, a new circle of friends; father-child ceremonies, a new stage of life. Ceremony marks the transition from one season to another. It says powerfully, forcefully, and *regally*, "From this point forward, life is going to be different!"

At the conclusion of Dostoevsky's classic *The Brothers Karamazov*, Alyosha consoles a group of boys who are grieving over the death of a friend. He says this about memories:

I want you to understand, then, that there is nothing nobler, stronger, healthier, and more helpful in life than a good remembrance from our childhood, when we still lived in our parents' house. You often hear people speak about upbringing and education, but I feel that a beautiful, holy memory preserved from early childhood can be the most important single thing in our development. And if a person succeeds, in the course of his life, in collecting many such memories, he will be saved for the rest of his life. And even if we have only one such memory, it is possible that it will be enough to save us some day.[3]

Life-changing memory is what ceremonies are all about. And yet, most men in America today lack a rich, masculine memory because, for them, there are no manhood ceremonies at all! Instead of *lasting* impressions, there are no impressions—no powerful, internal portraits etched in memory that call to mind our passage to manhood, no indelible moments that shaped our masculine identity and now compel us to pursue authentic manhood.

For years I have met with two good friends, Bill Wellons and Bill Parkinson, to research, discuss, and plan how to raise our sons into manhood. I remember a few years ago when Ann Parkinson asked me a question I couldn't answer. "Robert," she said, "how does a young man *know* when he has become a man?" As the mother of three teenage boys, Ann wanted to know.

The more I thought about the question, the more I realized my friends and I needed to do something to initiate our sons into manhood. Something tangible. Something memorable. With seven sons between us, we wanted to create something that would empower our boys. So the three concerned fathers got together and took tentative steps toward designing manhood ceremonies.

At our first meeting, someone mentioned the idea of creating a family crest. Bill Parkinson then independently researched the subject guide of heraldry and brought back some examples. Using these as a guide, we fashioned a crest that reflected our values. Then we took our idea to Nancy Carter, a graphic artist employed by our church. Nancy played with the concept and the colors and developed the finished product. We then had three copies matted and framed and placed in prominent locations in our homes.

Our crest is in the common form of a shield. The Greek words across the top say, "Fight the good fight," an allusion to Paul's admonition in 2 Timothy 4:7. The helmet symbolizes the fight of faith. The Greek phrase at the bottom of the crest means, "One Lord, one faith, one hope."

Three major sections make up the crest. The section on the left—with the sword in the shape of a cross—represents "conventional" manhood of selfish, earthly instinct that must be surrendered to Jesus Christ. The section on the right with the crown and wreath symbolizes our definition of *authentic* manhood. The crossed swords in the middle represent not only our three families, but also the ongoing masculine truths each dad offers a son to fight with for an honorable, noble life.

Commemorating Key Passages in a Boy's Life

We now had a major *symbol*, but we still lacked a *process*. As our discussions continued, the three of us identified some key passages in a boy's journey to manhood. With our own experiences as a plumb line, we settled upon these four:

1. *Puberty*—that great transition at the start of adolescence when a boy's body wreaks havoc on his mind.
2. *High school graduation*—when, for the first time, a young man experiences unbridled freedom.
3. *College graduation*—when a man must face the world and begin providing for himself.
4. *Marriage*—when a man assumes responsibility for a wife and the leadership of a family.

We then decided to craft ceremonies to commemorate these passages and to empower each of our sons with a vision for the next stage.

Puberty: The "Page" Stage

Age 13 is a pivotal time in a boy's life. At this stage in his development, a boy's body often outpaces his ability to comprehend the changes taking place inside him. Puberty is a confusing time for a young man. His sexual desires become intense and predominating. A boy needs a father's help to make sense of the confusion.

Recently, before my oldest son, Garrett, turned 13, I asked him to join me in listening to and discussing Dr. James Dobson's tape series called "Preparing for Adolescence." This seven-part study covers such issues as emotions, physical changes, sex, and self-esteem. We went to the church in the early mornings for our study, then concluded our times with breakfast at a local restaurant. Each session, including breakfast, took approximately two hours. It was a great time of preparing Garrett for this personally significant transition he was about to experience.

Our talks were lively, sometimes explicit (we talked candidly about sex), and relationally bonding for father and son. At the conclusion of our study (which I coordinated with his 13th birthday), I prepared a simple ceremony and took Garrett to dinner and let him order any meal on the menu. He chose his favorite: steak.

For an hour, the two of us sat and talked about adolescence and manhood and his growing responsibilities. At this time, I introduced him to the manhood definition symbolized on the crest by the crown and wreath. "A man is someone who rejects passivity, accepts responsibility, leads courageously, and expects the greater reward—God's reward." I explained these phrases and illustrated each concept in a simple way.

I then asked Garrett to memorize the definition, which he did almost immediately. I told him this would be the "North Star" for his manhood (as it had been for mine) and that I planned to refer to it often in the years ahead. To "spike" this special ceremonial occasion, I read a special tribute I had written to him, praising his character and abilities. I then finished the evening by putting my hands on my son and praying for God's blessing in his life. What an evening!

Since that time, I've been amazed at how many opportunities I've had to shape my son's behavior by referring back to our definition of manhood. This is the beauty of clarifying and defining values.

High School Graduation: The Squire Stage

A second ceremony occurs when a son finishes high school. This, too, is a pivotal time, fraught with potential dangers. Upon leaving home for college, a young man discovers a newfound sense of freedom. And unless he is well-grounded, he may choose to renounce the values of home.

Four of our sons—Bill, Ben, Daniel Parkinson, and Bill Wellons Jr.—have now been through our high school graduation ceremony. It has had a profound effect upon each of their lives. Together the three dads took each son as he graduated to a nice restaurant and celebrated over dinner this major passage in his life. Then, in a formal way, we talked with each son about a number of issues pertinent to leaving home and continuing his education at college. Each father openly shared about his own collegiate successes and failures; we described honestly and in detail the things we did wrong, the things we did right, and how these things impacted our lives later on. We also discussed what we would choose to do over if we could, with our wisdom of experience.

It was immediately clear that having *a group of dads* share with one young man like this dramatically increased the power of this moment. We emphasized the importance of beginning strong academically, setting goals and boundaries, and resisting the host of temptations that awaited. The son was given the opportunity to ask any question on any subject. The interaction was often spirited and frank.

Then the three of us brought out a picture of our families' crest and explained select portions of the imagery to him. For instance, we used the three swords to represent one essential manhood truth from each dad that we wanted him to take along to college.

One of the truths we always communicate to our sons at this juncture was that we will no longer treat them as boys. From now on, our relationship will be more like peers. They are on their way to becoming men now and can be expected to be treated as such.

The discussion usually lasted for two hours or more. Once this part of the evening ended, we returned to one of our homes, where all the other members of the three families had gathered. We then pulled everyone into a circle around the college-bound son. Each father talked generously about this young man's achievements and character, affirming his commitment to Christ. Other family members were invited to make special comments too. Then everyone laid hands on this young man and prayed for him. Awesome!

In describing the impact of this one evening, Bill Wellons Jr. said, "It was incredibly affirming. It made me feel important. It was really challenging."

College Graduation: The Knight Stage

This third ceremony is unique for three important reasons. First, it is here that we formally initiate our sons into manhood. Youth ends here. The ceremony, which we'd like to expand into a weekend, takes an evening of private interaction where we discuss in depth this new life of independence and the responsibilities that come with it. We spend time defining additional aspects of the family crest, especially the crown and wreath, which depict authentic manhood. More than ever before, we challenge him to aspire to it, for *now is the time*. Reject passivity! Accept responsibility! Lead courageously! And again, the son is given the opportunity to ask questions, with robust interaction often taking place.

This ceremony is also unique because of a special gift. At the appropriate time, the young man's father reaches into his pocket and presents his son with a powerful reminder of this moment. A ring. But not just any ring. A ring of great value.

Applying the first rule of ceremonies ("memorable ceremonies are costly"), we took our family crest to a jeweler and asked him to engrave this image on a gold ring. Like nothing else we do, this costly gift "spikes" forever in a young man's mind the importance of the occasion. It is his dubbing as a knight.

The college graduation ceremony is also special for a third reason. Once a son has been through this ceremony, he formally joins the dads as a "fellow knight." He is now to be included in their round table. For the first time, he becomes an active participant in the other manhood ceremonies with the younger sons as they reach these same milestones.

This particular ceremony is still evolving. Our goal is to make the college graduation ceremony a weekend event instead of an evening. We'd like to get away for at least two days and discuss some key manhood concepts in depth. During the weekend, we could also have time for some manly activities, like camping, hunting, and fishing.

Marriage: The Promise/Oath Stage

One of the primary responsibilities of real manhood revolves around "a woman to love." You may remember that a knight's promise—his word of honor—was the most important thing a knight possessed. Knights were the Promise Keepers of the Middle Ages.

A woman to love and *one's word of honor*. Both elements are central to this final ceremony that occurs the night before the wedding, at the rehearsal dinner.

In the one promise/oath ceremony we have conducted, Ben Parkinson was called forward before friends, family, and his bride-to-be and challenged in the ways of married manhood by each of the dads. Then, to "spike" this special moment, he and Aimee received a family crest like the one in each of our homes, for the new home they were creating together as husband and wife.

Two final exhortations concluded this ceremony. First, Ben was exhorted as a knight to keep the vows he would make to Aimee the following day. Second, he was exhorted to keep the vows he had already made to us: the promise of pursuing real manhood for a lifetime.

This is what *we* do. There is nothing sacrosanct about our ceremonies; you may choose to imitate aspects of these or develop your own. But the important thing is that you do *something* creative and memorable to initiate your son into manhood. Remember, too, that the power of ceremony is the *actual experience!* It is the lingering memory it makes and the potent vision it marks.

With great clarity and regal pronouncement, manhood ceremonies tell a son, "I notice you! You are important to me! You are important to the kingdom of God! You have an important masculine destiny to fulfill!"

A son will remember these special occasions *with you* as some of the finest days of his life.

Notes

1. Will and Ariel Durant, *The Story of Civilization: The Age of Faith* 4 (New York: Simon and Schuster, 1950), 572-573.

2. Richard Barber, *The Knight and Chivalry* (Totowa, N.J.: Rowman and Littlefield, 1975), 38.

3. Fyodore Dostoevsky, *The Brothers Karamazov*, trans. Andrew R. MacAndrew (New York: Bantam, 1970), 934.

Index

Yankelovich, Daniel, 14
Young Men's Christian Association
(YMCA), xii, xiii

Zondervan, 101, 107, 173

About the Contributors

David Blankenhorn is president of the New York-based Institute for American Values. He is the author of *Fatherless America* (Basic Books, 1995) and a co-editor of *The Fatherhood Movement* (Lexington Books, 1999).

Don S. Browning is the Alexander Campbell Professor of Religious Ethics and the Social Sciences at the Divinity School of the University of Chicago and director of the Religion, Culture, and Family Project, funded by the Lilly Endowment, Inc. He is the co-author of *From Culture Wars to Common Ground: Religion and the American Family Debate* (Westminster John Knox Press, 1997).

Dan Coats is a former U.S. Senator from the state of Indiana. During his tenure in Congress, Coats dedicated himself to examining the relationship of government to the family. Senator Coats chaired the Senate Labor and Human Resources Subcommittee on Children and Families and authored the Project for American Renewal, a legislative package designed to encourage the revival of civil society. Mr. Coats, author of *Mending Fences: Renewing Justice between Government and Civil Society* (Baker, 1998), is a practicing lawyer and is chairman of Big Brothers, Big Sisters of America.

Gordon Dalbey pioneered the Christian men's movement with his best-selling first book, *Healing the Masculine Soul* (Word, 1988), from which his chapter is adapted. Rev. Dalbey is the author of two other books, most recently *Sons of the Father* (Tyndale, 1996). He holds graduate degrees from Harvard and Stanford. A popular international conference and retreat speaker, Rev. Dalbey may be reached at Box 61042, Santa Barbara, CA 93160, or on the Internet at http://www.abbafather.com.

Barrett Duke is the director of denominational relations, conferences, and seminars for the Ethics and Religious Liberty Commission, the Southern Baptist Convention's agency for applied Christianity. Holding a master's degree in Old Testament Studies, Mr. Duke is a contributing translator for the new Broadman and Holman translation of the Old Testament. He is also the author of numerous pamphlets and articles on gambling and the environment.

Don Eberly directs the Civil Society Project in Harrisburg, Pennsylvania, a project committed to civic and democratic renewal, and is the founder and chairman of the board of the National Fatherhood Initiative. Mr. Eberly has authored or edited six books on issues of culture and society, most recently *America's Promise: Civil Society and the Renewal of American Culture* (Rowman and Littlefield, 1998). He is a former congressional and White House aide.

E. Bernard Franklin is vice president of the National Center for Fathering where he gathers data, gives direction for programming, and serves as spokesman for African American fatherhood. Holding graduate degrees in counseling, Dr. Franklin serves as consultant to numerous educational institutions and community organizations on leadership development topics. He is writing a book directed at encouraging African American men to be engaged fathers.

George Gallup Jr. is chairman of the George H. Gallup International Institute, a public charity designed to discover, test, and encourage application of new solutions to social problems. Serving on the boards of many organizations in the fields of health, survey research, education, children and youth, and religion, Mr. Gallup is also a prolific writer having authored twelve books, most recently *Growing Up Scared in America* (Morehouse, 1995) with Wendy Plump.

Wade F. Horn is the president of the National Fatherhood Initiative, an adjunct faculty member at Georgetown University's Public Policy Institute, an affiliate scholar with the Hudson Institute, and a member of the U.S. Advisory Board on Welfare Indicators. Dr. Horn is the lead editor of a compilation book entitled *The Fatherhood Movement: A Call to Action* (Lexington Books, 1999).

Diane Knippers is president of the Institute on Religion and Democracy, an organization dedicated to fostering the spiritual and political reform of the mainline Protestant churches. Ms. Knippers' most recent article, "Sophia's Children," appeared in the May 8, 1998 issue of *Wall Street Journal*. Ms. Knippers worked to promote resolution on fatherhood, marriage, and youth abstinence at the General Convention of the Episcopal Church in July 1997.

Richard Land is the president of the Southern Baptist Ethics and Religious Liberty Commission and host of "For Faith and Family," a daily radio show on current issues from an evangelical perspective, which is currently heard on about 200 radio stations in 34 states and Canada. Dr. Land is a graduate of Princeton University (B.A.), New Orleans Seminary (Th.M.), and Oxford University (Ph.D.). Married for 27 years, he is the father of three children.

Robert Lewis is a teaching pastor at Fellowship Bible Church in Little Rock, Arkansas. He has helped hundreds of men raise their sons with his unique approach through a seminar called "Men's Fraternity." He is the author of *Raising a Modern-Day Knight* (Tyndale, 1997), from which his chapter is excerpted. Dr. Lewis holds degrees from the University of Arkansas, Western Seminary in Portland, Oregon, and Talbot Theological Seminary in LaMirada, California.

Larry Malone is the national director of men's ministries under the General Commission on United Methodist Men and is the editor of *UMMen Magazine*. Desiring to ignite men's spiritual development, Mr. Malone considers himself blessed to speak throughout America. He holds degrees in systems management (M.S.) and aeronautics (B.S.). Mr. Malone is the married father of three children and two grandchildren.

Bill McCartney is the founder and CEO of Promise Keepers in Denver, Colorado, an organization dedicated to motivating men toward greater strength and Christlike masculinity. He is the former head football coach of the University of Colorado. Following the much-publicized 1989 season, Mr. McCartney received five Coach of the Year awards. During the 1990-91 season, Mr. McCartney led the Buffaloes to their first national football championship ever with a victory over Notre Dame in the Orange Bowl.

Michael J. McManus writes a weekly syndicated newspaper column called "Ethics & Religion" and is the author of several books, including *Marriage Savers: Helping Your Friends and Family Avoid Divorce* (Zondervan,

1995). As president of Marriage Savers, Mr. McManus seeks to inspire churches to recruit and train solidly married couples to become "Marriage Mentors." He has also persuaded the clergy of 88 cities to develop marriage strengthening strategies in their areas, called Community Marriage Policies or Community Marriage Covenants. Mr. McManus may be reached at 9500 Michael's Court, Bethesda, MD 20817.

John W. Miller is Professor Emeritus, Religious Studies at Conrad Grebel College/University of Waterloo in Ontario, Canada. Author of *Jesus at Thirty: A Psychological and Historical Portrait* (Fortress Press, 1997), Mr. Miller is also a lecturer in Old Testament at Waterloo Lutheran Seminary and active in developing and teaching in an ecumenical Bible instructional program for laity.

Anthony M. Pilla is the Roman Catholic bishop of Cleveland and, since 1995, president of the National Conference of Catholic Bishops. He has an M.A. in history from John Carroll University and several honorary doctorates. In addition to his religious leadership, Bishop Pilla is involved in the civic community through his service on boards and committees. He has demonstrated his dedication to Cleveland's well-being by his "Church in the City" initiative.

DeForest "Buster" Soaries is the senior pastor of First Baptist Church of Lincoln Gardens, in Somerset, New Jersey, one of the fastest growing African American churches in the state. An internationally renowned speaker and advocate for youth, Dr. Soaries is the author of *My Family Is Driving Me Crazy* (Victor Books, 1991). Dr. Soaries is also chairman of the Renaissance Community Development Corporation, a nonprofit organization committed to the redevelopment and revitalization of both human and physical capital, encompassing 880 acres.

Myron Stoltzfus is president and owner of Stoltzfus Meats, Inc., an enterprise begun in 1954 by his father. Mr. Stoltzfus is active in his church, Bethany Mennonite Church, and the community. While committed to guarding his evening hours for his family, Mr. Stoltzfus makes time to serve on the boards of Locust Grove Mennonite School and the Pennsylvania Family Institute and is a member of the Governmental Affairs Committee of the American Association of Meat Processors and the National Advisory Committee on Meat and Poultry Inspection.

W. Bradford Wilcox, a doctoral student in sociology at Princeton University, is writing a dissertation on religion and fatherhood focusing on Protestant men. His article reporting that conservative Protestant parents are exceptionally warm, expressive parents will appear in a forthcoming issue of *American Sociological Review*. He is a visiting fellow at the Brookings Institute and a former associate editor of *The Responsive Community*, a communitarian journal.

The National Fatherhood Initiative
One Bank Street, Suite 160
Gaithersburg, Maryland 20808
(301) 948-0599
E-Mail: nfi1995@aol.com

The National Fatherhood Initiative was founded in 1994 to stimulate a society-wide movement to confront the growing problem of father absence, and is dedicated to improving the well-being of children by increasing the number of children growing up with involved, committed, and responsible fathers.

A non-profit, non-partisan, non-sectarian organization, NFI pursues this mission through a variety of strategies and programs, including promoting responsible fatherhood via public awareness campaigns, organizing conferences and community fatherhood forums, conducting research and policy analysis, providing resources, training and technical assistance to organizations interested in establishing support programs for fathers, disseminating informational materials to men seeking to become more effective fathers, creating partnerships with members of the U.S. House of Representatives and Senate, Governors and Mayors and national civic organizations, and the development of state and local fatherhood chapters.